Praise for *Pretend They Are Dead*

"*Pretend They Are Dead* is a compelling story of fathers and sons. As a former major leaguer, the Tug McGraw chapter brought back great memories of having a catch with my own dad and being the dad playing catch with my kids. Don't miss this one!"

—**Mike Stanley, Retired MLB All-Star (1995)**

"Beautifully written with immediacy and candor, *Pretend They Are Dead* sheds light on the long-lasting effects of parental estrangement, childhood trauma and the crucial role that empathy plays in forgiveness."

—**Carol Bloomquist Mikulka, MD,**
American Board of Psychiatry and Neurology

"This book is a testament to courage and resilience in the face of abuse and neglect. It is ultimately a story of hope, that with persistence, determination and the right kind of help, healing and transformation is possible."

—**Patricia Coughlin, Ph.D., Clinical Psychologist**

"*Pretend They Are Dead* is a profoundly inspirational story of resilience, driven by Steven Eichenblatt's incredible determination to overcome the traumatic events of his past, which inspired him to focus on fatherhood, family, and serving others."

—**Michael Nitti, Author of** *The Trophy Effect and Mastery: The Art of Living on Purpose*

"Steve Eichenblatt has given readers an extraordinary gift: the language to express the unspeakable and the strength to uncover hope where it's hardest to find. *Pretend They Are Dead* offers a piercing, tender exploration of the unseen battles children endure when forced to navigate the chaos of adult struggles. With vivid storytelling and profound emotional insight, Eichenblatt reveals not just the lasting impact of these early wounds, but the quiet, powerful ways resilience takes root."

—**Christine Wolf, author of** *Politics, Partnerships & Power* **and Founder of Write to Heal Workshops and Retreats**

PRETEND THEY ARE DEAD

A Father's Search for the Truth

Steven Scott Eichenblatt

CHRISTMAS LAKE PRESS

Published by Christmas Lake Press 2025
www.christmaslakecreative.com
Copyright © 2025 by Steven Scott Eichenblatt
ISBN 978-1-960865-28-1

This memoir is based on a true story and reflects the author's personal journey and memory of his experience. He has made his best effort to recreate events, locales, and conversations, some of which occurred over fifty years ago. Names and identifying characteristics have been changed to protect privacy and maintain anonymity.

...

Interior layout by Daiana Marchesi

PRETEND THEY ARE DEAD

A Father's Search for the Truth

Dedication

To Jordan, Max, Sari, Zach, and Cody who, despite my imperfect fathering, know I love them. Remember, no retreat, no surrender.

To my wife, Melissa, who has taught me how to love and that it is OK to accept love. Her support and appreciation during years and years of early morning writing allowed me to finish *Pretend They Are Dead*.

To my mother, a survivor who earned my forgiveness and grace long ago. I love you, Mom.

And finally, I dedicate this book to the young Steven Nestle, who no longer hides in the closet, but rides his blue Schwinn Sting-Ray with the banana seat around my heart.

Acknowledgments

Ten years ago, I began writing this book and like any great relationship, it was a roller coaster of love and hate. It has been an emotional marathon, but despite moments of mental exhaustion, I never quit—because finishing is winning. There are many who helped me along the way. As part of my research, I contacted several former employees of Allen Nestle, former neighbors, and old friends, and spent hours staring at thousands of single-spaced typewritten pages on yellow paper written between 1960-1993. Steve Fayer was the source of many stories and spent hours sharing family history.

Sisters Sharon and Beth, and my brother Michael, helped to reconstruct some of the lost years. Cousin Dan Nestle whose dad, Jerry, was as happy as Allen was sad, spent hours filling in details about life in Bayonne with Pappa Charley and Grandma Annie. I acknowledge that several family members are not interested in revisiting the past, and I did my best to honor their boundaries. They each have their own stories to tell. My mother was an amazing source of support and details, despite the guilt she carries that even my forgiveness cannot erase.

I want to acknowledge and thank my close friend of thirty-five years and law partner, Gregg Page, who kept me moving forward during some tough times. I want to thank my friends who encouraged me during this journey. Thank you to Reid Berman, his sister Vicki, and his entire family. I also thank the following in no particular order: Bill Robbinson, Rex Hurley, Greg and Alexandra Band, Kevin Moon, Dr. Carol Mikulka, Michael Nitti, Frank Eidson, Teresa Finer, Daniel Wilson, Floyd Livingston, Tom Brown, John Bachman, Harlan Cohen, Bill Eberding, Lia Larea, and so many others.

Thank you to the multi-talented Christine Wolf, who wears many hats including writer, book coach, agent, mother, and now friend. I also must thank Nicole Guenther, a talented copyeditor from the University of Washington, who helped with edits and chapter placement.

Christmas Lake Press is an amazing publisher. Tom Fiffer and Julia Bobkoff spent hundreds of hours with me editing, reading each sentence out loud, and making sure, in Julia's words, that the words fit together like a symphony, because we are the orchestra. I cannot imagine a better team of people, which also included Erika Rundle for copyediting, Daiana Marchesi for typesetting, and Aaron Davis (with initial input from Maegan Sundlie and Sari Eichenblatt) for cover design.

Of course, I thank my wife, Melissa, and my kids for their mostly unwavering support and love.

I also want to recognize two great friends lost along the way, who each inspired me in their own unique way.

Frank Clark, aka Mr. Orange, left many voice and text messages encouraging me to step out of my comfort zone and to continue to do what is right, not what is easy.

Dan Moroff, a friend of thirty-five years, was a loyal supporter whom I miss every day.

"I can't think of any need in childhood as strong as
the need for a father's protection."
— Sigmund Freud

"The heart of a father is a masterpiece of nature."
— Prevost Abbe, "Manon Lescaut"

"When I look back on my childhood I wonder how
I survived at all. It was of course a miserable childhood: the
happy childhood is hardly worth your while."
— Frank McCourt, *Angela's Ashes*

"It is not flesh and blood but the heart
which makes us father and sons."
— Johann Friedrich von Schiller

Author's Note

Dear Dad,

You lived almost an entire life without me. Dying was your final selfish act—until it wasn't. I'm not a conspiracy theorist or UFO guy, but I now believe in ghosts. You want to know my story? Here goes, but it's a shame you chose to pretend we were dead.

I won't spoil the ending, but like any great book, it's a roller coaster of chaos, fear, inspiration, tragedy, love, and death—with a lot of shit to overcome along the way. *A lot!*

Maybe you can be forgiven, maybe not.

There is much to consider.

After all, it's easy to say I love you from the grave.

Steve

Contents

Prologue

Some accidents are no accident.

Today is one of those paralyzing New Jersey summer days when the unrelenting humidity casts a blanket of warm, moist air over my entire sixteen-year-old body. I am on my way to work, riding my bike, trying to avoid the cars speeding along Colfax Road like Mario Andretti. Mario won the Indy 500, and it's rumored that his cousin goes to my school. Colfax has no sidewalk. It's a winding, two-lane road with thick woods on either side punctuated by an occasional house. The turns are sharp, and I'm not supposed to ride this way because Mom says there's always accidents—but it's the fastest route. She says my hearing is selective. The truth is, I ignore my parents as much as possible.

Beads of sweat stream down the middle of my back, making the faded blue and yellow Los Angeles Rams number 18 jersey stick to my skin. The number belonged to quarterback Roman Gabriel, but he was traded to the Eagles, his new football family. Most days I wish my family could trade me.

Mom always threatens to trash the jersey. She claims it's glued to my body because I wear it so much. I'm a little husky, so I like the way the jersey hides my bulk. Besides, going shopping for new clothes is worse than going to Hebrew school. Riding my bike in today's heat might help me lose weight, but getting high every night usually leads to a late-night Carvel trip for a soft-serve vanilla cone dipped in chocolate.

No one wants to be outside today, but my job taking care of the Wayne Racquet Club tennis courts leaves me no choice. New Jersey won't give me a driver's license for another year, so my green Schwinn Varsity ten-speed takes me everywhere—including work. I bought it with cash salvaged from my bar mitzvah money and hidden from Richard, who showed up one day and proclaimed himself my father. Now I'm stuck with his complicated, impossible-to-pronounce last name. My life used to be simple with Mom and my first dad, but those days are long gone.

Richard doesn't pay attention to me unless it's to bark out orders or call me a loser. When friends and relatives handed me gift envelopes at my bar mitzvah, Richard grabbed them, daring me to react. Richard is the tennis club's president, and my boss—at work and at home. If I'm late for work, there's hell to pay in both places. Some of it is physical, some not. When he and Mom married, they told everyone how wonderful it was for their kids—his four and her three—to be a unified family, with two loving parents who love them equally, no matter the biology. We were dragged to temple events and strangers' houses so Mom and Richard could pretend we were brought together like one of God's miracles. They act like we are the Jewish Brady Bunch. But Mike Brady never screams at Carol or uses his belt on the kids.

My clothes are soaked when I reach the gravel driveway at the club's entrance. A small, sturdy oak tree nearby provides enough shade and cover to protect the bike. Once the Schwinn is secured, I walk along the slate path past the courts toward the aluminum equipment shed. Richard bought the shed directly from the Sears Roebuck catalog. It looks like an outhouse.

My job is to check the clay courts each day for divots and ensure a level playing surface. Loud-mouthed members love to blame the court conditions for poor play. Otherwise, their lousy shots are the fault of the sun, wind, moon, teaching pro, husband, ex-wife, ex-husband, kid in trouble, or President Ford. They're stuck as victims, even in their tennis games. No one whines louder or longer than Richard. He's the master of convincing everyone that nothing is ever his fault, including his terrible backhand. He thinks people believe him, but the truth is, few care what he says; they just agree to shut him up.

Today is the Fourth of July. No one is here. Holidays tend to be crowded in the mornings, and then people disappear. My strategy is to wait as long as possible to clean the courts. Going late increases the odds that no annoying people will be hanging around. Usually a few linger, telling the same tiresome stories of great shots and bad line calls, avoiding going home to nagging spouses or screaming children. I don't like talking to adults and answering their stupid questions. Today, solitude is a pleasant surprise.

Today, like every other day, there's a clipboard with a sign-in sheet that has a place for my name, arrival time, and departure time. Several others take care of the courts, though today it's only me. We're on the honor system, but Richard never hesitates to cut down the hours we've worked if he thinks we took too long to sweep or roll the surface. I'm pretty certain he does it to test whether I'll have the courage to question him, but that means a conversation—and the resulting punishment. His version of the honor system is not exactly honorable.

Workers are always quitting. No one wants to put up with Richard. I have no choice since he's my legal father. Looking for love or respect from Richard is a waste of time. He is an expert swordsman, wielding fear to keep me in check.

Since the parking lot's empty, the distant figures of swimmers at the private day camp next door are visible. The occasional shrill of a lifeguard's whistle pierces the air and forces the kids from the water. I can hear laughter from their direction but don't bother to look back toward the Olympic-size swimming pool. Sometimes I look for girls my age, but not today. The darkening gray sky, combined with the worsening humidity, motivates me to work fast. Pushing the wide broom before me, I start with Court 1, the farthest from the road, and continue moving through all six courts. Distributing each granule of the green Har-Tru clay evenly across the surface so that the court is level should keep the members from complaining.

Perfectly groomed courts bring to mind those winter mornings when fresh snow perfectly blankets our front yard and driveway. There's that point in time when each flake, like the granules, is positioned in its proper spot, only to be disrupted and displaced by the chaos of humanity. The absolute stillness of an early morning snowfall is much more calming than the quiet today. Later, there'll be Fourth of July fireworks to break through this wall of uneasy silence.

Court 6 is closest to Colfax Road. The only sound is my broom and its intermittent rhythmic vibration as cars approach and then fade into the distance. I'm relieved when no one slows down and turns into the club's entrance. Colfax has a long, tree-lined straightaway leading into a slight curve as it approaches the club. Today, with so few cars, they're easily heard from far down the road.

The swimmers next door have left. The lifeguard's whistle has gone silent. I don't even hear birds or see the squirrels running through the overhanging trees. I continue sweeping across the court's baseline, removing every speck of clay in a robotic, systematic motion. The symphony created by the straw bristles scraping against the white tape marking the tennis court's lines soothes me. Here, no one's yelling at me and my parents aren't fighting. My overactive brain finally begins to shut up and the voices in my head quiet down. I begin to relax.

Without warning, the furious screech of screaming car brakes and skidding tires disrupts my calm. The squealing yields to a horrifying crack, followed by the immediate crunch of a car slamming against the telephone pole just yards from where I stand. Metal collapses, glass explodes, and the pole splinters and begins tilting toward the ground, the way a sinking ship lists in the water. It's a slow process, but there's no question the outcome will be catastrophic. The sound is one I will never forget.

I drop my broom, run to the wrecked car, and the world disappears. My feet move too slowly, like lead, and the few seconds it takes me to sprint through the gate to the car feel like hours. My body feels disconnected from my mind. The smell of burning rubber mixed with gasoline fumes grows stronger and overwhelms me. Fluids pour out of the wreck. My tongue registers the artificial sweetness of chemicals mixed with fuel. Uncontrollable energy and adrenalin kick in. My heart pounds.

A middle-aged man is inside the car, his head pressed against the shattered windshield, blood streaming down his face. One eye is a bloody pulp. He is motionless. He might be dead.

My mind explodes. On the television show *Emergency!*, the actors rescue accident victims every week by performing heroic mouth-to-mouth resuscitation, but it's almost always for an actress who looks like a *Playboy* Playmate. Putting my mouth on that bloody guy's lips when I haven't even kissed a girl yet is not going to happen.

I turn away and run to the pay phone, four courts down, to call the police. My hands shake. I dig into my pocket and grab the coins resting there but drop one of my dimes. My mind races, questioning whether what I have witnessed is real.

I dial zero for the operator and hear a woman's voice asking if she can help me. But I'm not the one who needs help. I scream into the phone, babbling about a car crash and then dash back to the car, heart throbbing through my soaked shirt. The huffing and puffing sounds I hear of a person out of breath are coming from me. My chest heaves, but I feel nothing. People are gathering to help. *Where did they all come from?* There are a few houses close to the road, so I'm guessing the lazy afternoon quiet interrupted by the shocking and sudden sound of the car hitting the pole drew some attention.

I consider getting on my bike and riding away, but an irresistible force pulls me back toward the car. My brain is on high alert now. I fight the urge to leave.

Sirens grow louder and soon the police and an ambulance pull between the gawkers parked along the roadside. The paramedics pull the man out of the car and sit him upright against its side as they assess his condition. He is breathing. I shouldn't stare, but I've never seen a real car crash before. Blood is everywhere. No one is talking. I walk closer and catch a whiff of the last of the exhaust fumes, which are escaping the sputtering tailpipes, hanging on like someone fighting to take their last breath. The noise stops as the car shuts down for good.

Watching the paramedics work, a strange sensation creeps through my body, like an energy force that cannot be measured by any scientific testing device. Instinctively, I feel the stare of the bloodied man with a mutilated eye. I'm afraid to look because of what I might see, yet my head lifts to meet the forceful gaze of this crooked-faced victim.

All sensation leaves my body when I notice the left rear window of the crushed car has a decal with an insignia: "Doctor of Veterinary Medicine." My head spins. Time stops. The police officer is bent over, looking through the man's wallet. As he's loaded into the ambulance, the officer pulls a driver's license out of the wallet and reads his name aloud: "Allen Samuel Nestle, DVM." The officer looks around and raises his voice. "Does anyone here know this man?"

Does anyone here know this man? Should I say anything?

Dizzy, my brain shuts down, and I see a flicker of light before the black-and-white television screen in my mind goes dark. *Show's over.* I walk the few steps to my bike but don't remember mounting it or riding home. The sound of distant sirens fades from memory and I don't even wonder if he survived.

Does anyone know this man?

Now I'm in the garage, and worried about Richard and his questions if he finds out I witnessed the crash. I remember the adrenaline surges that forced my heart into overdrive. *Will I get in trouble? No, I can't tell anyone about the crash. I will just pretend it never happened.*

When I lean my bike against the wall, it falls to the ground. The noise sends another round of anxiety through me. My guts feel like they're going to burst through my belly button. *Is that even possible?*

I am confused but can't let Richard sense weakness. I'm always on edge, wondering which room he's in and whether he has his sights set on me. It's a bad feeling to live in fear.

I push the whole scene deep inside the dark, cold place beneath my memories, where I bury the bad stuff to die. I stay silent, because who would I tell? My brother, Robert, is too young. My twin sister Lori disappears for days before anyone notices she's gone. I shared my feelings with her in the pre-Richard days, but now we focus on survival. Although there are nine of us in the house, each of us is alone.

I retreat into my mind. *Maybe the crash is in my imagination. Maybe my brain is playing tricks. I don't know anyone who has witnessed a car crash before.* Then I'm standing in the kitchen as Mom yells for my brothers to stay away while she assembles hamburgers. I feel her eyes on me, but she doesn't say anything. Without warning, she grabs the sleeve of my jersey, pulls it to her nose, and inhales, causing her face to scrunch up. Her eyes register confusion.

Mom knows something's wrong but says nothing. She ignores most problems unless it's Richard flinging plates against the wall or the inevitable punches thrown when his temper lights the fuse for an explosion. She pretends we are that happy fantasy family she watches in her dreams. Her brown eyes used to brighten when she saw me, but their light keeps fading, and now they look dull and indifferent. I miss who she used to be.

She and Richard are leaving to go to a friend's house for a Fourth of July celebration. We are not invited. There are not many people willing to invite all seven children to their house. I consider this a good thing.

Mom leaves the burgers on a plate for us to eat later. She stands in the kitchen and looks down at Sam, our dog, who snores loudly, occasionally losing his breath, causing his body to rattle and vibrate like a car engine running out of gas. Sam lies like a piece of furniture next to his bowl. He doesn't miss any meals and will get his share of hamburger when we eat. He is impossible to resist when he stares with his soulful, sad beagle eyes. I love him much more than anyone else around here. He knows how to keep my secrets.

I discuss the crash with no one. There was more blood than I have ever seen, even more than when I cut off my fingertip. I'm churning inside as reality sets in. *Did the man survive? Did I save his life? Why did he stare like that? Did he recognize me? Why was he there? Was it a coincidence? Was it even real? I'm sure glad he didn't get his blood on my jersey. That would be gross.*

I keep hearing the police officer's voice saying the injured man's name and asking if anyone knows him. I can see his mangled eye staring into mine. *Why is he looking at me? What does he want from me?* His eyelid seems about to fall off his face, dangling down like a worm on a fishing hook. His flesh and blood are spattered across the windshield like disconnected puzzle pieces. Sadness hits me for an instant. Even though I refused to answer the officer's question, the man *is* someone I know. *Knew.* He used to be my father.

This is not the reunion I had hoped for.

CHAPTER 1

The Lost Save of Tug McGraw

Thick green blades of grass poke up between my toes while my six-year-old son, Cole, scrambles down the gravel driveway in hot pursuit of a runaway tennis ball—an optic green Penn Pro. The swift Florida breeze hurls pine cones off the trees like knuckleballs, which Cole sometimes tries to catch—without success. Telling him that catchers have notorious trouble handling knuckleball pitchers doesn't stop him. I think back to what I was doing on Saturday afternoons as a kid. My friends tell me my crazy childhood makes me interesting. They're not the ones who had to live it.

Watching Cole run with the innocence granted by a happy childhood helps to dull the events that keep me tethered to my past. His squeals of joy as he races to the ball, small legs pumping his black Converse high tops, are a world away from the shouts that still arise in my memory and scramble my brain.

Today, my four kids fuel the once empty chambers of my heart with happiness. Cole is the youngest of three boys. He is ten years younger than my daughter Sabra, and fifteen years younger than the oldest, Jacob. The older kids live with their moms, but we see each other all the time. They can't escape me. Cole's mom, a retired professional athlete, will become my second ex-wife.

The kids love to make fun of my disconnected thoughts and random stories that usually cause eye rolls or result in an emotional buffet of feelings, ranging from laughter to annoyance to genuine appreciation. When our eyes meet, we exchange the bright current of connection. Their subconscious does not carry the scars of pain. Parenting is a tricky business. I'm far from perfect, but growing up the son of a Vlad the Impaler wannabe will have that effect. As a kid, I read a story about the Romanian ruler and always loved the name, imagining how cool it would be to impale Richard someday.

Hopefully, my kids don't see the wounds caused by two flawed fathers. Someday, they will figure it out. I can no longer hide the abuse from myself but am an expert in compartmentalization. Hidden trauma, like lightning, can appear without warning, exposing Ghosts of Christmases Past. Cole doesn't know I perform a magic act every day, making my own childhood disappear so he can enjoy his. As I watch, Cole, still chasing the runaway ball, stops and shouts, "Dad, watch this!"

I nod and take a few steps across the lawn to get a better view. He looks over, face hidden under the garnet Florida State football hat that seems a permanent fixture on his head, and nods when his eyes meet mine. He stops to tighten his laces, then lines up to kick the tennis ball.

I yell, "Cole, just pick it up and throw it."

"Dad!" Cole looks toward me. "Let's play *real* catch. Not the tennis ball kind." I'm distracted, but saying no is difficult.

Therapy helps, but I haven't managed to share the truth about the car crash, the bloodied stranger, the impossible coincidence. It's been decades, yet the blood still looks fresh and the sound of screaming tires and scent of burnt rubber never leave me.

Now I stand in our front yard, feeling a gentle breeze. The trees sway in harmony. I'm attempting to teach Cole how to catch a baseball with his glove instead of his face. I tried the tennis ball first because it would hurt less, but he said that's for babies. Without warning, Cole suddenly flings his glove on the ground and runs into the garage. He's my only child with my second wife. One day he'll be thankful for her superior athletic genes.

Cole disappears, but I can hear him digging through mountains of old Wiffle balls, deflated footballs, three-wheeled skateboards, and basketballs flat as pancakes. By now, he's thrown everything all over the garage floor. He's not concerned about the mess, which will be left for me to clean up. We've discussed putting things away, but I'm not one to impose strict rules.

Cole's determined. He has a particular baseball stuck in his mind. While he's gone, I think about the countless hours I've spent playing catch, or basketball, or just hanging out with my kids. My favorite feeling in life is catching my kids watching me, making sure I'm watching them. I've seen everything from dance recitals to cheerleading competitions, football games to talent shows. Cole was born while my daughter was performing as a strawberry in her third grade play, and I still managed to see both.

Love for my children flows through my veins and gives me energy for life. Fathers protect their young; they don't leave them.

The screen door opens and Cole yells, "Dad, don't move. I gotta pee. Just wait, I'll be right out."

I smile. "No problem, buddy, take your time." He may be peeing or loading his pockets with forbidden candy his mom has hidden. Cole knows all the hiding spots. And he knows I'm a softie.

A few seconds pass and then the door creaks open. Bursting through the garage, Cole yells, "I found it!" He runs up to me, eager to play.

"Dad, heads up!" I notice that Cole has a baseball ready in his hand.

I yell, "Hey buddy, is that my autographed ball?"

"No, Dad, this has *my* autograph. Later, can you show me the Tugboat ball? Is that OK?"

I stare for a few seconds. "Sure, buddy. First hit my glove, bring the heat! C'mon!"

We all collect certain landmark moments in our memory's personal trophy case. These signal moments, both great and terrible, are the ones we can't shake. During Little League, a kid hit a home run off me that would have cleared Yankee Stadium. It's been stuck in my brain all these years. I still kick myself for giving him such an easy pitch. I remember my errors but forget game-winning homeruns.

Under the pines, it might be more accurate to call our game "throw and miss," instead of "catch," but Cole always wants to play. When I was young, it hurt to watch kids throwing with their dads, hoping to be invited. Today, I issue the invitations, so every kid is included.

"Parents and kids around the world play catch," I say, and tell him about the British and South American kids who play catch with their feet, and the kids in India who play cricket. I have to explain that cricket is not a game with actual bugs, and I find myself answering questions about the population of crickets in India versus the number of mosquitoes, and whether the local flea market has "really real fleas." Cole looks at me and says, "Tell me a story."

The kids love my stories. Exaggeration in just the right places to get their attention or a laugh helps, and they're always asking me to repeat them. I start telling my fish story, which has grown over the years from reeling in a largemouth bass to slaying a great white, but Cole rejects it. So I begin the story about being his age and having a fire-breathing dragon in my bedroom closet—but he stops me cold.

"Not *that* one, Dad, the Tug one, like the ball, tell me about the Tugboat, Dad. Tell me about *Tug.*"

Tug McGraw died before Cole first heard this story. I regret ever mentioning the word "died," because now he latches on to the death part, rolling out question after question before I can get to the real story. He asks about heaven and hell and who goes where and who decides, and whether there's a naughty-and-nice list like Santa's, and is hell where Santa gets the coal for the stockings, and is God a man or woman, and how do I know, and is his dead goldfish in heaven. He wonders a lot about a lot of things. He is too young to understand that some questions have no answers.

I do my best to respond and keep it simple so my Tug story comes out a little different each time.

Cole bristles and tells me the only baseball memory he has so far is the welt on his cheekbone from the last time we played, and that it was me who hit him in the face. He claims it was my fault. My twenty-plus years of legal experience argue that he has to accept some responsibility—but I catch myself when I start citing case law, recognizing I cannot win against my six-year-old opponent.

Cole persists, "Dad, just tell me the story. Please!"

It's impossible to say no. "OK, Cole, I'll tell it again. I'm ten and every morning I run out the back door and make a dash for the newspaper lying on the driveway's edge. It's also New Jersey and it can be freezing cold wearing just my tighty-whities. I sprint to read the sports section before everyone else tears the paper apart—or my mother uses it for toilet paper, which she's been known to do in emergencies.

"One morning, I open the paper and see the smiling face of Willie Mays, maybe the greatest player ever, taking up half a page in a huge advertisement for Builders Emporium. Below Willie, in the same ad, there's another player, but his picture is the size of a matchbook cover. His face is so small, it's hard to see. His name is Tug McGraw. I've never heard of him. I'm not interested in Tug McGraw. He's probably there to keep the great Willie Mays company.

"According to the ad, later today the players will be at Builders Emporium on Hamburg Turnpike, signing free autographs. Willie's at the end of his career. This could be my only chance ever to see him. I run upstairs, grab a ball, and draw signature lines in blue ballpoint pen on it. I get ink all over my hand because it's hard to make a straight line on a round ball without pushing my fingers against the ink..."

Cole interrupts. "Dad, why does your mom use the newspaper for toilet paper? That's stupid. And what are tighty-whities?"

I explain that I'm in the middle of the story, but he can't resist asking about the toilet paper.

He looks at me, deep brown eyes laser-beaming the joke that's coming. His smile displays five tooth-fairy dollars' worth of missing choppers. "Does your mom use the sports parts to wipe poop?" He lets out a high-pitched giggle.

Giggling like a kid is a joy I lost long ago. I miss it. I remember uncontrollable laughter when you're supposed to be dead quiet, like in the school library or during the rabbi's long, boring sermons. The librarian would send us to detention or force us to sit in some hidden corner. The rabbi would kick us out of the sanctuary, which was a victory.

I smile and shake my head. "You are a funny man," I say, and turn us back to the story, to the day when, as a determined kid—baseball in hand—I take off on my blue Schwinn Sting-Ray with the banana seat and baseball cards stuck in the spokes. I loved that bike until the day I traded it in for a Schwinn Varsity ten-speed.

"I ride as fast as my legs can take me to Builders Emporium. I don't even get tired riding up the hills, and once I get close, cars are everywhere. I hope they're dads buying supplies for weekend projects and not autograph seekers. Once inside the store, there's a huge line for Willie Mays.

"I walk past shelves filled with tools and try not to look. Tools are not my strength." Richard had screamed and thrown a flathead screwdriver at my head because he demanded a Phillips, and I handed him the wrong one. I had no idea there was a difference, and no one ever bothered to tell me. *Who was Phillips anyway?* I wouldn't dare ask Richard. He told me to get lost, which was a relief.

"From the end of the line, I watch as middle-aged men and women push kids aside and stick armfuls of pictures and buckets of baseballs in Willie's face. Most of the kids my age are with their parents, and their parents don't allow cutting. But more and more adults wearing Mets jerseys push ahead of me, claiming someone was holding their spot or they were in the bathroom. I'm not a kid who cuts in line.

"Even this far back, Willie's irritation is easy to see. There must be one hundred people in line. My gut begins to churn as a feeling of panic creeps over me. The worst thing is to wait for hours in line, and then get shut out. Willie and the Builders Emporium manager are whispering. Willie's patience must be running out. They should have a special line for kids, but that's not happening.

"One other time, I rode my bike to Atkins Chevrolet because Willis Reed, the star center for the New York Knicks—"

"Dad, what's a nick? Did someone cut themselves? Is that when you nicked your finger with the apple and it fell off?"

Laughing, I continue. "You don't forget anything, do you, Cole? No, my apple finger is a whole different story and that wasn't a nick, but a slice. Anyway, Willis Reed's basketball team was called the Knicks, K-n-i-c-k-s, and we waited in line for a long time. Then, while a bunch of us were still waiting, he walked out.

"Since that happened with Willis Reed, I decided not to wait for hours again. So I started to walk toward the exit. I'm thinking about getting on my bike and stopping by Kresge's for a banana split."

Cole stops me yet again, "Dad, a banana split? I love ice cream," he shouts, "Let's get one!" I smile and tell him that Kresge's closed years ago.

"Let me get back to the story. We haven't gotten to the good part." He smiles. I continue. "So, I take the first step toward the exit, when I see a man with a Mets hat sitting alone at a card table in the corner of the garden department. He's near the birdseed and the stinky manure."

"Dad, what's manure?"

"It's cow poop we use to brighten the flowers. I'll explain later."

He seems satisfied, but six-year-olds, like elephants, never forget. I wonder whether it's even true that elephants don't forget.

"I decided to investigate. There's a little name card in front of him that says, 'Tug McGraw.' I'd never heard of him but learned he was a left-handed pitcher. I felt bad he was alone so I walked up to him.

"He asks my name and tells me to sit down. He has a big smile, and I can tell he likes kids and isn't irritated like Willie. Of course, there aren't a million people screaming for his picture. He asks me about my family and about what position I play. He grabs my baseball and rolls it around in his hand like he's getting ready to throw a fastball. He pretends to whip it at me but doesn't let it go. I flinch. I can't help it. I don't like to get hit in the face.

"Tug just laughs, though, and tells me 'Don't worry. I would never hit a kid.' When other kids start to line up, Tug shakes my hand, signs my ball, and writes, 'Good Luck, Steve. Have a great life. Your Friend, Tug McGraw.' He tells me I'm a polite, nice kid. Tug didn't have kids then, but that would change."

I toss the ball back to Cole.

"The end," I say.

"Dad, that's not the end. Keep going."

"All right," I say, "And they all lived happily ever after. That's the end."

"Daaad," he says, "Please."

"OK." I continue where I left off, describing my ten-year-old self running out of Builders Emporium, hopping on my bike, and flying home to show off the signed baseball, not even stopping at Kresge's. "I became a big Tug fan and followed his career through several teams and World Series wins. Turns out, he becomes a great relief pitcher, and soon everyone knows him. He becomes famous for the catch phrase: 'Ya gotta believe!'"

"Dad? Believe in what?"

"That's a big question," I say. "For Tug, it was about belief in his team, belief in himself. It's about staying positive. I cherish the ball Tug signed because Tug treated me like his friend and smiled at me. It was like he knew me, like I was the only one there in the whole store with him. I saved the ball not because he was some superstar—he wasn't then—but because he took the time to talk to me, to make me feel important. He asked my name, wrote it down, and looked me in the eye. The signed ball holds those memories. It's not like a store-bought autograph, but about the thrilling moment you meet the player. The ball is a kind of time machine returning me to the past. Tug made me feel special."

It's getting chilly. Cole asks if he can hold the Tug ball. We head into the house, and for the fiftieth time, I show the signed ball to my kid. The words are now a smudge of blue ink. I can see "September 9," but can't make out the year. No sharpies back then. You can hardly make out Tug's name, but for me, the signature is as vibrant and clear as it was forty years ago.

Cole then informs me, "Dad, you forgot the part about Tug's son." I explain how Tug didn't get to know his own son well until his son was older. I tell him my own father left when I was a kid and we never did play catch. I see Cole is confused.

"Dad, is your Dad dead? How did he die?'

"Cole, one day you'll hear the whole story. Tug's son is like me and went to see his dad when he was a little older. His son became a great country singer named Tim McGraw."

"And you became a lawyer! What will you say when you tell Tug's son the story?" He asks the question as if it's a given we'll connect.

"I'd tell him his dad made me a better person and a better dad, but he didn't help my baseball."

Cole asks if it's OK to use my Tug McGraw ball to play catch. I tell him I'm sure Tug would approve and remind him to keep his eye on the ball. He pretends to take his eye out of its socket and rest it on the stitching.

I chuckle. "Ya gotta believe! Ya gotta believe in yourself."

He giggles. I grab the ball and pretend to whip it at him. Cole doesn't flinch. Instead, he looks and says, "Dad, *throw* the ball. C'mon, I'm right here. I can catch anything you can throw."

I grip the ball tight. Tug's name stares at me in faded blue ink, and I smile. The road to happiness has been bloody. I've been in a civil war with myself for decades.

Cole won't understand, but some kids are taught to swim by expert instructors hired by concerned parents. Others are thrown into the deep end—to drown or survive.

I think of the lifeguards blowing their whistles and then the unusual quiet just before the crash, like the calm before a storm. Sometimes you can sense the oncoming noise in your guts.

Cole's voice brings me back to the present. "Dad, stop messing around and throw the ball. Earth to Dad, c'mon!"

Someday, he'll hear the whole truth. I grip the ball and throw it toward the treetops. Cole takes off. He runs hard and then dives onto the soft green grass. For a moment, the ball disappears under his body. He screams and scrambles to his feet, flashing a smile.

"Dad, ya gotta believe, right?" Cole extends his glove and shows me the ball. He made the catch.

CHAPTER 2

Albany, New York, February 2014

*"It was, of course, a miserable childhood:
the happy childhood is hardly worth your while."*
— Frank McCourt, *Angela's Ashes*

Miserable childhoods produce turbulent adults. It's ironic that the worst memories sometimes provide the best entertainment. Growing up, for me, included an irresistible brand of unique torment that's perfect material for a binge-worthy Netflix series or best-selling beach novel, but lousy for the ones who lived it. When the past catches up, you either crash or find the tools to fight back. Tools weren't my thing as a kid, but now my continuing journey results in five kids, two divorces, and a perfectly imperfect third marriage to my first ever girlfriend. We are happy together, and so far, she seems to accept most of my many quirks.

Looking back, the writer in me appreciates the material created by my somewhat normal beginning and then a series of terrible decisions (not mine) and tragedies that turned our family upside down. For decades, I survived by pushing all emotion into the dark compartment of my mind and refusing to feel a thing—or deciding to feel nothing. Either way, it was what I came to know as "the feeling of no feeling." When reality became unavoidable, it dripped out of my brain, measure by measure, as if there was an IV controlling the recovery rate of repressed memories. Shameful secrets I thought dead and buried were alive and threatening. Action became necessary.

I think back to turning twenty living in Israel on Kibbutz Mizra, confused, alone, and hoping someone could guide me. When around others, my face hid the turmoil churning in my guts like a rogue wave. There was no such thing as a life coach in 1980, and many of the residents were Auschwitz survivors, branded like cattle with numbers on their left forearms. Most kept their distance or didn't speak English, but the sadness in their eyes exposed the pain that never left them.

On the kibbutz, there was a small library where I discovered self-help books like Dale Carnegie's *How to Win Friends and Influence People, and Napoleon Hill's Think and Grow Rich.*

On my one day off, I would find a corner, sit on the floor and read. I carried around a letter from Florida State in the pocket of my blue, kibbutz-issued work shirt informing me I was on academic suspension. Shame prevented me from sharing or processing the news I had flunked out.

One day, reading one of my "underdog overcomes adversity" books, lightning strikes. It hits me that self-help means I need to **help myself.** This seems like common sense, but I'm not sure it ever before connected in my tumultuous mind.

There was no big brother or dad to ask for advice on my future. And I knew I couldn't spend my life looking forward to the Saturday disco nights in the bomb shelter or chasing exotic women trying to get them to make out with me. It was time to wake up and plow ahead.

Living on a kibbutz, driving a tractor, picking fruit, pulling weeds, working six days a week, gave me time to think. That was decades ago. Today, they call it meditation. For me, my brain slowed enough and I decided to become an Israeli citizen and join the IDF. I wanted to fight for the survivors around me, to fight for myself, and to get a cool uniform with a beret to wear. The kibbutz-issued clothes resemble Americana prison garb.

My path changed though when I returned to school and earned my degree. Still, there was that moment, when you realize no one can do it for you...and no relationship will work until you decide to find help.

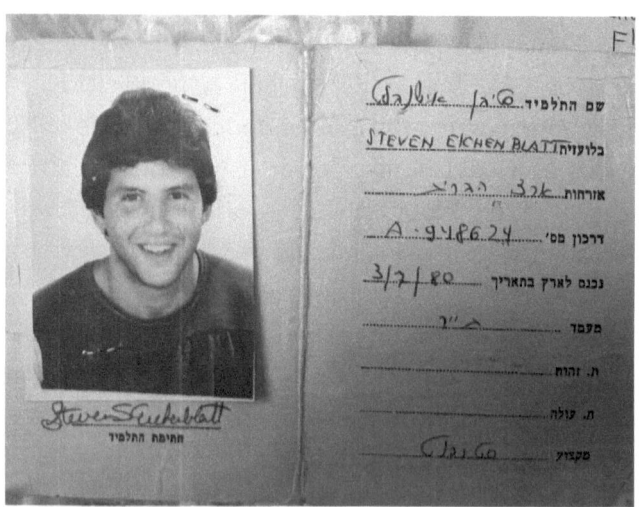

***

One night, I leave my home in sunny Orlando and board a plane bound for snowy Albany, New York. A few weeks back, I'd called a psychologist friend after another relationship ended with a partner telling me I'm "disconnected" and "incapable of emotional intimacy." More than once, I've been asked whether there has been sexual abuse. Two divorces and another breakup must mean someone is doing something wrong.

My friend recommends an evaluation with a leading expert in intensive psychotherapy. The psychologist is a well-known author who teaches at a university medical school. I am tired of being told I have no feelings. *Feeling nothing is a feeling, isn't it?* Regular therapy never works for me. I need an exorcist to get rid of the bad shit stuck in my brain. Desperation is flying to Albany in the dead of winter—voluntarily—to see a shrink.

***

The therapist's office is located in a small blue cottage on an Albany side street. My morning arrival means walking through snow covered sidewalks in my running shoes, and I've underestimated just how cold it gets in upstate New York. When I open the cottage door, a bell chimes announcing my arrival. After a few minutes, the inner door opens, and I hear a woman's sharp, confident voice tell me to come in.

Dr. Pearson greets me with little fanfare and points to a chair. She has a commanding presence and doesn't initiate small talk. She sits across from me in a nondescript skirt and blouse and tells me to "get comfortable." She explains the process and asks permission to tape the session for later use. I make some stupid comment about a sex tape, but she doesn't laugh. Bad start for me.

Dr. Pearson says, "The number one rule is to tell the truth. Transparency here is absolute because otherwise, you're wasting my time and your money."

For the first time, my eyes meet hers, which appear blue but are partially hidden behind reading glasses. She asks, "Do you always try to make jokes when you're nervous? You're nervous, right?"

I squeeze my hands and respond without thinking, "No, I'm great. Not nervous. All good."

I look downward to avoid her intense gaze. She's right, I'm nervous. Admitting it makes me feel weak. I lie instead.

"Steve, I have asked you two easy questions and you're not telling me the truth. We are less than two minutes into the session. You may think you're just lying to me, but that's not the point. You're lying to yourself."

Dr. Pearson isn't going to let me bullshit my way through this. She sees right through me. My limited charm will not work here.

My eyes again search the floor. She nails me with the hard truth. I'm always trying to defend myself. Everything feels like a personal attack. Even as a defense lawyer, other attorneys complain that I take things personally. This is a great trait when fighting for clients, but a terrible way to live—and to treat the people close to you. The chip on my shoulder grows larger.

She continues, "Of course you're nervous. That wasn't a trick question. You've made little eye contact since we met, you keep pulling at your jacket sleeves, and you don't know what to do with your hands. Now try to relax. You're here for a reason, and I need the truth. Be vulnerable and cut the macho act. It's time to let it go."

Dr. Pearson doesn't know about Richard's pathetic manhood code: Real men don't show weakness, never cry, and must be tough. His words remain tattooed on my brain. Feelings are forbidden.

The therapist stares in silence, her readers now pushed down to the bridge of her nose, urging me to share. Her gaze packs an energy stronger than words, while the rest of her face has no distinct expression. The noise in my brain betrays the quiet that has embraced the room. This is uncomfortable. I'm dripping sweat and feel anxiety fighting to become a full-blown panic attack. I ask to use the bathroom and she points with a knowing look. I splash my face with cold water and return.

She has my attention. I straighten up and focus. For hours, we talk about my childhood. She's like a champion marathoner who never changes her pace or shows fatigue. The woman barely blinks. I find myself sharing stories that have been buried or forgotten for forty years. After five brutal hours without a break, we reach the day in 1977 that decades of anger turned into violence.

"Tell me about that day, Steve."

Years of attempting therapy and considering exorcism have yielded no results, but now the collaborative process where therapist and patient are both engaged somehow makes sense. My hope is that this doctor will be different from my past therapists, whose potpourri-scented offices overwhelmed my sense of smell while their white noise machines drowned out the Led Zeppelin songs that my mind plays to help me cope with stress. Not much makes me more anxious than sitting in the waiting room of a therapist's office, praying no one will recognize me. To be fair, though, the urologist is pretty awkward.

We plow ahead. My arms tense up as I wrap them around my stomach. The quiet thickens as my clammy hands become clenched fists. Dr. Pearson continues to peel through the layers of scar tissue that protect me. My discomfort makes me fidget as I sit, exposed and stuck. The anxiety increases as I push away the feeling of claustrophobia trying to trap me.

I take a deep breath. Inside my mind, a pressure valve releases and I decide to trust this therapist and let almost everything out. *After all, this is one and done, and I will never see her again. Plus, she listens and challenges me to be open. I paid a lot of money to freeze my ass off in Albany so maybe it's time to grow up and concentrate on getting something out of this. Maybe I will actually listen to her and try to engage in the process. Stay connected...*

A story emerges that has been hidden for the last forty years. I explain that Richard adopted me when my father disappeared, and we eventually moved to Florida. She says we will get to everything later and tells me, "Just focus on what happened that day in 1977."

"Well, I lost my mind and beat the shit out of him is what happened. I clearly left my brain so my body could bloody him and shut him up for good. My six brothers and sisters all stood nearby watching, too shocked to move."

I look over at the therapist, expecting a surprised look on her face. She's ice, her face frozen without expression, and I consider some clever quip to humor her but realize that's what she expects. Maybe she is an exorcist, because there's some deep shit pouring out of my mouth. I can't believe it's my voice, but I accept that this is finally about me—and she isn't judging. She just nods for me to continue.

"I managed to get Richard under me. He's my legal father, but I refused to call him Dad. I had Richard on the ground and blood began flowing downstream from his broken nose. Drops even managed to land on my hand, now wrapped around his throat. Eventually, his movement began to slow, but he was still breathing.

"I was so angry, but I'd kept this anger hidden for decades. It probably started the day Richard showed up like a stray dog with his litter of puppies. That moment was particularly confusing, since I already had a father. I guess I'll be discussing *that* whole story with you later."

She nods. "Keep going. You were strangling Richard."

"It's hard to explain, but I was a spectator watching my hands as they squeezed his neck and he started to gasp for air. It was like my hands were doing the work and I stood by, feeling nothing and not caring what was happening. My speedometer had gone past anger into the zone of nothingness."

Taking a break, I glance again toward Dr. Pearson. Her face seems unchanged, but I detect a hint of sadness in her eyes. She tilts her head in an almost imperceptible encouraging motion.

Then she whispers, "Describe Richard. What does he look like? What's he wearing? What details come to mind?"

I look at her, then close my eyes.

"Old Spice. Richard smelled like Old Spice, the kind everyone's grandfather used to wear. It's weird, but I just remembered his smell. He was a lion marking his territory with Old Spice instead of urine. His voice was loud, in that Brooklyn way, so he was easy to hear. He was tall enough not to be considered short, but not as tall as he claimed. I'm guessing five-eight or five-nine, but I never asked. He liked expensive clothes, and his wallet was always stuffed with cash. Of course he wore a Rolex, but I'm not sure when he got it."

I pause and look at the therapist.

"Continue, Steve."

This is hard. I feel a warm sensation like my blood pressure's rising. My heart begins to speed up, anger starts to energize me, and I feel a sword of hatred pressed into my right hand. *Or is my left the sword hand?*

"Richard was tough. He had the angry, irate energy of a furious man who did not want to be bothered or touched. He walked and talked like he was moments from beating someone up. He mocked everyone around him. He was the anti-Dale Carnegie.

"He had blue eyes, with a gap-toothed grimace and broken nose. He looked like an old, bald boxer. Behind his back, we called him 'bald eagle.' I don't think he ever found out. He was a bully but had friends who loved his sarcastic humor and biting wit. Even I can admit, looking back, that he could be funny."

I stop and look up at Dr. Pearson. She tells me to keep going.

"Richard was still bigger than me, but at seventeen, I was getting stronger and would soon be much taller. He always underestimated me, and now he would pay. His suffering made me fight even harder. No one had ever before dared to fight him back. He seemed shocked that it was me who threw the first punch. I caught him by surprise. Then, I tackled him. When Mom's screams became primal, Mark, one of my three brothers, tried to pull me away. I released his throat, and all I could feel then was my own heart racing. Even now, my heart races. Fuck—the anger is returning."

Dr. Pearson interrupts me. "Steve, look at your hands. They were around his neck, right?"

I nod. "Yes, until Mark pulled me back. He saved me from myself. I love him like you would a biological brother: We don't distinguish bloodlines in our family. You know, Mark and I have never spoken of the fight... never."

"Forget about that part. What if Mark *hadn't* pulled you back? What would you have done? *Your hands were on his throat.* Predators kill their prey by pouncing on their jugular veins, squeezing their necks and choking them to death. You were going to kill Richard, weren't you?"

I consider this. It's a surprising question, one that had never before entered my mind.

I look over, then to the floor as the truth catches me by surprise.

Her gaze penetrates. "Steve. Would you have killed him?"

Suddenly my heartbeat picks up and anxiety from years past floods me as I relive the fight. This happened forty years ago, but the details are as clear as yesterday. I can still hear the contempt in Richard's thick New York accent as he calls me a loser. "You'll never amount to anything," he crows. His death might have landed me in prison, but at least the world—and I—would no longer have to tolerate him.

As a lawyer, I know that if this happened today, the new self-defense or domestic abuse laws might help me. However, this occurred in 1977. The laws were different, and physical discipline from parents and authority figures was often unquestioned. Many fathers took the belt out to inflict pain. And now, decades later, I'm trying to decide whether my goal had been to kill mine.

Again, I consider the question. Richard's skin still feels stuck under my fingernails. I can still smell his Old Spice. His head was covered with freckles and craters that looked like sunburn. Sweat covered the top where hair once grew as his brain seemed to throb under the exposed skin.

The therapist says, "Steven, you promised the truth. You know the answer and you're afraid to tell me. What is it? Think about it." My mind is mush. Five hours and counting.

The room is silent, but the voice inside my pounding head won't shut up. *The fucker deserved to die, but would I have killed him? It's stunning that the mere mention of him still changes my energy and demeanor. I wasn't born to be a violent, hate-filled teenager. It all happened so fast.*

I finally speak out loud. "He... he always told me, 'You're not tough enough to be a fighter. You're not tough enough to be a man.'" My own voice is unrecognizable as it cracks. "He lives on in my head, unleashing poisonous thoughts. I guess everyone thinks they could have been better. It's not like he wrecked my chances to become a professional football player, though I had some talent. But he did destroy any confidence I once had and kept me fearful and assuming I deserved the worst. Turns out, he was wrong about the fighting."

The therapist interrupts. "You're struggling. Let's take a break and you can answer the question when we return."

Half smiling through my daze of memories, I nod and stand. She has already dragged far more history out of me than any of the therapists I've seen over the years. Some trauma is buried so deep, it's taken me years to figure out if the event actually happened or is merely a fictional story. Denial has been a coping strategy that has kept me safe from the reality of the trauma. Now the only safe path is sharing my secrets. But it's agonizingly hard.

It's a good time for a break. I push open the door and feel the chilly air embrace me.

***

No one in Albany knows me. Every close female relationship I've ever had, including two marriages, has imploded. My first girlfriend, Melissa (Missy), who I dated as a senior in college, told me years later she knew something was wrong. I never spoke about my childhood or allowed myself to be vulnerable. I don't like to be touched, and letting anyone get emotionally close was impossible. Missy was perceptive enough to recognize there was baggage and always suspected I was the victim of sexual abuse. She had the abuse part right.

My sleep was lousy last night. I had no idea what was going to happen. This morning, I let the hot shower pound my head. When it was time to step out, I switched the water to its coldest setting, gasping for air when the freezing stream hit me, then grabbing a towel. Drying off, I was afraid to look in the mirror. I'm almost sixty, fit, and athletic. For years, running has been my therapy, and I work hard to stay lean. Still, when I dropped the towel, I couldn't make eye contact with myself. My fear? That the reflection would reveal a husky, sad boy with a David Cassidy haircut, the same boy wearing the faded football jersey pedaling away from a bloody car crash. He's the kid who lives within me and needs protection.

During our break, I head for a coffee shop. My body is drenched with sweat even though the temperature is below freezing. The crunch of my sneakers on the ice-lined sidewalk reminds me of predawn mornings when Richard would wake us up to shovel snow off our driveway. He never shoveled; he supervised from the warmth of his running car while we breathed in his exhaust. He did teach us the value of hard work, even though we had no choice.

Thinking back to the fight still causes my heart to pound. My biological father chose not to protect his children. In nature, lions kill to protect their cubs. They jump their prey by chomping down on the victim's jugular vein. I'm a father now, with five children of my own. There's no question, I would kill to protect my kids. A father's true love is a force field that should be impenetrable. My thoughts turn again to the damaged boy inside. *Am I too damaged to feel love?*

My behavior the day I fought Richard was not what anyone expected from me—a quiet, shy teenage boy who spent hours reading books in the closet and staying out of the target zone. I was never a troublemaker. But the stranger living inside my skin was much tougher and stronger than anyone ever imagined— including me. That husky kid is a survivor.

Leaving the coffee shop, I'm determined to finish the session. Walking back to the office, the pieces in my brain start to fit back together. It's like the moment when you're working on a jigsaw puzzle and you realize just where those last few pieces belong. Dr. Pearson waits for me, already seated in her solid, wingback chair, legs crossed with perfect posture.

She smiles and welcomes me back. I notice the reading glasses are resting on her chest, attached to a silver chain that reminds me of my fifth grade teacher. She claps her hands.

"Steve, you with me? Focus! Back to the question, Steve. Do you kill him or let him go?"

I smile and joke, "You mean like The Clash's song? Should I stay or should I go?"

She stares and doesn't crack a smile.

My mind wanders. I need to focus.

She doesn't know that I'm haunted by two different dead fathers who both stare with bloodied faces, bad memories burned into my brain. She doesn't yet know that a year or so before the fight with Richard, I saved my biological father's life. She doesn't know that when one father died, his failed heart was broken by hate, while the other died of a heart broken by love. It's sad that hate won while both were alive.

I speak with confidence now, and my voice is strong. "KILL HIM. I should have killed him. That's the answer. He deserved to die."

She doesn't seem surprised, and in a gentle voice, says, "OK, Steve, then just do it. Kill him. Take me through it step by step.

Tell me what you would have done if your brother hadn't stopped you. I want you to feel it."

This is new.

I look at her and she nods that it's OK. My mind takes me back to that moment when I had my hands around his throat. "I push my brother away and regain my grip. I squeeze Richard's throat as hard as possible. I keep my hands coiled around him until he stops flopping and becomes... still. He's no longer moving; it's... over." My eyes close and I fight tears. *Tears of sadness? Tears of joy?* I feel my heart pounding, and then listen as my breathing begins to slow. I open my eyes and look at the therapist.

She lets me absorb the moment. She nods and asks how I feel.

I think through what just happened, then stop thinking as some emotion finally breaks through. *Forty fucking years consumed by anger and hate for this man—that's what fuels the energy necessary to end this. I see the teenage boy disappear.*

I nod and embrace the moment. "He deserved to die. He was such a fucking bastard."

She nods back. "Now you'll need to release him from your mind and bury him. Give yourself closure by sinking him deep into the past, under the earth so he disappears. I want you to picture the hole, to feel the weight of the earth you pile on top of him. How far down will you bury him?"

I see it in my mind. "He's at the bottom of the Grand Canyon, under the Colorado river. A place so deep, you can no longer hear his voice. Maybe even the Everglades where the gators can gnaw at his bones. His payback for moving us to Florida."

I meet her gaze, and then close my eyes. Breathing deep, I nod my head as if agreeing with my own decision. And he's gone.

I smile but am no longer nervous. Dr. Pearson has freed something inside me, released the chokehold Richard had on me all these years. I've been his prisoner, caged in an emotional cell, and I'm now free to move past him. Maybe his voice will disappear from my mind forever.

Maybe.

"Now that I've killed him off, it's time to figure out who I might have been if my first father had remained my dad."

Dr. Pearson asks, "What does Steven really want?"

Meeting her gaze, I respond, "I want to feel something, I want to feel love. That way, I can give it."

She smiles as I leave her office. My mind feels lighter, and my body relaxes. Richard can no longer hurt me. His loud voice, once mocking me, goes silent. I've killed him. And buried him. *And* he's dead. He's nothing. Nothing. The feeling of no feeling must be what killers feel. It's like a page with no words, or a wall without color, a blank slate of nothingness.

Goodbye, Richard.

CHAPTER 3

Apple Finger: West Orange, New Jersey, 1965

Mom and Dad are asleep. The only sounds are the hum of the refrigerator and my socks slipping along the hallway floor. I'm careful not to fall, because my parents made me promise to stay in bed until they got up. I'm always the first to wake, so I try to remember to keep quiet. Mom says Robert looks up to me because I'm six, so I shouldn't teach him to get up early. He's three, though, so I'm taller and he *has* to look up to me.

Sometimes I run down the hallway and slide like I'm ice skating. Mom doesn't like it. Sometimes Dad takes us to skate for real when the lakes freeze. Dad isn't around much these days because he works a lot, and Mom gets mad. He hasn't taken us skating for a long time.

Once, I fell and hit my head on the table. Mom was happy the table wasn't broken but was mad because I had to get stitches. Dad is an animal doctor and said he could stitch me up the same way he does the animals. He tried but Mom said his stitches looked crooked and brought me to the hospital. It took a long time, but not as long as the time I drank liquid aspirin and my stomach had to get pumped. That was bad, because first Dad tried to get me to puke by sticking his finger down my throat. There was a lot of yelling.

Mom says I don't pay attention, and that's why I get in trouble. She tells me I'm spacey, but being a spaceman is cool. My mind wanders a lot, and sometimes I think about what happens next instead of what's happening now, so it seems like I'm not paying attention. My body doesn't always keep up with my brain and sometimes my brain isn't in the same place as my body. That's when trouble happens.

This morning I hear the newspaperman's brakes squeak as he stops before each stoop. The car grumbles louder as he gets closer. I have never seen his face, just his arm when I peek out the window and watch him pitch the papers. He is deadeye accurate with his throws, except for Sundays when the paper is too big to toss. On Sundays, he has a kid helper who takes each paper and runs like he's going to score a touchdown. I am a sports kid and love it when someone is around to play catch. Sometimes my grandfather comes over and tries to throw, but usually it's my grandmother or Mom. My parents haven't let me start Little League yet, even though I'm six. Dad doesn't play sports with us. He said he played baseball once, but he hasn't with me. I don't believe it. He did buy me a Mickey Mantle Louisville Slugger Little League bat and claims someday he will show me how to swing level. Otherwise, he would play catch, so maybe he doesn't know how. Or maybe he's embarrassed because he throws like a girl?

When I'm up super-duper early, the milkman is still making deliveries. He doesn't come to our house. Mom says it is too expensive, and that's OK because I hate milk—except when it's chocolate. The milk truck says "Van Paulen Dairy." I can hear the glass bottles being placed in our neighbor's metal milk box.

During Christmas time, I've seen pee-colored milk delivered. My mom says this is eggnog, which Jews aren't allowed to drink. Mom says Jews don't believe in Christmas, so Santa doesn't bring us presents. Mom also says we are God's chosen people, but she never says what we're chosen to do. We have a lot of rules about things we can't do and food we can't eat. I don't pay much attention to the rules.

Besides, we don't have a fireplace. I wonder how Santa knows which families are Jewish. Mom says that's why we put a candle holder with eight candles in our window, but Butterfly our cat knocked it over, so now it's broken. Maybe Santa will show up anyway this year.

I'm hungry, but no one else is awake. Lori and I are twins. Mom tried once to dress us up in the same clothes, which is stupid. Some people think we are identical, but she has girl parts. Lori cries a lot and I never cry, so Mom spends most of her time with Lori. She says Lori is more demanding, and I never ask for anything. Mom gets mad because she thinks I don't know my ABCs.

We live in a garden apartment. I don't understand why it's called that; the only flowers are dandelions growing in the cracks of the walkway. My friend Patrick never steps on the cracks because he says that's how you break your mother's back. I step on the cracks sometimes to see what happens, but my mom's back seems fine. Besides, I don't want to hurt her.

I like to play with the bugs that live in the dirt, but Dad gets mad when I bring them inside. He knows a lot about bugs, even though he's an animal doctor. Once he brought home a tick in a jar that jumped on him from a dog. My mom yelled at him but he must not have heard her. He said they carry diseases and he had to go to the hospital when one crawled under his skin.

Mom tells me every night not to get out of bed until she wakes up because she worries I am going to open the door and let some scary murderer in the apartment. Dad tells the story of some guy with an axe who killed a bunch of kids. Some kid didn't listen to his parents and let the guy in the house. That kid lost his head, and no one ever found it. I'm not sure it's a true story.

Dad told the same story when we went on our Cub Scout overnight camping trip. When I ask Dad how much blood there was and whether their heads got cut off, he always has different answers. Plus, he says *axe* one time and *hatchet* another, and my friend Patrick's dad tells the same story only it's a *sword*. Adults are always trying to scare us so we behave.

I'm not sure it counts as camping, since Dad locked himself in the car. We could see him sucking on his Camels enough to create a red glow from the ashes. He'd crack his window to tamp the ashes on the ground while the cigarette smoke circulated through the camping area. His radio was playing Frank Sinatra and Andy Williams. I waited for him to come inside the tent like the other dads, but he didn't. It was scary to sleep alone because some axe or hatchet or sword murderer might be waiting outside the tent.

Eventually, I fell asleep dreaming about the dead kid's head being used as a bowling ball at T-Bowl, the bowling alley next to Dad's animal hospital. When Mom discovers that Dad slept in his car, she stares with the same look of disgust she gets when she catches him sneaking a smoke. Mom is easy to read. Her facial expressions range from smiles to frowns to anger, and the worst is disgust.

Dad told Mom it wasn't his fault I was scared, and that I should have knocked on the car door. He said, "He has to be tougher; it was just a story. How is he going to learn to be a man if he's scared of a silly story?"

Mom said, "You don't understand your own son. He wants you to act like the other dads. He wants attention. You never spend time with your own son."

I told Mom the Cub Scouts weren't for me anyway and the uniform is stupid. She let me quit right after the camping trip. Most Sundays, we drive forty minutes to Bayonne to visit Dad's parents. They live in a tiny apartment that Mom says should be knocked down because it's old and it smells. Mom and Dad always argue about who's driving. Dad tells Mom she drives too fast and will get us killed. Then Mom yells because Dad drives too slowly and is going to get us killed. Since they both are going to get us killed, I say we shouldn't go, but that gets ignored. My dad's dad Pappa Charley drives a bus, so maybe he can drive us. Pappa Charley is fun and sometimes he burps to make me laugh. Once he took me on his routes in Jersey City and Newark. He always tells all the passengers I'm his grandson.

My parents can't hear us when they're fighting. Sometimes they fight about Mom's parents, Nana Ruth and Pappa Ben. Other times, they fight about Grandma Annie and Pappa Charley. They yell until they get tired. Then they grow quiet the way songs slow down on Dad's record player, until all you hear is the static of the needle scratching the grooves. Dad will light a cigarette and then the smoking argument starts. Mom says smoking is disgusting and she doesn't care if he wants to kill himself. Dad says she sounds like a broken record. I think that's funny, since Dad loves his record player and records. I once asked, "Dad, if a record is broken, then what does it even sound like?" He tried to explain that she keeps telling him the same thing over and over.

Sometimes we go to Nana Ruth and Pappa Ben's fancy country club. We're forced to dress up and are paraded around like we're in a dog show. Nana says things like, "Oh, don't you love his chubby red apple cheeks? Aren't they delicious?" or she says, "He's one of the twins. Don't he and Lori look identical?" My cheeks are always sore because Nana squeezes them each time we meet someone new, and then demands that her friends squeeze, too. The parts of my face that aren't sore get smeared with shades of red lipstick from all the fake kisses.

Once, we went to the club and Nana Ruth gave me a tongue sandwich. I loved it until Lori told me it was real cow tongue. I didn't believe her but the next time Nana offered me tongue, I peeked under the rye bread and the tongue looked like a tongue. Lori was right. I never ate a tongue sandwich again.

Grandma Annie, my dad's mom, is always giving us dead whitefish with their heads still attached. Sometimes the eyes stare at me but I try not to stare back. We always go to their apartment and I eat whatever Grandma Annie tells me to, because she won't let me have her fresh, hot cinnamon cookies if my plate isn't empty.

This morning, I might as well go look for the newspaper or sneak into the kitchen and see what I can eat without Mom catching me. We are not allowed in the kitchen unless Mom or Dad are around. Mom doesn't want us eating her Hostess Cup Cakes or drinking Yoo-hoo for breakfast. I know all her hiding spots and will check for candy bars. She says we have to eat a healthy breakfast like apples or bananas or some boring cereal like bran flakes or cornflakes. I beg her to buy Cap'n Crunch or Cocoa Puffs, but she says those are bad for me. The bad cereals taste good and the good ones have no taste. My mom also thinks I'm going to turn on the stove and burn down the house or set Robert on fire.

Robert is three years younger than me, which makes him three years and eleven minutes younger than Lori, who is eleven minutes older than me. Dad tells me I'm a gentleman because when I was inside my mom, I let my sister leave first. He says I took so long that the doctor almost closed the hatch. He said we almost forgot you were there. I'm not so sure I was being nice to Lori by letting her climb out first. I may have pushed her. I don't remember living inside Mom, but when Robert lived there, we could feel his kicks.

We all lived in Michigan until a year ago. I was almost five when we moved. Dad went to school at Michigan State and all three of us were born in a town called East Lansing.

I was just a baby when I was born, so I don't remember much. Mom says it was a big deal when my dad graduated because he won some award for having the best grades. Dad studied all the time and even when we were born, Mom says he was studying. She says it was hard for her to take care of us since she was only twenty-one.

When Dad stopped studying, Mom had a party, and he became an animal doctor. Then we got on an airplane. I remember my ears hurt when we landed. We got out in New Jersey, the Garden State. I had my fifth birthday in our garden apartment without a garden.

One time, Dad gave me this cool James Bond 007 gun. Mom didn't want me to have a gun, but it wasn't even real. I lost the gun in this huge dirt pile but I couldn't tell anyone where I lost it because then I would get in trouble for being there alone, getting dirty, bringing dirt in the house, and of course, losing the gun. Then my parents would fight about me having the gun in the first place.

Guns make Mom nervous, because she was never a soldier like my dad. He was in the army and was in France, but didn't get to kill anyone. Pappa Charley killed bad guys in the war, but we aren't allowed to say anything. His two brothers died on a beach in France. They were fighting and Charley went looking for them and both had died. I've seen pictures of Pappa Charley in his Marine uniform with a big gun.

Once Mom got mad when we went to the store and she told me to watch Robert while she went to the bathroom. I got distracted and lost sight of him. Mom got mad and said I never pay attention and am just like Dad. That made me proud, even if she was mad.

My stomach makes hunger noises. Butterfly, our cat, tiptoes down the hallway. I can hear her paws hitting the floor. Dad says the black markings on her white fur look like a butterfly. I think they look like a black blob of nothing.

We used to have a goldfish, but I fed it to Butterfly by accident. It was a mistake even if it was on purpose. I just wanted to introduce them since they are both pets. Once I realized Butterfly wasn't playing, I was able to get the fish out of her mouth. Dad tried to put his mouth on the fish's lips and blow air in to save him because he is an animal doctor and good at saving things, but it didn't work. I saw this with my own eyes, but Mom says I made it up because my father doesn't kiss anything.

Dad even treats horses, and sometimes lions from the zoo. Mom says he is the only one in the whole state who can save the big animals when they are sick. Sometimes my dad gets bitten and comes home with bandages. She seems proud that he gets called if the circus is in town and one of the animals is sick. We even have a picture of him with a lion.

Still, he didn't save the fish. I thought about crying because I felt sad. My dad says the fish is happy swimming in fish heaven, even though I saw him flush it down the toilet. The fish did not look happy; it looked dead. Besides, heaven isn't in the toilet bowl.

I'm really hungry. Dad is snoring, and Mom is asleep. She just rolled over. She wakes up at even the softest sounds, and if she sees me, she'll force me back to the room I share with Lori. I am six and don't like sharing with a girl.

It's boring being the only one awake. When the milkman leaves and the newspaper gets delivered, it's too quiet. Sometimes I play my own game of hide and seek, which is not easy to do. Or I play army and shoot the bad guys. One time, the noise of my gun woke Mom and she told me I was a crazy kid and needed to go to bed. I shot her with my finger gun, which had no bullets.

My stomach keeps growling. I better get some food. In the kitchen, there's a fruit bowl with apples and bananas above the drawer where Mom keeps the silverware. I'm not in the mood for a banana. They make the insides of my ears itch. Dad says I was a monkey before I became a kid, and monkeys like to scratch themselves. I'm pretty sure I was never a monkey. He worked with sick monkeys that bite. I don't bite unless Lori gets me super mad.

Dad makes jokes sometimes but almost never laughs. When he does, he sounds like he's swallowed a box of rocks. He must be out of practice. Mom says smoking makes his throat hurt, so he doesn't laugh much. Still, sometimes the other dads will be outside smoking and laughing loud enough for us to hear in the apartment. Dad never goes out to join them. He says he likes animals more than people.

Mom tells him to smoke outside because one day he'll burn down the apartment and we'll all die. Moms are big on death. Mine always thinks we are going to get hit by a car or drink laundry detergent and die. Even her hair has died. It's red, but my dad says it's really black and she "dies" it. I don't know how hair dies. Everyone says Mom's pretty, and once I overheard a man say she has "big boobs," though I thought he said "boots," which didn't make sense because she doesn't wear boots.

When I asked Dad about this he just laughed and said, "Son, someday you'll understand."

Understand what? That she has big boots?

Dad has brown hair and is tall, according to my mom who is tall for a woman, according to Dad. He looks like a scarecrow because he's so skinny, and his hair always sticks up all over. Grandma Annie says he doesn't eat much because he's too busy smoking or drinking coffee. She says things in Yiddish when she doesn't want me to understand. The red apple in the fruit bowl is shiny and doesn't look real. Nana Ruth has fake apples in a bowl, and once I thought they were real. I don't understand why anyone wants fake apples. When I tried to bite one, my grandmother grabbed it out of my hand and told me I would quickly die and that would upset my sister.

Mom won't even know I've eaten this apple until it's too late. If Mom were awake, she'd cut this apple into small slices and remove the skin. I like the skin, but it can get caught in my teeth and make me spend the whole day with my finger in my mouth trying to get it out. Mom loves to cut everything into little pieces. She worries a big piece will choke us to death. She cuts our hot dogs into a million pieces. Death is always looming.

Mom will be happy if I eat the apple because apples keep the doctor away. I go back to my parents' door and listen, hoping to hear the toilet flushing, but they're still asleep. I check her hiding spots again: no chocolate.

I don't feel like waiting. The apple is so red and shiny and juicy looking. My dad says the apples come from trees a few miles away. I have never seen an apple tree.

I'm standing at the edge of the kitchen where the wood floor ends and the white floor begins. The kitchen floor is important to Mom because she's always washing it with soap and telling us to keep it clean and stay off it. I can't wait to bite into a sweet apple.

I look over at the bowl again, and step onto the white tile. I hear the patter of tiny feet and freeze. Suddenly, I feel the fur rubbing against my pajamas and can hear Butterfly purring. I reach down to pet her. She stares at me with eyes like green marbles. She must be hungry, too.

Butterfly licks herself with her sandpaper tongue. When she licks me, it feels scratchy and dry. The fruit bowl is close. I am not allowed in here without Mom. She always complains about how she can't move around and feels like we are standing on top of her when we're all in the kitchen at the same time. There's a small wooden plaque over the sink that says "Elaine's Kitchen."

I open the drawer where Mom keeps the knives. She always tells us not to touch them because we can cut ourselves and die. But I'm just going to cut a small piece. I pull a couple of knives out of the drawer and try to decide which one to use. The silver shines across my eyes from the bigger knife with ridges and bumps along the blade. I think Mom uses this one for bread. It's longer than my whole arm. The other knife is smaller and Dad uses it to cut steak. I don't know which knife to use to cut the apple. I don't even know which hand to use.

Mom doesn't know if I'm a lefty or righty. Lori uses her right hand for everything. My teacher says using both hands means you have two brains, even if you don't have two heads, and that means you're smarter. He tried to get me to write with my right hand and realized I was bad as a lefty but worse as a righty. My handwriting is sort of backwards. I swing a baseball bat righty and lefty. Forks go in my left. I throw righty. When I'm sitting, I do everything lefty.

Knives confuse me. I need to figure it out right now. With one knife in each hand I imagine I'm a pirate using the knives as swords, getting ready to fight Captain Hook from *Peter Pan*. Mom wants me to be Peter Pan for Halloween, but I want to be a pirate with swords and a pirate hat.

Butterfly nudges me again and I put the knives back into the drawer. I'm scared I'll get caught, but part of me talks in my head and says to go ahead and don't be a scared baby. I can cut the apple so fast Mom won't know. I stop and listen. Mom and Dad are still asleep.

My hand pulls open the drawer. I'm going to use whichever knife my hand touches first. My fingers grip a handle and I pull out the big, long bumpy one. I hear cars outside starting their engines as the neighbor dads leave for work. I'd better hurry.

I grip the apple, squeezing it hard, while resting the long shiny blade against the spot where I will make my first cut.

I press down with all my strength. Dad does it this way at Thanksgiving when he cuts the turkey. I am surprised how easy it is to cut through the apple's skin. It worked. Now all I have to do is make another cut.

But this time the knife slips.

Ouch! I drop the apple.

I'm in trouble. Mom's floor is no longer white.

I scream, realizing I have cut off more than a chunk of apple. The whole top of my finger is on the floor!

My finger burns and blood is pouring all over my mom's clean kitchen and my new Batman and Robin pajamas—the ones I promised to keep clean—and I'm still screaming. There is a chunk of meat on the floor that used to be attached to my finger! Blood is everywhere.

I just wanted an apple.

Lori is the first to come into the kitchen, and she screams like it is her fingertip floating down the red river on the floor.

Dad walks out to see why my sister is screaming. I shut up.

Mom bursts into the kitchen, looks at the floor and says, "Allen, help him!"

Dad tells her to calm down and jumps into action. He grabs my hand and puts my finger under the cold water while he tells my mom to get ice. He wraps my finger with the tip together in a bandage around my finger and tells me to raise my hand high. I am afraid to look but can't help but see the bloody pulp where my fingertip used to be. A piece of the mangled tip still hangs from the bone.

Mom keeps saying my name over and over. "Steven, Steven, Steven, what have you done now?" I am pretty certain she knows the answer so I don't answer.

Dad doesn't talk. He is calm and just keeps pressing the tip to the rest of my finger. My heart calms down a little. The pain isn't as bad. It's nice to have him near me.

"Dad," I say, "I'm really hungry." I see a slight smile on his face but he just shakes his head.

Dad and I jump into his car and we drive to the hospital. He doesn't even light a cigarette on the drive and keeps telling me to hold my finger together in the bandage and keep pressing the ice on it.

At the emergency room, the doctor asks what happened, and Dad explains. The doctor tells me how lucky I am that my dad knew what to do, because I might have lost my finger. I'm not sure how I could lose it since it was right there on the floor. He gives me a shot to numb my finger and then sews the piece back on the top. He says he's unsure if it will work right. I lose all feeling in the tip. I never do get to eat breakfast.

Dad and I go back to the car. I'm still wearing my Batman pajamas. He pulls something out of his pocket. It must be a cigarette. He throws it to me and I catch it. It's the apple.

This is not the last time blood will connect us.

CHAPTER 4

A Fish Tale, 1966–67

Dad shows me an old picture of him holding a big fish. There's no joy, not even a little smile on his face. The fish looks happier than he does.

Dad does take me fishing on occasion, but he mostly reads the newspaper and smokes cigarettes. We haven't gone for a long time because he works almost every day saving animals—and not just pets. He saved a porcupine once and gave us some of the arrows that come shooting out of its body.

Today we are fishing for the first time since I turned eight. Dad was going to take me on my birthday, but someone's dog got smashed by a car. That was a few months ago. Lori doesn't fish, and Robert's too young. Mom worries Dad doesn't pay attention and Robert will fall in the water.

Dad takes me to Pompton Lake, which has a waterfall that crashes over a dam into a swirling pool below. The lake is near our house at the end of Colfax Road. I rode my Sting-Ray here once, but Mom hates it because there have been accidents, and she says kids like me who don't pay attention wind up smashed on the side of the road. We see cars slide off the road during winter. I haven't seen a crash when there wasn't snow or ice on the ground.

When we fish, we stand close to the waterfall, where the mist sprays down and we hear the roaring water pounding over the rocks, rumbling forward toward the base where we stand. Some days the foam at the bottom turns gray, but today it's a green color.

The area near the falls stinks from the water treatment plant on the other side of the lake. The wind carries the sour milk smell in different directions. Today is not bad. Dad explains that the water here starts in our toilet bowls. When we flush, the poop goes to the plant, where chemicals are mixed in to dissolve it. He says the mist we feel is poop landing on our heads. I can't tell if he's joking.

Dad calls me "kiddo" today, even hugs me, and strokes my head like he does with the sick dogs in his office. Mom says he doesn't like to touch people, not even his kids, so it's strange that he hugs me. I'm not used to hugs. Mom says we're not a hugging family. Dad seems more distracted than usual. Mom complains he's spacey, but I know he's not an astronaut.

The first stop today is his clinic, so he can check on a sick cat. Chicken Galore is next to Dad's office. The window sign advertises fried chicken with french fries and has a cartoon of a smiling, bony chicken. Sometimes Dad brings home fried chicken and jokes that while he saves animals on one side of the wall, Chicken Galore cooks them on the other.

Whenever we fish, Dad first takes me to the Sweet Shop where he buys me a bottle of cold chocolate Yoo-hoo and Yodels. Yodels are chocolate rolls with vanilla creme, wrapped in foil. Mom doesn't let us have chocolate snacks at home. The Sweet Shop is smoky and smells like the huge cigar that Mario, the owner, always has in his mouth. Dad takes care of Mario's dog, so they talk about the dog and the Yankees.

Mario hands me a grape Tootsie Pop, a hard candy lollipop with a chocolate Tootsie Roll inside. I'm too impatient to suck the shell and wait for the chocolate, so I bite down, which means the hard candy winds up stuck in my teeth. Mom yells at me when I do this, but Dad doesn't care. Yoo-hoo is my special drink for fishing. Dad claims Yoo-hoo and Yodels will bring us luck. Once, there were no Yodels, and I ate a Devil Dog. Dad says we got skunked, but I didn't see or smell any skunks. We just had no luck that day.

Mario sells us fat nightcrawlers for bait. He says, like always, that the fish are biting.

Dad compares baseball to fishing, because we spend most of our time waiting. Just when we get bored, a hitter slams a home run or our fishing pole bends when a fish bites. Dad says I jump when the red-and-white bobber gets pulled underwater the same way fans jump out of their seats when a batter crushes the ball. Mom wonders how I can sit for hours in one place waiting for a fish to bite but can't pay attention in school for ten minutes.

Even though we go together, Dad doesn't fish. He says he likes watching me. Besides, he jokes that if he fishes, too, the fish will choose his bait over mine.

Mostly, he reads his paper and smokes. Dad started smoking in the army. No one tells me what Dad did in the army. Later, I heard he did top-secret experiments in France, but he never tells me anything about the past.

His brother, Uncle Jerry, is more fun than Dad and still plays baseball in local leagues. We drive each Sunday from Wayne to Bayonne where Uncle Jerry lives to visit him and Grandma Annie and Pappa Charley. Uncle Jerry has kids who are my cousins, but he doesn't see them because they live in Ohio. Grandma Annie gets mad and says it's a shame.

Dad told me Jerry was a military police officer. He thinks it's funny since Jerry is the one who needs policing. Mom complains that Dad should be fun like his brother.

Today, Dad buys his paper and we walk the two blocks to our fishing spot. Our spot is near the bridge down from the falls, where there are big rocks we can sit on. We walk down a steep hill and try not to slip on the green algae near the water. The sound of the falls pounding the rocks and the gurgling sound from the spinning at the bottom is loud enough to drown out our voices, so we don't talk while we walk.

We fish close to the bridge where it's quieter, and the falls flow into the Ramapo River. The smell and mist aren't so bad here. Dad helps me tie the hook to the line without taking the cigarette from his mouth. I don't really need his help.

He's distracted, probably thinking about saving people's pets, so he isn't watching me. I stick my fingers into the cold, black dirt where the worms are hiding, trying to grab the fattest, squirmiest one. My index finger and thumb feel a wiggler, and I squeeze as it tries to escape my grasp. I feel bad, but that doesn't stop me from sliding it onto the sharp hook, hoping a fish might like my choice. It's probably tastier than the lousy cafeteria food they serve at Pines Lake School.

The worm feels like Jell-O on my fingers. I don't like the school's Jell-O because they put fruit in it. Mom's is better. The school's chocolate pudding stinks, too, because it tastes like chalk, which I tried in first grade. Sometimes they burn the pudding and force you to eat it anyway.

I'm not paying attention and realize my finger is stuck on the hook instead of the worm. It's the same finger I cut trying to slice an apple. Dad doesn't even look up, but I imagine Mom telling me to pay attention to what I'm doing. She says I don't pay attention to anything. I lick the blood off and wipe it on my pants. There's a small hole where the hook entered, but the fingertip has been numb since it was sewed back on. Dad says the doctor did a bad job, but the scar is cool. The first worm has found freedom, so I grab another one and am careful this time as it slides onto the sharp hook.

I watch the red-and-white bobber for signs that a fish is near, and every few minutes change out the worm. When a fish bites, the bobber goes underwater and then you set the hook. I wouldn't dare take my eyes off the bobber, because that's the moment a fish would bite and I'd miss my chance to set the hook.

Dad smokes and reads, and when it begins to get dark, he says, "Kiddo, time to go. Fish don't bite in the dark." He finishes his cigarette, throws the butt down, and smashes it into the ground with his foot. He doesn't want to start a fire, but Mom says he's littering. Dad's car ashtrays are filled with cigarette butts.

I plead, "One more cast, please, just one more? Fish eat in the dark, Dad!"

My arm is in motion, and I cast, not waiting for his answer. The bobber lands far downstream behind a big rock.

The line doesn't move so the hook must have caught on the rock. Dad's irritated and yells that we have to go. The hook is snagged, so I yank hard on the pole. When nothing happens, I pull again, and in that moment, I feel a slight twinge as the line begins to move, and something big is pulling at the other end. I watch as the bobber disappears under the foamy suds on the lake's surface. *What's happening?* My heart leaps. The line peels off while the reel screams and makes a sharp zinging sound. I can't believe it.

I yell, "Dad, I have a fish, it's a good one!" He must not hear me. I yell louder, "Dad, come quick, Dad!"

He keeps moving toward the car. I can smell the freshly lit cigarette as the wind blows the smoke in my direction.

My rod bends and I can feel the fish pull out even more line. Yoo-hoo spills on my new Bob Cousy black high-top Converse All Stars. Mom will be mad because I promised to wear my old sneakers but forgot. The sound of line being stripped off gets louder, which causes my heart to pound even harder. The fish fights for his life. I wonder what happened to the worm. *Has it been eaten, or did it swim away? Can worms swim?*

Dad says worms can't feel anything. When I ask if he ever treats worms, he laughs and says only when they get in a dog's tummy. Sometimes he's hard to understand. Mom says he mumbles because his brain moves faster than the words coming out. The fish pulls harder. We have only caught small fish here so we didn't bring a net. I'll dive in if that's what it takes to land this fish.

The fish tires and I'm able to pull some line back. It's almost close enough for me to grab. If Dad were here, he could help me land it. I yell for him one last time: "DAD, DAD, COME HELP," but he's gone.

My stomach's in knots... I can't lose this fish now.

I walk closer to the river's edge. Without warning, the water explodes and plowing through the foam, a huge largemouth bass hurdles its body into the air. The bass swings its head toward me and spits out the hook. There is nothing I can do. The empty line falls into the water and the fish has disappeared. The reel no longer zings, and the lake returns to its usual state, reclaiming the fish and leaving me alone on the bank.

The bobber has vanished, and who knows where the worm went. The fish is gone. My head sags. I trudge back up the bank and walk back to the car, head down, defeated by a fish.

"The fish is gone!" I cry out. "I lost him!"

Dad stands, leaning against the car, a smoke resting in the corner of his mouth. The radio is on and Frank Sinatra sings "Fly Me to The Moon." I decide then to hate Frank Sinatra, because he caused Dad to ignore me, and I lost the fish.

"Son, it's OK, he's back with his family."

I look down and don't say a word. *But it's not OK, and he should have helped.*

Tears crowd the corners of my eyes. Dad seems sad and stares at me. Neither of us speak.

Decades later, I still wonder what I did wrong. *Did I set the hook right? Did I pull too hard? Should Dad have brought the net? How big was it? Would we have kept it?* It's taken me a long time to forgive Dad, but it turns out much worse was soon to come. I did forgive Sinatra but remained a hard rocker.

At least I have my own fish story, like Pappa Ben. Pappa tells the same story all the time, about a salmon he caught in Maine like a hundred years ago. He claims it was a world record but his friend convinced him to eat it instead of measuring it. Each time he tells the story, the pain of fresh regret fills his eyes, as if it had just happened.

Mom says it's the memories that matter, not whether you catch the fish. I don't care about the memories. Catching the fish is what counts. Otherwise, it's just a fish tale that anyone can tell. Pappa remembers the fish, but not his friend's name.

Dad says I can pretend it was a world-record bass. But pretending is like lying, because the fish is alive, living down the street in Pompton Lake.

We return home from fishing and I tell Mom how the fish got away. She seems irritated. "Mom, it was a world-record bass, maybe bigger than Pappa Ben's!" That gets her attention, but she looks upset. She snaps, "Steven, that is just some fish tale. Did your father tell you anything special today?" Dad has his head down. "Anything you can remember?"

My confused brain tries to think if Dad told me to remember something, since I have a history of forgetting things even when I'm told not to. I'm not sure it counts as forgetting if you weren't listening in the first place. Mom glares like she's mad.

I blurt out, "Dad told me it was OK the fish got away because now it gets to stay with its family."

Mom shakes her head without saying anything. She glares at Dad and says, "You *didn't* tell him that, did you?"

Dad looks away.

Mom says, "I figured. Go ahead. Make me the bad guy. You were supposed to have a father-son talk with your son. What kind of father are you?"

Dad says nothing. Mom turns to me. "Steven, your father's moving out. Lori knows and Robert's too young to understand. Dad has an apartment and you'll stay with him every other weekend and Wednesday afternoons. We love you, but we're getting a divorce."

Silence. This seems important. But I can't stop thinking about the bass and how it spit that hook out. Mom says, "Steven, do you have any questions?"

"Mom, can I have the Yodel left over from the fishing trip?"

She shakes her head and tries to hide the teardrops escaping from the corners of her eyes. "Ask your father."

I still don't understand how that fish got away. It was just... gone.

When I turn to look for Dad, I see the taillights of his car as he drives away. He's gone, too.

CHAPTER 5

Yours, Mine, and Ours, 1968–69

Nana Ruth and Pappa Ben show up a few months after Dad leaves and announce we're going on a trip. Mom needs some "alone time." This is exciting news because we never go anywhere, and this is the first chance to tell Pappa my fish story. It's weird that I lost the fish and Dad on the same day. It's become hard to think of one without the other. Pappa never asks about Dad. I don't think they like each other. It's been months since Dad has seen us. The weekend visits mostly never happen. I wonder if Dad knows about the trip. Pappa loads the car while we climb into the back seat. Mom and Nana are talking in the driveway. I hear my name: "STEVEN!"

Mom is yelling, but not a mad yell.

I look, "What, Mom?"

"Pay attention to your grandparents."

"I will."

Nana and Mom stare at me. I hear Nana say that Pappa isn't happy about Mom's decision. I don't know what Mom's decision is, but I guess we'll know soon. Mom hugs Nana, and I hear her say she's excited about her new life. Mom rarely hugs us the way some of my friends are hugged or kissed by their moms. That's embarrassing anyway.

I wonder, *Is someone dead? Is that the news?* My brain circles around bad news and I think about the Abraham Lincoln book we read in fourth grade. *Who told the Lincoln kids their dad was dead? What about the Kennedy kids? Why am I even thinking about dead presidents? Is Dad dead? If not, where is he?*

My mind drifts and I can't control its direction. Mom still says I never pay attention and never listen. *Is it not listening if I hear her voice but am not paying attention so I don't know what she's saying? Or, what if I hear her voice, and just ignore her? Does that make me a poor listener or a good listener who decides not to listen?* Random thoughts churn around inside me about fishing, or the Mets, or this girl named Annie who sits near me in class. Or Lincoln. Or Tug McGraw. Last year I liked a different girl but never spoke to her. I haven't had the courage to say anything to Annie.

The big test will be Valentine's Day, and whether she gives me my own card. I'm doing nothing and will see what happens. It's embarrassing to give a girl a card if she doesn't give you one. Last year nothing happened, which means something did happen, but it was nothing.

Mom yells goodbye, and says she loves us. She has an odd edge in her voice. I am listening but don't respond.

Nana Ruth swivels her head and stares from the front passenger seat of Pappa Ben's new silver Cadillac DeVille. Lori, Robert, and I sit in the back seat. Robert is the smallest, so he sits in the middle. We haven't been told where we're going, only that we're going somewhere. *Somewhere isn't like going to the Milk Barn for ice cream or the International House of Pancakes, because they would tell us. So somewhere must mean somewhere else.*

Nana knows I'm almost nine but still treats me like a six-year-old. Lori asks where we're headed. Nana just gives her the mean-eye stare and says it's a surprise. Pappa's eyes meet mine, and he nods with a slight head movement meant for only me. I understand he's telling me not to ask any questions.

Every year, Pappa Ben buys the newest Cadillac, drives to our house, and takes us for a ride. Only one other person in our neighborhood drives a Cadillac, but it's an old one with wings. Dad has an old Chevy Impala that smells like cigarette smoke and cat pee. Sometimes, he has a sick dog in the back so there's newspapers all over the place in case it poops or vomits.

When we lived together, Mom said she wished he would pay as much attention to his kids as he did to his animals. It's been months since he moved out. Mom yells at him sometimes through the car window and Dad says nothing. I don't miss the arguments when Dad lived with us, but I do miss him.

Nana hits the power button on the electric seat to create more space. I hear the whirr from the motor as the seat moves. Nana gazes toward us with piercing dark eyes, her lipstick lips always seeking the cheek of her nearest grandchild. Usually it's Robert, because he's her favorite. She likes me, but not as much as Robert.

I know because she tells me. Dad says her face was lifted, but he didn't tell me how high. Nana tells me to take the Kleenex she is now shoving toward me. This is the fifth time she tries to wipe my nose, but there's nothing to wipe. She worries green snot will come running out and mess up Pappa's new leather seats. She's covered the entire back seat with plastic, like she uses in her house. The plastic smells like plastic, which stinks because I love the leather smell.

Nana says smokers will never be allowed in the car. She means Dad will never ride in the Cadillac. He says that people buy Cadillacs to show off and act rich. He will never buy one, even if he's rich someday. Then he says being rich isn't a bad thing.

Pappa is unhappy about what Mom's doing but still won't tell us. Kids are the last to know anything. Like, when Dad left. Everyone knew except us, and then he was gone. He had a new place before we were told he was leaving.

Nana has forbidden us from playing with the electric windows and won't let us press the button that moves the seat. She's still mad because I pressed all twenty-two floors when we rode the elevator in her high rise building. She used to live in a condo on the ocean. Some old people got mad and complained to the building managers. Nana said we'd be kicked out if it happened again.

Kids understand more than their parents realize. I knew Santa wasn't real before Mom told me. I shouldn't have told my best friend because he's Catholic and cried and it became a big deal. His parents won't let him come over anymore. Santa is cool, even if he's fake. It doesn't matter anyway because he skips our house. Dad says Pappa Charley has a Santa belly but we haven't seen Charley for a long time.

We wind up going to this fake town in Sturbridge, Massachusetts, where people dress up like Revolutionary War times. At Sturbridge, I go to the bathroom and pee right next to George Washington. He was President of the United States. The real one's dead.

George Washington seems surprised to see some kid peeing next to him and says in this stupid voice, "I pray ye are enjoying our village." I roll my eyes and stare down without saying a word. I'm not stupid and know he's fake. I don't look toward his privates because Pappa Ben yelled at me once and said to keep my eyes on the family jewels, but when I told him there wasn't any jewelry to see, he just laughed.

I look at George. He has white stuff that looks like powdered sugar running off his wig, and he's wearing a Red Sox shirt under his Washington coat. He pulls out a silver lighter like Dad has and lights a cigarette. He starts talking to a fake British soldier who wears a big red coat and is also lighting a cigarette. I thought they were fighting the war against each other, but they get excited talking about Carl Yastrzemski, the Red Sox star player. The British guy doesn't even have an English accent.

I like the Mets, but they didn't have a team during the Revolutionary War. I know the real George Washington wasn't a Red Sox fan. Still, I will tell my teacher because she likes history. Not many kids get to pee next to a president. Lori, Robert, and I have been with Nana Ruth and Pappa Ben all weekend. It's strange because we never take overnight trips with them. Nana complains we're too much work. She says she already raised her kids.

Since Dad left, we haven't gone to Bayonne. Mom drives us to the dentist or Hebrew school. Sometimes she brings one of her dates to the house when she thinks we're sleeping. I spy on them, but nothing happens. She did introduce us to one guy who likes sports. Then he had a heart attack and died, so they stopped dating.

My grandparents take us out to dinner, but don't force us to drink milk like Grandma Annie does. Nana nags us to eat vegetables, but she's easy to fool. I fake her out by telling her to look in one direction and then slide the vegetables into my napkin or put them in my pocket. They let us have dessert even if we don't eat our whole meal.

Now I stare out the Cadillac's window, inhaling the leather smell, and my mind drifts. I spent most of the trip from New Jersey to Massachusetts playing with the electric windows until my grandfather figured out how to lock them.

Pappa never raises his voice but he did when he kept telling me to stop playing with the windows. He even threatened to let Robert have the window seat. He tried to scare me by telling me horrible stories. His first story was about the handless kid who stuck his hand out the window just as a motorcyclist was passing and it got torn off. Then, there is the headless kid whose head was chopped off when he stuck his head out the window and a motorcycle hit him. I asked my grandfather if the same motorcyclist ripped off one kid's hand and another kid's head. He just looked at me and shook his head no.

Adults like to scare kids with stories about limbs getting chopped off. I have never seen an accident, except for my own finger. Well, one morning I jumped on the table and fell off and had to go to the emergency room to get head stitches.

Nana gets mad because a fake Martha Washington yelled at me for touching the wooden teeth on the display table. I just wanted to feel them to see if they were Washington's real fake teeth or a fake of the fakes. Plus, one kid at school told me Washington's teeth were made from whale bones and another said they were elephant tusks.

Pappa Ben pretends to get mad sometimes because my grandmother will tell him to tell me to stop doing something, even though she's standing right there. Then he says, "Steven, your grandmother wants you to stop doing whatever it is you are doing that she doesn't want you to do." Then she glares and says he's making her look like the bad guy, while I stand there trying to figure out what I am doing that I am supposed to stop. Pappa Ben is tall with black hair and a mustache that twitches when he gets impatient. He plays golf almost every day, loves to fish, and likes to go to Mexico and paint. Mom says he gets to do anything he wants. Pappa is a businessman and used to own grocery stores. Mom says he still owns the stores, but not the groceries in them. That seems stupid to me. Pappa wears colorful clothing and everyone smiles when he says hello.

My grandma plays a game called bridge that has nothing to do with bridges. She talks about matches while we're driving but never teaches us how to play. My grandfather is some kind of bridge master, but I don't know what that means. Pappa has dark brown skin and Mom says I get my skin from him, because his mom's from Siberia. She looks like the Eskimos we see in the school picture books who live in houses made from ice cubes.

Nana still plays tennis and golf. She says she will play with me when I get older. Mom plays tennis and likes to dance and wanted to be a ballet dancer. She had to quit when she hurt her knee. Sometimes my grandmother or my grandfather will play catch with me. Dad isn't around, but he never would play catch even if he was.

Pappa continues to drive on some boring highway, and it feels like we've been driving for years. Every time I ask if we're there yet, Nana says another few minutes. She thinks I don't know she says this to shut me up. I keep asking now to bother her and see how many times she'll say the same thing. Every car in the state has now passed us because when Pappa goes even one mile over the speed limit, Nana tells him to slow down. They argue but their arguments don't seem like arguments, since no one is screaming or slamming doors.

The good thing about Dad being gone is he and Mom don't fight. Maybe it's because he's not around. The house is library quiet. I don't miss the noise Mom and Dad made when they fought. When Dad lived with us, he and Mom would fight until Mom would lock herself in the bedroom. Dad would then walk outside to smoke a cigarette. Dad never raised his voice but his eyes would darken when he was mad. Sometimes, Dad would get mad and slam the front door. When that happened, he was going to his office or just leaving. I never asked where he went. The driveway is below my window so I can hear when cars are coming and going. I recognize Mom's car sound when she comes home and even the smooth running engine hum of Pappa's car.

Dad's sputtering engine sounds are easy to identify. When he first left for good, I would lay in bed and wait, hoping to hear the rattle of his car or the creak when he opened his door. If it was cold, he'd sit in the driveway, smoke coming out of the car's exhaust pipes, and you could see a tiny red glow as he sucked on his cigarette. He sometimes would come home late from an emergency and finish his smoke before walking into the house. When they used to fight, he would disappear and then my mother would go look for him.

One night, Mom woke us up and said we needed to find Dad, so we drove to his office. I had been listening for his car but had fallen asleep. His parking lot was empty, so she drove around the back where the special garbage dumpster is kept that holds the dogs he puts to sleep. When I asked him if they were sleeping, he said they go to doggie heaven. He always says they don't feel pain. Dad is always uncomfortable when we talk about this part, and I can tell it makes him sad. That night, he is nowhere to be found.

A garbage dumpster in the back corner of an empty parking lot is not heaven any more than the toilet bowl with my dead fish. Dad's long gone and sometimes I forget he's alive. Maybe *he's* in heaven.

One time when we stayed with Dad, Robert had been invited to a birthday party. Dad thought the party was on Sunday, but it turned out we were a day late. The people were nice and gave Robert leftover birthday cake and a goodie bag, but Mom was embarrassed. She yelled because Dad got confused which happens a lot.

The steady hum of Pappa's car tires rolling down the highway makes me tired.

My eyelids close and I start to fade. Lori and Robert are quiet. My head rests against the Cadillac's window. I imagine being propelled into space on a magic carpet, like on *I Dream of Jeannie*. I always wondered if every girl genie is named Jeannie, or just the television one. I think it would be cool to have a magic carpet. I'm half asleep and half awake, though I'm not sure which half. I'm bad at math but begin to imagine teeth falling from my mouth.

It would be great if Jeannie was the tooth fairy, but Mom likes doing it. The tooth fairy will have to put a ton of quarters under my pillow because my teeth dangle from their stringy roots like dead leaves about to be torn from a tree. I have all baby teeth except for my two front buck teeth. They make me look like a chipmunk.

I know Mom's the tooth fairy, but she either doesn't know I know or acts like she doesn't know that I know even if she does. Either way, I'm happy to take her money.

Once, I tied one end of a string around my loose tooth and the other end to my bedroom door handle. I told Robert to shut the door, which jerked my tooth from the root. However, it didn't come out, so Mom yanked it out with pliers. It's hard to admit it, but that hurt. I tried to bargain for a raise, but Mom laughed and told me to go to sleep. When I woke up, there was a note from the tooth fairy saying plier removal is not approved by the tooth fairy.

Robert nudges me and I realize everyone except Pappa, who is driving, is staring at me. We are still in the Cadillac. My brain drifts again and Nana tells me to wake up and look outside the car as we drive by an apple orchard where cider is being sold. We're always raising money to buy trees in Israel. *How many trees do they need?*

One day the rabbi drops by our Hebrew school class and gives me a blue metal box with an Israeli flag on one side and a picture of the desert on the other. There's a slot for quarters. He wants us to raise money for the Holy Land. My great-grandmother lives in Israel. Any time Israel is mentioned, Mom says, "You do know we have relatives in Israel."

I say, "Yes, Mom, I met her when the rabbi cut my privates off." When I ask her why that happened, she says, "That's just what Jews do." When I ask her why we don't celebrate Christmas or Easter or eat ham, she says, "That's just what Jews do." So we Jews do and don't do lots of things because that's just what Jews do or don't do.

I don't understand. My grandparents never talk about temple or God or anything. yet they are concerned about this. *What does cutting my pecker have to do with Judaism anyway?* So many things don't make sense. Rules seem to show up out of nowhere. My teacher jabbers on about spelling rules, like when you have to use one letter even if it sounds like another letter or has no sound at all, because it's still part of the word. I still don't get why two (to, too) is spelled three different ways. Or why "why" has a "wh" instead of just a "y." It's a long list. My brain gets stuck sometimes, like it's in quicksand. My teacher says I overthink things. Other times she says, "Steven, please plug in your brain." Sometimes my mother thinks I have hearing problems and yelling louder will help. When things don't make sense, I ask questions.

In Hebrew school, the rabbi and teacher both yell in Hebrew. I'm forced to learn Hebrew with upside down and sideways letters that you read backwards. To confuse things more, the Jewish year is different than—then?—our year because my teacher says there is no Jesus, but I know—no?—there—their?—is, because one—won?—of my favorite baseball players is named Jesus. I even have a friend named Christian, but no friends named Jew.

I remember Dad finally explaining why he was moving out. "Kids," he said, "Your mom and I love each other and love you, but we have decided it's better for me to leave the house and get my own place. Sometimes parents have trouble getting along, but it's important for you to know it's not your fault. We are still a family and always will be."

My brain raced. I never considered it might be my fault, but now that Dad says it's not my fault, I realize it must be. Why does he think it's my fault?

When Mom told me they were divorcing, it didn't register. I figured Dad would return home. He couldn't just disappear. We're his kids; I'm his oldest son. Besides, Dad still has my chocolate Yodel. I wonder if he put it in his fridge. Mom and Dad always have secrets swirling around so it's hard to keep up.

"Steven, Steven, Steeeven, Steven, what are you doing?" Lori pounds my shoulder. My head is pressed against the car window. My eyes are closed but I'm wide awake, my mental gymnastics flipping around like an Olympian. We are still driving home, and it seems like it's taking forever.

Daydreaming in school is a problem. If a class is boring, it's impossible to waste time paying attention. My brain travels in time and from one country to the other. My mind never shuts down and I'm awake sometimes when I'm asleep.

Adults don't get it. Sometimes they talk in front of you like you're a piece of furniture. Mom tells strangers embarrassing stories even when I ask her not to. She slapped me once after I hit Lori in the face with a basketball, and then she told everyone. She was more upset than I was about the slap. It didn't hurt, anyway.

Mom always tells everyone how I didn't know my ABCs because Lori would always help me finish. It started when my teacher sent a note home one day asking Mom and Dad to come to school for a special parent-teacher conference. They were upset because no one else's parents received a note. When I gave it to Mom, she asked what the conference was about. Then she said maybe I'm getting left back. Mom stared at the teacher's note and said it was because I didn't know the alphabet and was in the lowest reading group.

I responded, "The teacher says I'm a special student and don't need a group."

Mom looked at Dad. "See, Allen, he has special needs so is getting left behind. She's going to tell us he will have to repeat the grade. That's your fault. I asked you to help your son."

When the conference started, Mom wanted me to stand outside the classroom door. I saw a note Dad wrote telling the teacher to give me extra assignments. I wasn't worried about reading.

When they returned, Mom was upset and asked me to stand next to her. She handed me the newspaper she was holding. "Steven, read the front page and don't stop until I tell you."

I look up at her and Dad. Both stare with weird, puzzled looks on their faces. I begin: "Vice President Hubert Humphrey said tonight that during his European trip Pope Paul VI told him with 'tears in his eyes'..."

Mom tells me to stop and both are quiet. She says, "Steven, Miss Bosland was shocked when I told her that you don't know the alphabet. She asked Dad and me if we realized that you are reading at the highest level she has ever seen for a seven-year-old and can read *The New York Times* from start to finish. How can you do this? You *embarrassed* us. First, I was embarrassed because you didn't know your alphabet and now, instead, I'm embarrassed because your teacher tells me you read better than almost anyone in your school. But you never finish the alphabet. Lori always has to finish it for you."

Miss Bosland is right. I read *The New York Times* every morning before my parents get out of bed. I didn't know it was a crime. They don't talk much to me. They are always either fighting or taking care of Lori or Robert. It's not like I'm perfect. I've gotten into some fights and once had a neighborhood kid hit me with a stick and splinters got stuck in my head. Mom was furious and the doctor had to shave part of my head to get the splinters out. I wouldn't tell who did it, so that caused more trouble.

My daydream ends when Nana asks what's been my favorite part of the weekend. I blurt out, "Seeing George Washington pee." Nana Ruth gives me a "that's nice," but no laugh. My grandfather chuckles but seems nervous. "Steven," he says, "Nana has something to tell you kids."

CHAPTER 6

Wild Kingdom, 1968–69

Pappa pulls into our driveway. A strange station wagon with brown wood-trimmed side panels is parked in the driveway. The tailgate is open and there are suitcases and diaper boxes covering the back seat. I look toward the garage and become even more confused. My blue Schwinn Sting-Ray is lying on its side, the banana seat touching the floor. Someone threw it to the ground and didn't bother to use the kickstand. The baseball cards I attached with clothespins to the spokes are scattered on the concrete. They aren't my best cards, but they make my bike sound like a motorcycle. I only use unknown players or Yankees, because I'm a Mets fan.

Whatever this is, it feels bad. Words form but no sounds emerge from my throat. Standing on the front porch is Richard. The man

Nana just told us Mom has married. Behind him is Mom, who stares at her feet. Richard doesn't acknowledge me. He has an intense glare that burns through me when our eyes briefly meet. Behind him on the porch are his four kids.

I watch as Mom picks up the crying little girl. Richard says she needs a diaper change and Mom scurries into the house. The others stare at us, and for a few seconds there is silence as we all try to understand what's happening. I feel like an exhibit from the Turtle Back Zoo, which is the only place I ever saw these kids who are now moving into my house.

The oldest boy, Mark, has my football in his hands. Maybe he's the one who threw my bike down. I turn away and wonder if Dad knows what's happened. He's been gone over a year, and now Richard's car is in Dad's spot. There are strange bicycles leaning against the garage's side wall, the same place my bike usually stays. My stomach begins to ache, which happens when I'm nervous.

Richard stands on the porch like he owns it. Cramps kick in and I need the bathroom. I start to move past Richard to go inside when he stops me. "Where are *you* headed?" I mumble, "To the bathroom," and begin to move. Richard blocks my path, and now I'm in pain.

He snarls, "Kids can't use the front door. You either walk around to the back door or shit in your pants. It's my house now, so my rules."

HIS house? I thought this was my house. Or at least Mom's house since Dad left.

I say nothing and turn to walk around to the back door. He shouts behind me, "Your mother and I are married now. Things are going to change, so wise up." My stomach is churning. There'll be a volcanic eruption soon. I hurry to the bathroom.

Richard's energy feels like bad weather. My brain switches channels. Every Sunday I watch *Wild Kingdom*, starring Marlin Perkins and his faithful assistant, Jim, who's usually shoulder deep in some chocolate pudding-colored swamp on the eastern border of the western side of some exotic country. He describes the horrible smell and how the mud is thick enough to swallow a kid. Jim will be wrestling some killer fifty-foot, two-headed crocodile while Marlin sits in the Jeep and narrates like it's a football game. "Now Jim is going to stick his head in the crocodile's mouth. Kids don't try this at home. But first, Jim, hold your position—we will be right back after these commercials from Mutual of Omaha." I worry Richard won't let me watch Marlin and Jim.

The commercials always come just when Jim's about to be choked to death by a rare albino python or crushed by some massive lion defending her cubs. I have no idea what Mutual of Omaha is, but Dad says it's in Nebraska. *Does Nebraska have crocodiles?*

Marlin says animals can sense when a killer storm is coming long before humans can. He says by watching animals, you can see the signs. They know to seek shelter when Mother Nature sends trouble their way. I sensed danger the instant we pulled into our driveway. My grandparents were trying to pretend everything was great, but that just made it worse. George Washington was pretend because he's dead. Richard is real.

When I return to the porch, Richard orders me back in the house. My grandparents have left. The other kids are already inside, sitting on the floor of Dad's den. Mom says everyone's names and ages. There are seven kids, and we are all within five years of each other. Mom says we are having our first "family meeting." I'm confused by the word "family," and recall that the last meeting in this room was when Mom told me Dad was leaving. There's still some daylight left, and now I want to leave.

Dad's stale cigarette smoke still stinks up the room. I can see coffee stains in the carpet where he dropped his cup. His bookshelves are bookless, like a sad tree whose leaves have died. His hiding places where he'd stash extra packs of cigarettes and *Playboy* magazines are empty. The walls, once covered with family pictures and diplomas, are bare.

Richard stares at us from Dad's chair, while sitting at Dad's desk. Mom sits motionless, her eyes half closed as he talks. Richard glances over at her, which must be her signal to nod in agreement, which she does.

I look Richard over. He's a stocky, mostly bald man with a thick mustache. He's taller than me, but I'm a kid. He's not tall like Dad, who Mom says is six feet. When I was little, I used to think she meant he had six feet. And when I asked if that meant he had three pairs of shoes, Dad actually laughed.

Richard has hair that reminds me of Bozo the Clown, who's also bald on top with hair on the sides in a horseshoe pattern.

Richard has a few loose strands combed over from one side to the other, but they don't move when he does. Maybe they're glued to his head. Dad still has his hair. I think it's brown, but I'm starting to forget.

Richard speaks with a heavy Brooklyn accent and has a loud voice. His nose is flattened like it's broken, and his nostrils look unusually large. There's a gap between his two front teeth that reminds me of Vince Lombardi, the famous football coach. Everyone says Lombardi yells a lot to get the players to do what he wants. They must listen, since his team, the Green Bay Packers, won the Super Bowl last year.

Richard continues talking but that doesn't stop me from fading away. *I imagine getting my Sting-Ray off the garage floor and maybe asking Lori to ride with me to get ice cream. Lori has a girl's Sting-Ray with a flower-trimmed basket attached to the front.*

Once we tried to take the basket off, but Lori decided she could use it to carry Butterfly, our cat. It was a good idea until Mom ran Butterfly over one day and we never saw her again. Butterfly, not Mom. Dad was living with us and said butterflies like to fly away but always return. Mom got mad because she said he's joking and it's not a joke. Dad probably knew Butterfly was dead and wouldn't tell us

My brain stops and I realize the voice I hear is no longer the one in my head. Mom is talking to me. "Steven, pay attention!"

First, Richard goes over our new room assignments. Mom says nothing. I look toward her, but she doesn't look at me. She must know this isn't right. Richard does this like he's announcing the starting lineups for the World Series: "Now occupying room number one... Robert Nestle and Larry Eichenblatt." I guess family members, like baseball or football players, can be traded without notice. He continues: "Sharing room number two... Steven Nestle and Mark Eichenblatt."

Larry and Robert are both six and will share Robert's room; Gail Eichenblatt is nine, the same age as Lori and me. Sometimes I forget Lori is my twin.

The girls will share my parents' old bedroom, while Cindy, who's in diapers, gets her own room. Richard and Mom are going to be turning Dad's office into a new master bedroom. When Mom says this, I speak up and ask about Dad. Mom just looks at me and shakes her head. She seems afraid to say anything about Dad. It's weird: she acts like he's dead.

Mom finally answers, "Don't worry about him, he doesn't worry about you. This is your family now. The subject is closed."

No one asked about sharing my room. Richard says Mark is now my brother and I will need to make space for him.

Later Mom will tell me that Mark has a history of trouble in school and likes to fight.

I have nothing against these kids. It's not their fault. They seem as shocked as we are. I wonder if they were invited to the wedding. I'm stunned Mom didn't tell us. My brain shifts again, and I wonder what Dad knows. Later Mom will tell me I need to accept things as they are and not question everything. But all I have is questions and no answers.

I look over at my "brothers and sisters" like they're the new kids in class. A few weeks ago, when we all went to the Turtle

Back Zoo, they were just regular kids. Mom never mentioned they were to become family. This makes me wonder what else she might be hiding.

I'm not stupid. She did say something on the drive home from the zoo about Mark's school troubles and how their mom got sick and died. I didn't really listen but know she felt sorry for them and Richard, who would have to raise four kids alone. Maybe I should have known something was up, but Mom never mentioned them again—until today.

Gail is only one month younger than me. She's the oldest in their family, and a year older than Mark. She doesn't talk much. I hardly know what her voice sounds like. She seems sad, and her eyes always focus on the floor. Larry and Mark seem happy, even though their mother died. I saw them laugh at the zoo.

Gail carries Cindy around and changes her diaper like she's her mom. That is gross. No way will I ever change some kid's diaper.

Richard is still talking. He never stops. *Nine people now live in our house. Seven kids between two and seven years old. My mind races on a circular track with no finish line. What is Mom thinking?*

I'm not happy about sharing my room. Nothing against Mark, but I don't know him and now he's my brother *and* my roommate. I would rather have roomed with Robert, since he's been my brother longer. But it's not Mark's fault, and he likes sports, so maybe we'll play catch.

I had just gotten used to living without Dad. He was like a ghost when he was here, but at least he was here. I knew he'd protect us if aliens attacked. When he moved out, my stomachaches got worse and so did the nightmares. I stay out of his den because it's sad looking around the vacant spaces where his books and typewriter used to be. Sometimes, I only knew he was home because there might be cigarette smoke lingering around or I could hear his typewriter clacking or the burble of hot coffee brewing, but he didn't leave the den. Dad has his own Dad smell, but now it's hard to remember. Some days, I even forget what his voice sounds like. Dad's not scary like Richard when he's in the house. He mostly kept to himself.

Richard doesn't feel safe. I'm not saying this just because he will live in Dad's house and sit in Dad's chair and park in Dad's spot in the garage and turn Dad's den into another bedroom, or because he's going to be in Mom's bed. I wonder what's going to happen when I have a nightmare and need Mom. I will *not* go into her bedroom if Richard's in there.

I don't see why we need Richard. Robert, Lori, and I get along without too much trouble. My grades are all As and Bs and I can even read *The New York Times*. Mom says I take after Dad because he's a great reader and his handwriting stinks, too.

This is turning into a long meeting. It's boring, and I want to disappear. But there is no escape today. Richard lays out the rules. "Kids, we are one family now. You are brothers and sisters just like you have the same blood. You call me 'Dad,' or 'Richard Daddy,' but not 'Richard,' and Elaine is to be called 'Mom.' I expect you to keep your rooms clean, and... "

Blah, blah, blah. His droning voice fades and my brain turns its channels. I'm worried about the places in my bedroom where my prize Mickey Mantle baseball card and money and fake guns are hidden. I even have *National Geographic* magazines my grandmother gave me, with bare breasts. Mom brags to her friends that we are easy kids. I don't understand why all the rules.

Maybe, after this family meeting, I can go play stickball or see if any of the big kids will let me play baseball with them—I can already hear the crack of the bat. Or maybe we can play hide-and-seek in our living room and I'll squeeze under the couch.

My body senses there is abrupt silence, and Richard is yelling my name. "Steven, *Steven!* Are you paying attention?"

My mind goes blank. Richard says, "You're my oldest son and I expect you to protect your brothers and sisters and set a good example." He stops talking, but I forget to listen and don't notice until his voice changes. "Steven, what did I just say?"

I look around but my brain churns in confusion. *How can I be this man's oldest son when he's not even my dad?* Everyone looks away except for Mark, who giggles. Mark doesn't seem bothered by Richard's tone and continues to laugh but keeps his freckled face hidden from view. Mark's eyes meet mine, and for the first time I see they are bright blue. He makes a face and I try not to laugh. We both giggle, but I stop because everyone is staring.

The heavy pressure on my shoulders tightens, like when my teacher asks me a question and I don't know the answer because I don't know the question. I feel a knife-sharp glare coming from Richard.

Mom yells, "We're all waiting for you, Steven."

I stare at her and Richard but have no idea what he's asking me. *Wow. Mom's never spoken to me like that. Her tone throws me off. She seems irritated with me.* I don't know what to say and stare at the ground.

Richard smirks repeats a little louder, "OK, what did I just say?"

The silence is agony. He's not going to let up. I don't know what to say, since I don't know what he said.

His eyes burn a hole in my forehead. "We'll wait for you to tell us what I just said. I have all day."

Mark laughs again. I'm going to puke.

Richard hears the giggle and screams. "Mark, you think this is funny? I don't think you'll be laughing when you I hit you with my belt!"

The room shifts to the absolute silence that must happen at funerals. Or like, when at school, the teacher looks for someone to answer some horrible grammar question and everyone drops their pencils to bend down and pick them up and avoid eye contact. The worst is getting called up to the blackboard to do a math problem that involves multiplication, subtraction, and division all in one equation.

Richard waits for me. Hours may have to pass before I answer. Mom is looking down, and the forced quiet increases my feeling of defeat. I mumble, "First you said, 'OK, what did I just say?' And now you said, 'We'll wait all day if we have to for you to answer.'"

I know this is not what he wants to hear, but it's the truth. I'm not sure what to expect, but my senses tell me it won't be good. Richard snarls, his voice taking on a dangerous tone.

"Oh, you think you're a comedian. Elaine, did you know your son's a comedian?" His face changes color like a light bulb switching off, and then there is no color. He roars, "Steven, get your fat ass upstairs and wait for me! I will not put up with your back talk in my house!" Marlin never yells at Jim, even when Jim does something stupid like sticking his head into a huge crocodile's mouth. Richard's words paralyze me. No one has ever yelled at me like this. My heart pounds and I'm scared. It hits me that this house is no longer my home.

Mom looks down, frozen in place. Richard's words don't seem to bother her. She doesn't say or do anything.

Mom will not look at me. My "new brothers and sisters" hide nervous giggles under their small hands. Robert and Lori look scared. I stand up and move toward the stairs, only to hear Richard yell, "Steven! Get back here and try again!" *Now what?*

I turn around and Richard has his hands on his hips, his nostrils flaring. He has a sly smile on his face and I notice the space between his front teeth is wider than I thought. He needs braces. My mind begins another lap around the track...but my wandering is interrupted. "Weren't you listening to me?" Richard yells as if I'm a mile away. "You're not allowed to walk in the living room! Get back here and walk around instead!" *What is he saying? I don't understand where to go.*

Tears form in the corner of my eyes, but I fight them off. He won't see me cry. I stare at Richard and tell him I don't understand what he said. He explodes. "I don't care. If you had paid attention you would know the new house rules. Do you even know what you don't know? Do you have any idea what I'm asking? My kids are not, nor will I let them be, losers. This is the last time you kids are going to hear the rules," he yells. "I will say them again because Steven here thinks he's too important to pay attention. You will listen now, right Steven?"

I nod my head but am confused and just want out—out of this family that is not my family, out of this house that is not Mom's house or Dad's house but *his* house, *Richard's* house. *How did this happen?*

Richard begins: "Number one: You must walk in the back door and are never allowed on the front porch. Never, ever use the front door. I don't care if it's snowing or raining. Front door is out!

"Number two: No one is allowed in the front yard. I don't care if you used to play football or what you did before. Go to one of the neighbor's yards and ruin their grass, not mine.

"Number three: No one walks into or is allowed in the kitchen unless it's mealtime. The living room, den, my bedroom, dining room, and downstairs bathroom are off limits. If you have to go to the bathroom, go upstairs. Same for your friends.

"Number four: You are not allowed to sit on any of the furniture in the living room, dining room, family room, or in the downstairs bedroom—ever. You can sit on the floor in the family room when I am there, but you cannot watch television without permission.

"Number five: You will not enter the kitchen when your mother and I are eating. Your mother will serve your meals, and if you miss dinner, you will not eat. When we're eating, I don't want to hear you, or see you, so stay away unless it's an emergency. You do not enter the kitchen without asking permission.

"If you break my rules, you will be punished by me or your mother! Also, tell your friends to use the back door. I don't care if they ring the front doorbell. You tell them to go to the back door next to the garbage cans. When your friends are in the house, they must obey the rules or they'll never be allowed in again." Richard looks around. "Elaine, you need to add anything?"

"Kids, just listen," Mom responds. "I know it will take a while to get used to the changes." I mumble to myself that he's not my father.

Richard snarls, "Steven, if you have something to say, be a man and say it to my face. I expect my kids to be tough. And stop sniveling. Now get to your room and wait for me." Without thinking, I blurt out, "You aren't my dad." He stares.

"Well, your dad is no dad. He hasn't bothered to visit you, has he? He doesn't even pay child support. Forget about him, he doesn't give two shits about you. He's gone and never coming back."

I'm stunned but walk away. Again, Mom says nothing. I go sit in my room that is no longer my room but the room I will share with Mark. The seconds pass over my body, but they feel like hours. It's the same feeling I had sitting outside the principal's office waiting for my punishment after pushing this kid and he started crying. At least then, I knew the punishment would be something stupid like cleaning toilets or helping serve food in the cafeteria.

Waiting for Richard is a punishment worse than any punishment. Who knows what he will do. The punishment possibilities are endless. I picture torture scenes like the dunking machine in *March of the Wooden Soldiers*, or wooden stocks, like in Sturbridge. He's probably going to hit me with the belt. I think of various kung fu moves to defend myself. Maybe I can pull a James Bond trick or be like Cato in *The Pink Panther*.

Eventually, I lay on my bed and pull out a Horatio Alger story, *Ragged Dick*, about a poor boy in New York who fights to overcome bad things and becomes a rich man who does good. The book has someone else's name written on the inside cover in black ink. My dad bought it for me at some dead people's sale. The pages smell old. I always feel better when I read it, but I do so now with one eye on the door. I listen for Richard's footsteps coming up the stairs. He never shows up. I crack the door open and hear him yelling at someone else.

Richard tortures me by not torturing me. He knows I'm waiting, but that's just part of the punishment. I'm a long way from eating apple pie made in the Sturbridge Village bakery by fake Martha Washingtons. It's only been one night, but I even miss the sound of Nana asking me to name the New England states or singing silly songs during the long hours of driving in my Pappa's Cadillac. That drive back to what I thought was home seems like years ago.

I fall asleep that first night, below Mark in the new bunkbed he sleeps on top of, remembering Dad's only baseball advice. The words replay from somewhere in my brain: "Swing level, Steve, swing level. Steve, choke up, keep your eye on the ball." Dad loves baseball, but I've never seen him throw a ball or swing a bat, so he must have heard someone say this once. I dream of taking my 28-inch Louisville Slugger Little League bat, lifting up my elbows, taking a couple practice swings, and then, imagining the freckles running along Richard's head are the red stitching on a baseball, swinging as hard and level as I can. *Dad, I swung level. Aren't you proud? You can come home now. I kept my eye on the ball.*

Come home, Dad. Game's over.

Come home!

CHAPTER 7

A New Life, 1970–1973

Since Richard moved in, my friends stopped visiting. Sometimes, their parents pick me up to play. I stopped asking Mom for rides because she's always distracted. I refuse to ask Richard anything. Most of the time, I jump on my Sting-Ray and bike to the park or Preakness Shopping Center. There's a movie theatre there, and a candy store where I steal Hershey bars.

Sometimes, I ride miles away to K-Mart or Builders Emporium and walk around, staring at fishing lures or sneaking a Tootsie Roll. Once, I took a pocketknife but had to hide it from Mom. But I hid it so well that my brain didn't register where I put it, and it disappeared.

Mom rarely talks to me anymore. Sometimes she stares with desperate eyes, as if she wants to say something. I can see her pain. Everything I tell her goes to Richard, so our conversations are short.

Richard talks to me, but that's only when we're stuck in the car together or alone in a room. He never says anything about his first wife who died, but he must be sad. I don't even know her name. She's dead, and it feels like my dad is dead or dying, too, since we rarely see him. We all pretend they never existed.

Mom spends most of her time handling Richard's kids or fighting with him. Then she spends hours on the phone telling her friends how horrible he is. Sometimes I listen to hear my name, but she never says it.

Most of the time, I steer clear of Mom and Richard. Sometimes, I wander the street looking in the houses, wondering what a loving family feels like. *A dad who played catch and joked with me or took me to games would be nice. Or just one who didn't scream all the time. Or smoke.*

My friend Patrick wrestles with his dad, and once they invited me to play hockey when Pines Lake was frozen over. It was fun, and they even laughed together. It's like they were friends, except when Patrick said "shit" and his dad said he could eat some when they got home. His dad winked at me when he said it, so I don't think he meant it.

Maybe I shoplift—stealing candy bars—to get caught. Any place would be great to live besides here. Out in the wild with Marlin and Jim would be the best. Maybe Marlin would let me ride in his safari Jeep. Or let me stay in one of his African huts.

One Saturday morning, a steady, pounding rain wakes me up. I can hear Richard's voice, and alarm bells ring in my head. He's not supposed to be home; he plays golf on Saturdays. The rain hasn't let up, though. This makes a dreary day even worse.

Mom says it's raining cats and dogs, which makes me think of Dad. He's been gone for months now. He doesn't show when he's supposed to and hardly calls because Mom will answer and they'll fight. Sometimes Mom and Dad argue for hours and nothing ever gets better. Once she saw me listening and hung up.

"Steven, your father is stubborn and makes everything difficult. He makes it very hard for this family to function. This has to end."

I asked in a low voice, "Well, is he coming to get me?"

Mom shakes her head, her lips tight, and stares in frustration.

"No, he's not coming. I don't care if he ever comes. He makes my life impossible. Steven, he's so selfish and thinks our life should revolve around him."

Staying here with Richard today is not an option. Maybe I'll sneak out the back door. That's not a rule violation so Richard won't care. No one will notice and it's worth getting wet to avoid spending the day in Richard's target zone. But then Patrick invites me to his house. Maybe today will be a good day after all. I put my sneakers on without tying them and run from the back door toward the front porch. It's off limits but worth the risk to stay dry until my ride comes.

Patrick's mom better get here soon. Richard's voice is creeping closer and he'll be angry if he sees me on the front porch. I see headlights through the rain and hear the car as Patrick's mom pulls into our driveway. Waving, I take one step off the porch when, without warning, I'm kicked from behind and launched like an Apollo rocket over the stairs, sending me face first into the bushes. My head slams against the dogwood tree that Dad planted with me.

Stunned, blood starts to flow from my nose. Soaked, I sit on the wet ground while the downpour continues. My jeans are drenched and it's cold. My head throbs. Looking back toward the flight path, my eyes meet Richard's. He laughs. "Use the back door next time. Toughen up, son."

He slams the front door and disappears, but his voice chants in my head, *loser, loser, loser,* and then my brain shuts down. He leaves me still bleeding from my nose. *I won't cry, though. And I'm not his son. No way will he see me cry. I can't let him win.*

Patrick's mom has backed out of the driveway and is parked down the street. I don't dare look back as I run to her car. My pants weigh a ton, but I'm not going back in the house. Patrick sits in the front seat and asks if everything is OK. His mom drives a few feet and then stops the car and turns her head and looks toward me.

"Steven, we have dry clothes at our house for you. Did he just kick you? Does he do that a lot?"

Kick me? He launched me!

I'm stunned by the question and take a second to decide how to answer. My eyes drift toward her face. She seems concerned.

Patrick's mom has lots of freckles, with green eyes and real red hair, not the fake red Mom has. Mom says she's Irish and Richard calls her Mick, but I don't think that's her name. She's Patrick's mom is all I know. She smiles a lot, but not today. I hope she'll still make us Nestlé's Quik chocolate milk. It's much better than Hershey's syrup, but there's no way Richard wants any Nestle in our house.

She waits for an answer to her question. I shake my head from side to side. *Technically, he hasn't launched me like a rocket ship before.* But she knows the truth.

Patrick says we might go bowling, which is around the corner from Dad's office. I feel safe being close to Dad, even if he won't see me.

Sometimes, Richard laughs with Mom, but it happens less and less. They've started playing tennis together. When they come home after playing, Richard might tell us how great she was, or, if they lost, call her fat and worthless. Mom stays quiet or walks away when he starts up calling her names. I think it hurts her feelings, but she never fights back. At least Dad didn't call her names, but it's hard to remember them being in the same room together long enough to fight.

We wind up bowling, but no Dad sighting. Patrick doesn't know Dad's car was in the parking lot. Sometimes he parks behind his office near the dumpster he shares with the chicken place. It's confusing that he doesn't pick us up since he works so close. Someday I might just walk into his office and ask where he's been.

CHAPTER 8

Yours, Mine, and Ours–The Reality

One Rosh Hashanah, the Jewish New Year, we attend services and dress up in uncomfortable clothes—collared shirts, clip-on ties, jackets, and fancy dress shoes. Richard and Mom want everyone to see our "happy" family. The synagogue is packed with families dressed in new outfits. Everyone acts like it's the National Dog Show and they're competing for Best in Show. I know about this because Dad has a poster in the back of his office (where the dogs are kept) showing the prizes for classes and breeds. I sometimes have to sit and wait for him, so I memorized each dog breed.

When we show up for services our seats are in the back row. Neither Richard nor Mom knew we needed tickets. You pay more to sit up close, like at a baseball game. The rich are up front and the poor are in the bleachers. (To me, the back is better, because escape is easier.) When the old usher with the long beard and yarmulke explains this, pointing toward the back row, Richard begins arguing. He doesn't care that he's causing a public disturbance. Richard will never back down, and despite hundreds of people watching, he commands us to follow him. Mom is beet red, embarrassed, and stares at her feet while we walk behind her. Richard spies second-row seats and pushes aside the reserved sign.

"Sit down here," he growls like an attack dog.

Dad says you can tell a dog's about to bite by the way they snarl and bare their teeth.

Richard is seething—scowling while his eyes darken. Rage causes his body to tense up. A man, who turns out to be the temple president, explains we can't sit there. Negotiating with Richard is a mistake. Richard starts to push him, but Mom grabs his arm.

The man shakes his head and says, "That's fine, the seats are yours for a $5,000 donation."

Richard looks at him. The entire congregation stares. For once, his bully tactics don't work. Mom, her face still flushed, tries to calm him.

"Richard, it's OK, we want the kids to be close to the bathroom anyway. Seven of them going back and forth to pee will cause a disturbance. Plus, Cindy is just out of diapers. She still has accidents."

He seems to calm, and his snarl becomes more of a bark. He stares at the temple president and repeats what Mom just said as if it's his idea.

"Elaine, let's go. It's better to be closer to the bathroom than here." We stand up, the congregation quiet as everyone waits for us to leave. Seven pairs of feet shuffling along the wooden floor like prisoners with leg irons is all that can be heard.

Richard snaps, "Jesus, can you pick your fucking feet up when you walk?"

I think we're going to take the seats near the bathroom. Richard slows, but we don't stop until we get to the car. *Great, I think, no services. We get to skip services!* It was totally worth the humiliation.

***

A dark cloud of fear follows me. My safe place is the basement closet or the woods behind the house. The entire family breathes a sigh of relief whenever Richard leaves. There is no joy when we see him pull into the driveway. Mom and Richard fight every time Dad is supposed to pick us up, because he's never on time. Richard is early for everything and quotes Vince Lombardi, who tells his players, "If you're five minutes early, you're already ten minutes late."

Richard's right. Dad's always late to pick us up, and sometimes he brings us home earlier than planned. He seems erratic and likes making Mom mad. A few times, he said there was an emergency, and if no one was home, he would leave us at the neighbor's house. He has a lot of emergencies. He shows up less and less and our visits get shorter and shorter.

Dad sometimes even forgets to pick me up from baseball practice. Richard's right about some things. For the rest of my life, on time will mean ten minutes early.

It's taken a year for the house rules to sink in, but I've accepted that the Eichenblatts are here to stay. Dad is no longer referred to as "my dad." He's called "Allen Nestle" or "the Nestle father." Mom begs me to call Richard "Dad," or "Richard Daddy," but I refuse. Robert and Lori started calling him "Dad" soon after he moved in. I can't do it. That's admitting defeat.

Sometimes Mom yells, "Steven, you must call him something. He's angry, and it's disrespectful. You're the only one in the whole family who refuses. His kids call me Mom. Can you at least try?"

"Why? I have a dad. Richard's not him."

"Steven, just try. OK?"

"OK," I say, but we both know it won't happen. Something inside my brain won't allow it. She keeps trying. My guess is that Mom tells Richard she's trying. She wants me to give him a chance. *Why? He doesn't ever give me one.* She suggests I ask him to play catch or go down to the basement and ask if he needs help.

Richard spends many nights putting together a Lionel train set with actual engines and a railroad crossing with a bridge and a red caboose. The set has a real train horn. He's rebuilding the trains for Mark, and no one else can touch them. He caught me trying to run them and screamed that the trains have been in *his* family and aren't for me. I started to say, "Aren't I your family?" but I don't want to be his family. The trains are cool, but I never go near them again. When Mark offers to let me play with them, I refuse.

To make Mom happy, I try my best. Richard will be at his workbench and I'll ask if he wants help, but he usually ignores me. Sometimes, I go back upstairs without speaking.

There's also a big room with old toys in the basement with a storage closet in the corner where I keep my books. My favorites are sports books about football or baseball players, and Horatio Alger stories. I read biographies from the library about Babe Ruth, Lou Gehrig, and Jim Thorpe. Reading keeps me safe. My mind hides in their pages, which protect me from reality. Within their words, I learn that to become a hero, and save others, I need to survive.

One book I read is about John F. Kennedy and patrol torpedo boat *PT-109*, and how he was a war hero. He dove into dangerous waters to save his men after a Japanese destroyer sunk their boat. He risked his life for his men, and they trusted him to keep them safe. Those soldiers were fighting for a cause. I'm trying to stay safe in my own home. There is no way Richard would risk his life to save anyone. If our house caught fire, he would run away from the flames.

The closet is the perfect place to read. Neither Richard nor Mom know when I'm there and won't look unless it's important. The basement is unfinished, with a concrete gray floor. It's cold and dark. Mom spends time there washing and ironing everyone's clothes.

Richard doesn't want me there any more than I want to be there. It always feels like he's going to punch me in the stomach. He barks, "Go grab me the Phillips head screwdriver and a 3/8-

inch socket wrench. Be quick about it. Might as well try to use you."

I have no idea who Phillip is and can't remember which socket size he wants. He never has explained the different tools and sets me up to fail. I bring back two tools. He rolls the wrench and screwdriver around from hand to hand, like they're weapons.

"What the fuck is this? Are you stupid? Your mom says you read big books. She says you love books like some librarian. You aren't even smart enough to grab the right tools!"

He sticks the screwdriver about an inch from my face, then throws the tools across the basement. They hit the wall and crash against the dryer. "Do you even know what a Phillips head is?"

I hear the basement door opening. Someone steps down the stairs. "Is everything OK down there?" Mom asks.

"Everything is perfect, Elaine," Richard shouts. "Just your son screwing up the screwdrivers. This boy knows nothing about tools—even less than his sisters."

He keeps her on edge. I wait for Mom to come down, but she moves back upstairs. *Why doesn't she defend me?* The door at the top of the stairs slams shut, and it's just Richard and me again. He tells me to grab some specific size nut or bolt, or screw or nail, but I'm not listening. I can't deal with the pressure.

Instead, I tell him I'm going to the bathroom and run out the back door. Pines Lake School is close, and Mr. Palumbo might still be there. He's the janitor. He lets me play basketball in the gym. Sometimes, he lets me help him mop and even asks me to fetch tools but is always nice and says thank you. He won't let me use the waxer because he says it's dangerous. I'm not sure he knows my name. He calls everyone "kid" or "kiddo."

My new brothers and sisters only know Richard as their father. We never talk about Allen Nestle or their dead mom. There are no family pictures anywhere and I've never seen a photo of their first mom. Mom's pictures are on the walls of Nana and Pappa's house. They live in Florida now, so we don't see them much. Mom looks happy in her pictures. She's tall with dark black hair, and always has a nice smile. Her wedding picture to Dad is there, and she wears a white dress with girly fringes and some princess-looking things in her hair. Mom says she has big boobs, but that's embarrassing. She used to laugh and tell me that boys at school would run into her on purpose to touch her chest. She doesn't laugh anymore.

We kids begin to unite, like an army squad thrown together in war. Our kid dinners force us to sit together; we even attack the food like soldiers. The seven of us eat dinner apart from Mom and Richard. Mom cooks a bunch of hot dogs or sometimes chicken. She makes good lasagna, but feeding seven kids means a lot of food, and Mark will grab huge chunks with his hands before anyone else can get a piece.

Mr. Palumbo tells me his wife and kids eat dinner together every night, and that on Sundays, they eat a huge Italian meal with the grandparents, aunts, uncles, cousins, nieces, nephews, and anyone else who shows up. He invites me, but Mom won't like it. When I mention this to Mom, Richard hears and says he's just a janitor.

Richard comes home most nights as we finish dinner. We're all seated at the dinner table, relaxed and even joking, until we hear his car. When he pulls in we get quiet and hope he doesn't storm into the kitchen. Mom reports to him when he calls for her. When he's not home, she stays in her bedroom with the door closed, or on the telephone. She fights with Lori because Richard says Lori causes trouble and Mom needs to "handle" her. Mom tells Richard the bad things we've done, and then we wait, hoping he won't explode. Our house used to be calm, and other than when Mom and Dad would fight, no one yelled.

Now, it seems like there are always explosions. Mom yells like she never did before, unless we deserved it. For instance, she yelled when Mark threw a baseball at Larry's head and broke the front window, or when I snuck into the kitchen and broke a glass milk bottle. When Richard's home on the weekends, we're forced to do chores. Mom is not the same mom. *Where did that Mom go?* She's always bothered or in a hurry when I try to talk to her. She locks herself in her bedroom for hours some days—just like my father did.

With seven kids, someone's always in trouble. Most days Richard saves his big anger for Mom, Mark, or Lori. Mark fights with Larry almost every day. Larry's scrappy, but too small to be a threat. Mark and I have had a few short scuffles.

Since we share a room, I avoid fighting with him. We get along better every day. It wasn't until Richard moved in that I started fighting. He keeps saying I'm not tough enough. Gail and Lori fight, too, but they mainly yell and cry. Richard expects Lori to introduce Gail to her friends, but Lori thinks that's unfair, and it leads to big confrontations.

***

One day, Mom decides to take all seven of us clothes shopping at Stern's in her new green Ford LTD Country Squire station wagon—which I later learned was a gift from Pappa Ben. Stern's is one of those fancy stores that doesn't even have a sports department. No fishing poles, lawnmowers, or knives. Just boring clothes and smelly perfume.

As Mom gets ready to pull out, Ton-Ton, who lives next door, dives into the back seat of the wagon, the one facing the back window. He ducks down so Mom never sees him. He's nine and plays most with Larry and Robert. His actual name is Antonio, and he's one of six kids who live next door. There are thirteen kids between our two houses, and they don't have rules like we do. Sometimes, I wander over to see what's in their fridge or what they're watching on television. Their dad died, so it's just their mom and she's nice. They are a nice family.

Mom is proud of her wood-paneled wagon until she realizes half the neighborhood moms have some version of the same car. Decades later, the wagon will be replaced in every neighborhood by the "soccer mom minivan."

Watching pretty girls try on clothes is one thing. But watching our sisters is pure torture. I'd rather be in prison. Mom might have let us stay home, but she doesn't trust Mark. It's a mistake for the girls to try on clothes with the whole family watching. We yell silly things and call them stupid and try to make each other laugh. We don't tease Cindy because she cries. Larry and Robert laugh, too, and Mom gets angry. She knows bringing the boys is a mistake. While the three girls are changing clothes, she twirls to face us, pointing her long index finger, and beckons us to come closer. Larry and Robert have disappeared, probably looking for Ton-Ton.

"Come closer, you two." She's trying to control her temper.

I ask, "What do you want, Mom?" *Getting too close could be dangerous.*

She addresses us like a coach giving us a last-minute pep talk.

"Listen, you two are the oldest boys and I expect you to behave. Set a good example for your younger brothers. Otherwise, you'll both have to sit in the car while we shop."

Mark says, "I'd love to sit in the car. Anything's better than shopping for girls' underwear and listening to you discuss whether they need bras."

There had been some debate between Mom and Lori about whether girls her age wore bras.

Because Lori's tall, we go to the women's section. Mom doesn't notice that Robert and Larry are missing. I can see them playing hide-and-seek in the baby section. I see a flash of Ton-Ton's dirty white Keds disappearing around a corner. Mom still doesn't know he's a stowaway.

Lori and Mom fight about what she can wear to school. Lori wins, because otherwise we will be here for months. Lori wants the boys to notice her and always has a crush on someone. It's taking forever.

The girls love trying on clothes. They would try on every dress in the store if Mom let them. When Mom takes me shopping, we argue because I hate trying on clothes and parading around wearing jeans that are plywood stiff and two sizes too small. She says I must be color-blind because the clothes I wear never match. *Who cares? Just get me out of the store.*

Gail never tells Mom what she likes so Mom shows her different clothes, while Gail just looks at her, the braces on her teeth the brightest part of her expression. Gail's funny, though, and rolls her eyes at Mom and even the shop clerk when they aren't looking. She says she doesn't care, but she takes forever. A couple of boys at school like her, but she's too shy to talk to anyone. Gail has curly brown hair, deep blue eyes, and freckles. She can be fun and tries her best to protect everyone from Richard. She even tries to keep Mark in line. She's Richard's favorite, his oldest, and a quiet child. He never yells at her. She's the one person Richard seems to like.

Mark and I are bored beyond belief. The other boys are still running around the baby section, and I see Ton-Ton headed up the escalator toward the bathrooms. Mom tells me to keep an eye on my brothers, but instead, I ask Mark if he wants to play hide-and-seek. Of course, she doesn't tell me to watch Ton-Ton. Why would she? She still doesn't know he's here. We begin running around through the different departments, laughing. Mom says we are not to touch a thing or jump on the furniture.

We ignore the other customers giving us dirty looks. We hide under the clothing racks in the women's underwear section. We both throw bras on our faces and make booby jokes and crack up at the nude mannequins. *What does bra mean anyway? Is it short for something else?* The black bra I grab is big enough to fit over my nose. Mark has some pink, lacy one that looks like it could be worn by a Sears Catalog model. Mom asked me once why I had the catalog under my bed. I told her it's to look at the tools.

When it's finally time to go, Mark hides. Mom yells for him to come, then sees him as he takes off running through the dresses, knocking some off their hangers. He knocks over the half-naked mannequin and squeezes its breasts as he passes. He's quick and avoids tackles like a running back. The sales clerk tries to catch him, but she's too old. Mark just laughs, loving the game. Gail makes a half-hearted effort to slow him down. Mom yells for him to stop. All of us stand and watch like it's a movie. Mark scampers to the furniture section, where he executes a perfect swan dive onto a king-sized bed with fancy sheets and multicolored pillows. An old woman screams. He then takes off in a full sprint for the door. Mom yells "Catch him!" to me, but he's faster—plus, I'm enjoying the excitement. Mom leaves behind the pile of clothes my sisters just spent hours picking out. She tells them, "Forget the clothes."

Shopping's over.

Mark's in the parking lot now, and Mom's screaming for us to get in the car. My sisters cry, and Gail tells Mark to stop acting like a baby. He finally jumps in the car, landing on Larry's lap.

Mark laughs and I begin to giggle. I'm laughing, but I'm not sure why. I can't stop giggling, and every time I try, Mark starts up again. Soon my stomach hurts—and then it hits me.

"Stop! Stop! Ton-Ton's not in the car!"

Mom swerves over to the side of the road. She's as mad as I have ever seen her, and her voice cracks like she's going to cry. "Everyone, shut up!" She sounds like Richard. I've never heard her say this before. I sneak a nervous smile at Mark, and he smiles back, and soon we're giggling again. Mom turns around to stare at me. "Steven, do you want to be punished with him?" Then it hits her. "Wait, what do you mean "Ton-Ton's not in the car?'"

Everyone's cracking up now, and Mom begins to yell even louder. "*What* are you talking about?"

"Mom. Ton-Ton came with us. He jumped into the back at the last second. I think he went to the bathroom, and... we *forgot* him."

She takes a deep breath, "Are you kidding me? You think this is funny?" She hits the gas and the tires screech as she whirls the car around and speeds back to Stern's. When we pull up, Ton-Ton is waiting outside the front door, hands in his pockets, a smile on his face. He's a quiet, dark-haired kid who is big for his age. His brothers say he weighs a ton. So, his nickname became Ton-Ton. I don't think he weighs a ton because we're studying measurement in school and that's two-thousand pounds! He's a nice kid and I'm sorry we left him.

I swing open the back door and Ton-Ton thumps in like nothing has happened. He just grins, and we all try not to laugh. No words are spoken. Mom is burning with anger. We reach a stop light, and she turns to look at Mark. "This is all your fault. You are in BIG trouble."

I blurt out, "Mom, can you give Mark a break? You know his dad is going to hurt him."

Mom looks at me. "Steven, he's *your* dad, too." As the light turns green, she accelerates into the intersection while snapping at Mark, "When we get home, you're going straight to your room until your father comes home." I notice she says *his* room. It used to be *my* room. I stay quiet but can feel tingling in my skin. Nothing's the way it used to be. Every day seems worse than the day before.

When we get home, Mom follows Mark and makes sure he closes the door. She grabs a chair and sits down outside our bedroom door. "I'm not letting you out until your father gets home," she yells through the closed door. "Forget about dinner. I don't care if you starve to death."

Mark laughs behind the door. Mom sits and waits, determined.

The house becomes quiet, so the rest of us go outside. I check occasionally, but Mom never moves. I walk into the hallway and hear her sobbing. I ask if she's OK.

"Oh, Steven," she says, "I've made a big mistake."

"Yeah, Mom, forcing us to shop with the girls was a big mistake."

She looks away, trying to hide her tears. Mom doesn't cry much, so I'm not sure what to say. For a few seconds, the silence is broken only by the sound of her opening her pocketbook and grabbing a tissue. She dries her eyes and whispers, "I never should have married him. I thought Richard would be a good father. Your Dad was no father and you needed a man." She has said this before, but nothing changes.

Staying hidden works for me most of the time. From the basement, I hear the front door open, but Richard doesn't yell when he walks in the house. He doesn't say anything. His heavy-soled shoes thump toward the coat closet where I hear him removing his jacket. He drives from the South Bronx daily and complains about traffic and slow drivers. He's been in a few accidents and claims he hurt his back.

The silence doesn't last. Richard's shoes creak toward the stairs. The vibration can be felt all the way in the basement. He's now pounding up the stairs like a stampeding elephant.

Marlin's voice pops in my head: *"Jim, before we take a commercial break, do something about that damn elephant before he hurts someone. He missed his cue."*

Jim's too late, but *Wild Kingdom* is made for television. I make my way upstairs to watch the action. Richard walks past Mom and opens Mark's door. Mark's screams then pierce the uneasy silence. Richard must have the belt out. I picture him hitting Mark. Each whack brings a cry. Richard yells, "YOU FUCKING IDIOT." He's out of control. I hear the noise, but I'm not listening. Then Mark begins to laugh. WHACK! The louder Mark laughs, the madder Richard gets and the harder he will hit. WHACK! WHACK! WHACK! Mark needs to shut up.

I decide to take a chance and sneak out the front door and grab my bike from the garage. It's getting dark but I decide to head toward Pompton Lake. I haven't been there since the day I lost the bass. The Sweet Shop is nearby. Maybe Dad will be there buying cigarettes.

When I get home, Mark and Richard are moving around upstairs in my room. I can't make out any words, but Richard's still angry. This was once my house, but now everything and everyone belongs to Richard. He's taken over and there's nothing I can do.

***

On the weekends, Richard makes us work. Mom says it's good for us, but she's not the one raking every single leaf out of the backyard or picking weeds until it gets dark. We're not allowed to take breaks or go inside until every leaf is gone. We load up plastic bags and then dump them in the woods behind our house. When Richard gets mad, he brings the bags back and dumps the pile back on the grass and tells us to start over.

Richard says work unites us as a family, and his kids must learn to get their hands dirty. He lectures me about protecting my brothers and sisters and how he's going to teach me to fight like a man. We're not allowed to hang out with some neighborhood kids because they don't include Mark in the street hockey or Wiffle ball games.

Richard and Mom always fight. One day, some neighborhood kids are standing outside with me when we hear Mom's screams and then glass breaking. I run inside and see her running to her bedroom.

Richard storms out the front door and screams, "Fuck you, Elaine," and jumps in his car. Broken plates are all over the kitchen floor. I hear him peeling out of the driveway. I hope he crashes his car into a tree. Then we'd be free. I picture him... *Oh shit. He's back.* I hear his car door clang, followed by the BANG of the front door. Then the final slam of the bedroom door. He and my mother are talking in low voices. This isn't good.

When Mom fights with Dad, he mumbles and then gets quiet. He isn't a screamer like Richard. I never worried about Dad hitting me. These days, I worry all the time.

Mark and I are about to go to sleep one night when we hear the front door slam with enough force to cause a wall mirror to crash to the ground. We hear Richard's feet as he charges up the stairs. His routine is to walk in and put his jacket in the hall closet. Today, he just charges up the stairs. Those footsteps now pounding their way toward our door are a bad sign. Mark hears the same thing. We've gotten closer despite Mark's problems, and I'm learning to share my thoughts as well as my room.

My bed is the bottom bunk and Mark's on top. He's been in the room for a few hours because he talked back to Mom during dinner and she got upset and screamed, "Mark, if you don't behave this second, I'm calling your father at work and he will be mad."

Mark doesn't listen to her and winds up being punished. The sound of stomping feet stops and our bedroom door opens. Richard's in the doorway but doesn't say a word. He yanks Mark out of the top bunk and watches as he falls to the ground. When

Mark lands, Richard begins to kick him. He grabs Mark by his collar, drags him toward the stairs, and tells him he's going to apologize to Mom.

"My thumb!" Mark screams, holding his hand up at the bottom of the stairs. "My wrist!" Mark begins to cry. It must be bad, because Mark never cries.

Richard turns to me. "Steven, you want to be next?"

The following day, Mom takes Mark to a doctor. Mark has a broken thumb and a cracked wrist. Mom tells us that Mark is being sent away to a special school in New York where he gets to ride horses. He disappears.

He's my brother and I didn't protect him. Richard wants me to stand up for my brother but he's the bully. Someday, his turn will come.

CHAPTER 9

Wednesday Bored Game, circa 1968–69

Divorced dads pick their kids up on Wednesdays. When I ask why, Mom shrugs and says that's just the way it is. My friends don't know why, since none of their parents are divorced. I don't ever talk to anyone about the divorce, but sometimes I overhear kids talking about us.

I look forward to Wednesdays, though sometimes Dad's busy and runs late or doesn't show. He does have emergencies. People love their pets almost more than their kids, and he's the one who either saves their pets or has to tell them their dog or cat or guinea pig is dead. He always tries to save animals, even if it means giving mouth-to-mouth to a goldfish, like he did for me, even though it didn't work.

We'll be sitting on the curb, waiting for the clunking noise from his broken muffler and the squeals from his fan belt as he gets closer. We watch as he pulls in with his beat-up Chevy Impala. His car can be heard from miles away, but when he doesn't show, the silence is louder than his muffler. He shows up less and less these days.

When Dad does come, he takes us to fun places because we're bored sitting around at his apartment. Sometimes he has an animal emergency and leaves us behind. Sometimes we get to stay overnight. If he doesn't make it home, we eat cereal or cook eggs. We eat the same food for breakfast, lunch, and dinner. I convinced him once to buy Cap'n Crunch and Sugar Smacks cereal, too. Lori likes Trix, which has a white rabbit on the box. Dad's kitchen never has much food, but there's no Richard waiting to pounce when we break one of his rules. Mom's house is where Richard insists he's Dad, but he's not. You can't have two dads. This apartment is Dad's place, and he makes his own rules, though I'm not sure he has any.

Dad lets us sleep in his one bedroom, and he stays on the pullout couch. When we sleep over, Robert and I like to play Maxwell Smart and spy on him. It's a small place, so we crawl on the brown shag carpet and peek around the corner to watch. He listens to music or watches television. He reads books all the time, the kind with no pictures and thousands of pages long.

Sometimes, we go with him to the kennels and help clean the pee and poop. I don't mind, because there's always dogs and cats to pet and Dad tells us their stories. He even has a large tumor in a glass jar that he removed from a dog's stomach. He calls it Freddy.

Mom says Dad is uncomfortable around people. He says animals understand him. He mumbles unless he has a cigarette, and then he just takes long inhales without saying much. Other times, he acts confused and seems dazed. The only time he speaks clearly is when he's mad about Mom or is talking about the Yankees.

When Dad lived with us, he never made friends or even knew our next-door neighbors.

Mr. O'Brien told Mom that he had brought Precious, their dog, to Dad for treatment. Dad didn't recognize him—even though they used to stand outside and smoke together. He said Dad looked confused and said nothing when Mr. O'Brien asked how the kids were doing. Mr. O'Brien asked Mom if anything was wrong, but Mom didn't say anything. She just shook her head like it wasn't a surprise.

We have a dog now, too. Sam is a fat beagle mutt who snores and can only run a few yards before he has to lay down and sleep. Everyone loves him, and he walks the neighborhood searching for leftovers. Mom and Richard won't bring him to Dad for treatment. They take him far away to an out-of-town animal doctor.

***

We see Grandma Annie when Dad takes us to Bayonne. Grandma Annie doesn't like Mom. She and Dad fight about Mom, and

Grandma Annie gives Dad money because he owes child support. Richard yells at Mom about money and how worthless Dad is, since he doesn't support his own kids. My head spins anytime Richard insists we're *his* kids; if so, why does he need Dad's money? Real dads support their kids.

Sometimes Dad works for free—like when he has to put dogs to sleep at the animal shelter. Dad and Mom and Richard all complain about each other, and about money. We get thrown into the middle during their arguments, mostly when we're getting picked up at the house. Mom will sprint out the front door and down the driveway and snarl like a rabid cat. Dad told me once about treating a rabid cat, and the way it screamed and tried to bite him.

Mom will get to the car, her chest heaving, out of breath, and yell like we're a hundred miles away: "Allen! Allen, look at me. Where's my child support? Where's the money to put food on the table for your kids?"

He usually tries to ignore her, and then will mumble, "Calm down. The money's coming, I promise."

Mom will just shake her head, tell him he's pathetic, and then glare at us all sitting in the back seat, like we're the problem.

Sometimes Mom will stick her head in the window and ask, "Steven, am I right or is he right?"

This question always makes me squirm. Dad's sitting right there, and she acts like he's invisible. It's best to pretend I'm not listening and look out the window instead. My eyes stare without seeing anything except the words in my mind. *She isn't interested in my opinion unless it's to agree with her, but then Dad's mad.* Best to keep quiet.

The discussions usually end with Mom saying Dad will be hearing from her lawyer, and Dad calling Pappa Ben a rich Jewish prick. When I try to get them to stop, they both tell me to mind my own business. They need to fight in private, and not in front of us every time.

Our family is the only divorced one in the neighborhood. No other parents fight in front of everyone. Dad doesn't say much about Richard, but once he called him a "low-rent loudmouth from Brooklyn." Richard always brags about his fighting skills and how he was on his Army and college boxing teams. I told Dad this once because I was afraid he might try to punch Richard someday. Dad says he's not afraid of a loudmouth who brags about how tough he is. He said bullies like Richard are loud on the outside because they're weak on the inside, and they know it. I believe him but would never test his theory.

Uncle Jerry says Dad is tougher than anyone knows. He said that Dad would fight with Pappa Charley and some neighborhood bullies. Dad never talks about it but Uncle Jerry said he was in some special top-secret Army unit in France. No one knows what he did. It must have been scary because Mom doesn't even know.

Today, Dad slows down and we jump in. Our house is at the top of a hill and, as usual, I hear the car before I see it. His car sounds like it's being tortured. Richard knows about cars and says the fan belt needs to be changed before "that piece of shit car" breaks down. The exhaust stinks, the muffler drags, but Dad pays no attention to the noise. His car breaks down a lot. Once we were with him and a tow truck had to come. His nurse, Jill, who works in his office and used to babysit, drove us home. When I mentioned that Richard knows about cars, Dad shot me a nasty look and told me he didn't want to hear about Richard.

Dad never asks about our home situation. He might ask about Sam, or Snoopy, our new cat. He's seen Sam in the driveway and tells us he's fat and needs a special diet. When I mention this to Mom, she says he would lose weight but all seven kids need to stop feeding him table scraps and cookies.

Someday, I want to be able to tell him that Richard kicked me down the stairs. I want to tell him Mark is always fighting with Richard and getting beaten, even having his bones broken. Mom pretends it's not happening, but no one can stop it. I want to tell him that sometimes Richard's kids wait with us to see what *our* father looks like. Mark is the most curious. When we go to our dad's, Mark gets jealous and has asked many times to come with us, but Richard says no. I want to tell Dad that Mark complains it's not fair we get to have two fathers and he doesn't.

Richard yells at me sometimes about how "your father's" behavior is not fair to this family, and Mom needs to "take him to court." He complains that Dad is a deadbeat, as if there's something I can do about it.

Dad is goofy. He doesn't try to be funny, but he makes us laugh. Mom says he has "disabilities" related to his personality. He always forgets where he parks his car or sometimes takes me to the wrong baseball field on the wrong day for games. Dad always looks rumpled and can be a scary driver. Mom says he doesn't sleep much and drinks too much coffee. But if he doesn't drink coffee, how can he stay awake?

These days, things seem worse. It bothers me when Dad shows up later and later, or just doesn't bother coming. He's upsetting everyone, and Richard's losing patience. My stomach gets bubbly with nerves; it's the worst when we wait and don't know if he's coming or not. I wonder why he can't just call.

One winter Wednesday, Mom and Richard took Richard's kids somewhere for the day. When Dad didn't show, we waited outside, locked out of the house in the cold until Mr. O'Brien saw us and took us inside his house. Another time, Dad didn't show even when, for once, he did call and promised he was on the way. Everyone else had gone to a movie except for Lori, Robert, and me. This time I broke open the basement window and opened the door so we didn't get stuck outside again. Richard and Mom were furious. I knew I could forgive Dad. Still, why hadn't he shown up?

I am a veteran of parent wars. When Dad moved out, Richard replaced him, but the fights continued in the same house with the same rooms and the same mother, just different men.

As time passes, Dad shows up less, and we spend most of the visits we do have listening to him complain about money, business, Mom, and Pappa Ben. He seems unhappy and bitter whenever he's with us. He hasn't taken me fishing or to the Sweet Shop in a long time. Plus, he has a girlfriend now and is getting married.

Unlike Mom, he tells us about it, but we're still not invited. He's marrying Jill, his nurse.

Sometimes I don't want to go with Dad. I have friends who invite me places, but I can't go—because Dad's coming. Then he doesn't show, and I'm stuck doing nothing. Once, Patrick invited me to my first ever Mets game and I was super excited. Dad said no because it was during his time; and then on that day, he didn't even show up.

I know the neighbors feel sorry for me, because they always ask how Mom's doing. My response when adults ask about Mom is that she is doing fine, even though she isn't. I avoid eye contact with the adults. The neighbors haven't said much since Richard and his kids moved in. I don't want the entire neighborhood feeling bad for me. I can handle myself. I pretend like everything is great, and the neighbors act the same. We have an unspoken understanding to act like everything is great even though it's bad. More and more, Mom will drop us off at Dad's office. She does this when she and Richard have to go somewhere and she doesn't trust Dad to show up. Dad never seems happy to see us.

The receptionist is an older woman with glasses and gray hair. She swings open the little window and peeks out, never letting us look too far into what's happening behind her. The waiting room has a tiny desk and a painting of dogs playing poker. Dad says it's a Norman Rockwell. Years later, I would find out he was wrong. There's also a cool picture of Dad treating a lion. He says lions look cute but are predators and kill by grabbing for their prey's neck.

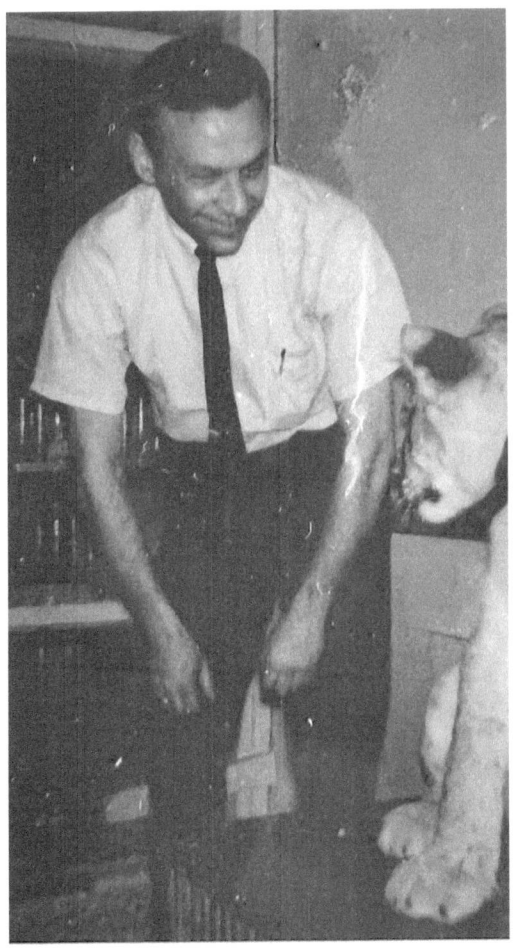

Sometimes he's doing surgery, and we must sit in the hard wooden church pew that's in the waiting area. He's so proud to own it, but he never has to sit on it. I get why church people stand so much while praying.

When Dad is in a good mood, we walk to the T-Bowl, the bowling alley a couple doors down, and eat at the snack counter. The dessert is the best—homemade chocolate pudding with a layer of chocolate skin on the top. Well, they claim it's homemade, but a bowling alley isn't a home, and I've watched them make it right in their kitchen. Robert and I like the bar stools that can whip you around in circles. We sit and spin each other until someone tells us to knock it off.

There's a jukebox, and sometimes Dad gives us money to pick songs. It mostly has boring Frank Sinatra and Bing Crosby music, but there are some Beatles songs and even The Monkees. Dad will sit at the counter watching us, smoking cigarettes and drinking coffee.

I love the smell and noise of T-Bowl. Our family—when it used to be our family—would come here together before Dad left. The stuff they wipe on the lanes to make them slippery smells sweet, like gasoline. I like hearing the crackling of burning grease when the cook drowns the basket of fries. I like hearing the thwack of the bowling balls hitting the wooden lanes and then the sharp noise when pins get knocked down. I can even tell when the ball goes into the gutter because you hear seconds of silence waiting for the pins to crash down, but nothing happens.

If we bowl, we get shoes with cool colors and stripes and a number on the back, like my baseball uniform. I'm number seven like Mickey Mantle, so I always try to get the number seven shoe. I'm not a good bowler, though I once bowled a 182.

We used to go to the movies, but since Lori told Mom we saw a naked lady in *The Prime of Miss Jean Brodie*, we don't go much.

I liked seeing the naked lady but told my mother I didn't notice her. My sister tells Mom everything, so I have to be careful. When the day is over, we usually spend the night at Dad's apartment in Pompton Lakes. He always forces us to be in bed by nine. My dad calls his apartment "the Nestle bachelor pad," and says he's like Joe Namath, the quarterback from the Jets. I hate the Jets. I like Fran Tarkenton and the Giants. I like the brown shag carpet and the soft sheepskins on the bed. Dad says they're real and you can tell because there's white fur on one side and the other side is the skin, which stinks.

Robert and I wrestle on Dad's carpet, which is squishy and doesn't hurt if we hit our heads. The last time we went home after wrestling on the carpet, Mom said it smelled like our clothes were washed in cigarette smoke. One time we were running around and I fell and hit my head on a stone coffee table. I did my best to hold my breath. Dad says boys don't cry. I wound up back at the hospital to get my head stitched up.

Dad has a poster of Raquel Welch almost naked in a caveman outfit on the inside of his bathroom door. Dad says people think he looks like Frank Sinatra. I know they grew up close to each other near Bayonne, because Grandma Annie repeats the same story about meeting Sinatra's grandmother. She says Sinatra's aunt comes into her yarn store. She tells it like it's the first time, but she's told us at least fifty times. Dad says it's probably not even Sinatra's aunt but some distant cousin who never even met Frank.

Sometimes we head to Bayonne. Grandma Annie loves to watch us eat and is always cooking something, usually pot roast with carrots and potatoes. She also makes noodles with cinnamon and cream cheese. I don't like the pot roast, but she makes me eat it. I've gotten good at spitting it into my napkin when she isn't looking and throwing the napkin away.

Grandma Annie's place smells like mothballs and the heater and toilet always make lots of noises. Pappa Charley takes us out on his boat and we float by the Statute of Liberty. He flies an American flag and a Marine Patrol flag, and we stop and help other boaters. I love being with him. Mom is afraid the boat's going to sink, but so far it hasn't.

Pappa Charley has a huge belly that he calls his "beer baby." He burps a lot and we laugh because it sounds like he has frogs inside him. He pats his gut and says it takes a lot of work to get this size and that it's his pride and joy. Grandma Annie says he's disgusting, then hugs him and says she loves him.

When Dad takes us to Bayonne, there are rules about who we're allowed to mention and who we aren't. One time, "Uncle Bill" met us at Dad's apartment but I know that wasn't his name because my dad kept calling him Gus. I learned later that Uncle Bill is Dad's real father, who left him when he was a teenager. He doesn't want Grandma Annie to know they are in touch but wanted us to meet him. He is afraid we might slip and tell Grandma about Gus, so we call him Bill. I don't get it but Dad says he will explain someday.

Anyway, I can't always keep track of who we're allowed to tell what to, and which person hates who, so I don't mention anyone's name to this person or that person, and I don't tell him I saw her, or she saw him, and on and on.

Adults make things complicated and confusing when they tell you not to tell someone one thing but to tell some other person another thing. Dad is insistent we not tell Mom who we saw or where we went or who was there. When we get home, Mom first asks who we saw and where we went and who was there. It's hard to keep up, and then Mom will ask questions I won't answer about Dad's girlfriends.

Dad has Battleship, the game, at his apartment. I love to name the enemy ships. The Battleship Richard gets blown up first, and next, the Battleship Mr. Schimmel gets destroyed. He's our Hebrew school principal, who yelled at me in front of the whole school. He didn't like the peace signs and drawings I made in my prayer book. He called Mom to tell her I'd been disrespectful to God. How can God be mad about peace signs? It's not right either, since we fight wars and blow people up to find peace.

Since I refuse to share a bed with Robert or Lori at Dad's, I wind up using a floor air mattress. I like throwing my sleeping bag on the thick shag and creating my own area. I don't like to share my space. Dad sleeps on the couch, which opens up and turns into a bed. When we get up in the morning, we find him sprawled out, sleeping with the television on and a half-finished Camel in a dirty ashtray on the coffee table. He is cranky in the morning, so we try our best to keep quiet.

Mom calls him a night owl. He stays up long after we go to bed. I like to lie awake and listen to the sounds to see if I can figure out what he's doing. Some nights I can hear Johnny Carson and *The Tonight Show*. I like when the announcer says: "Heeere's Johnny!" I don't know what Johnny looks like because I only hear his voice and laugh and the music.

Other nights I can hear the stereo and feel the vibration on the floor if he's listening to rock. Most nights, he types for hours and the tap-tap-tapping only stops when the bell sounds and he resets for his next sentence. Other times, he pulls out the paper in one long motion and it sounds like he's unzipping his jacket. When that happens, I can tell he's throwing the page away because the chair will squeak and his feet shuffle toward the garbage can.

The typewriter has a lingering oily, sweet smell, and when Dad changes its ribbon, the scent gets stronger. I can imagine the ink is wetter and darker on the pages. I can always tell when he decides to correct or replace a word because the room's odor, already mixed with the scent of the typewriter, cigarette smoke, and his coffee, is invaded by Wite-Out, which smells like paint. He uses it to cover up his mistakes.

Dad never tells us what he's writing. The typing paper is yellow. Once I tried to read what he wrote, but it was weird. Dad likes strange poetry and artists. He talks about movies and hangs poems by Rod McKuen up on his wall. Dad listens to sad orchestral music, chanting rabbis, and songs in Yiddish. It's all boring noise. I do like Glen Campbell, and so does Dad. He has a television show and sings songs like "Wichita Lineman," "Galveston," and "By the Time I Get to Phoenix."

One day, Dad takes us to New York. We're walking down the street and Dad says we just walked past Woody Allen. He says he knows Woody from his writing school in New York. He's excited. I have never heard of Woody Allen. He asks me if I saw the guy wave at him like he knew him. Dad acts like it's a big deal, but it's not like seeing Mickey Mantle or Willie Mays. I didn't see Woody Allen, but I pretend I did because that seems to make Dad happy. Plus, I might have seen him but didn't recognize him, because

I've never heard of him so I don't know what he looks like. When Dad describes him as a short balding Jewish man, I tell him that it might have been Richard.

At Dad's place, we play imagination games. Sometimes, I crawl on the ground like G.I. Joe and grab the game Operation from his closet. The idea of the game is to play surgeon and remove body parts from Cavity Sam, a body with a nose that lights up and a buzzer that screams if the tweezers touch metal edges as we remove organs.

A surgical mishap means a loud buzzing noise like an entire bumblebee colony has been unleashed, followed by an angry father who's been woken up out of a sound sleep. We dive under the covers.

One morning, Dad's different. The buzzer goes off when I try to take out the heart, and Dad looks upset and I worry he's going to yell. Instead, he scans the room like he's filming a movie and looks confused. Something's off, because he doesn't say a word about my using the game without his permission. His eyes have a faraway look. He tells us to get dressed because today he's taking us to see the movie *Oliver!*. I tell him it isn't my fault that the game made noise.

"Dad, can I please bring the game home? I will bring it back next week when we see you. Please!"

He says, "Stop asking about the game. Don't you have games at home? Operation stays here. Plus, you never know what next week will bring."

I figure his answer will be the same next week and the week after that. He knows I'll forget about it. My thoughts speed around my brain so fast that I'm on to the next one before I finish the last. It's like my brain finishes a sentence before I can even finish saying it and then I start a new one. Maybe the reason I talk so fast is so I can race my brain to finish the thought. Mom doesn't understand when I try to explain.

Dad's saying something, but I'm not listening. I'm thinking about the movies. *Oliver!* should be good, and I'll get to eat Whoppers, which are malted milk balls, my favorite Dad-movie-candy. I never eat Whoppers except with him at the movies. It's like my Yoo-hoo rule with fishing.

When we leave the movie theatre, it's snowing hard. *Oliver!* is a great movie and has a happy ending. Hamburg Turnpike has turned into a frozen road covered by a crispy layer of snow that crunches under the tires. The car slides, and the wind moans as it blows the snow sideways and tries to force our car into one of the growing snow banks. My father works hard to keep us straight on the street.

I steam the window with my breath and then write, "Steve Nestle the Great," but my sister keeps reaching over and erasing it. Dad tells us to keep quiet because he has to concentrate. He lights a cigarette and rolls the window down an inch. The wipers squeak as they lose their battle to keep the windshield clean. They only create a hole so Dad can see the road.

Outside my frosted window, I start to count the snowflakes but all I can see is one big snow wall being dumped from the sky. I imagine space aliens with pointy ears like Spock from *Star Trek* using giant buckets to get the snow off their own planets. Or maybe we're a speck, like in the Dr. Seuss book about Horton the Elephant who carries the town of Whoville around in his trunk. The roads are quiet; only a couple of others are crazy enough to be out driving. I see a few cars stuck in the snow banks. I'm hoping the snow will get bad enough that the siren will sound tomorrow at six thirty in the morning, canceling school. I love it when that happens. There's money to be made shoveling driveways.

Oliver! is a movie about an orphan boy who escapes from the bad guy, finds his aunt, and is adopted, so now he has a new family. I'm embarrassed to admit I have this good feeling from *Oliver!*, even though I know it's just a movie. It's like the Horatio Alger books I read. I normally hate musicals, because just when a cool part is about to happen, someone launches into a song that takes forever. Like, when Oliver wants more porridge and instead of the teacher just saying no, the whole orphanage has to sing a song and dance about it. James Bond doesn't stop and sing about killing the bad guys; he just shoots. The movie is good for a musical, but it would have been shorter without the songs and I could have gotten home earlier. Plus, maybe what happened wouldn't have happened if it ended earlier.

When the story ends, there's no chance Oliver will have to return to the workhouse and Mr. Bumble, the horrible man in charge of the orphanage.

The snow continues, and the sky has darkened as we veer off Hamburg Turnpike. We drive down Colfax road with its trees, telephone poles, and mailboxes close to the edge. Our house is off Colfax and close to the Wayne Racquet Club. My school is Schuyler Colfax Junior High School. I wonder if Colfax Road is named after the school—which is named after some dead vice president—or the great Jewish pitcher, Sandy Koufax. Probably not, since their last names are different...

Dad says you can tell where the Jewish people live because their houses are dark, so Santa knows not to deliver there. The Christmas lights on some of the houses are bright enough for Santa to see from the North Pole. Sometimes I wish we could get a tree and maybe just a couple of colored lights. This way, Santa might be faked out and will bring us a toy. But we don't celebrate Christmas. Some Jewish people like the whole Santa thing and even get a tree. Richard mocks Jews with Christmas trees or lights. He says they're ashamed to be Jewish so pretend to be goyim. My friends say we have Hanukkah, which is like Christmas, but they're wrong.

I stare at the decorations and think of kids and families by the tree singing songs, like on *The Waltons*. Most houses have the tree near the window so you can look at the ornaments on it and the presents under it. Sometimes, I go next door to the O'Briens' to see their tree, and the train set that circles the whole room. The fireplace is always lit and the wood crackles, while Mr. O'Brien moves the pieces around with a black fireplace poker.

I might ring the O'Briens' doorbell when we get home and ask if I can see the train.

Just then, the car starts to slide and my heart jumps as I hear Dad yelling for us to hold on. He turns the wheel like crazy, fighting to control the car, then throws his arm across us like he's trying to keep us from getting hurt. The car is out of control. He grips the steering wheel again. We sail across somebody's front yard. My stomach lurches, like when a roller coaster drops down and your guts are in your throat for a second.

We slam into a small tree, then a mailbox, and the high-pitched scraping sound of metal scratching the car surprises me, like the way a scary movie scene makes you jump. Except this is not a movie. The car keeps sliding until we finally smash a jolly Santa who's been standing with a big bag of toys over his shoulder, his lights sparkling in rhythm to the sound of "Jingle Bells" and his voice bellowing, "Ho, ho, ho, Merry Christmas!" from some tape recorder in his fake fat gut.

We've killed Santa, who lies in pieces on the snow-covered ground. His lights, however, keep flickering, though his reindeer is nowhere in sight. Things become quiet for a moment, and then I hear, "Ho, ho, ho, Merry Christmas!" Santa survived, but I don't think he'll be making many stops in his current condition, though he did stop our car just as we were about to crush the Baby Jesus in his manger. Santa has saved Jesus, which saves us the guilt of killing Santa and Jesus on the same night.

Dad checks to make sure we're alright and then tells us to wait as he opens the car door and gets out. I see his cigarette get flicked off his finger and into a snowbank. He rings the doorbell and stands with his hands in his pockets and rocks back and forth. He waits a minute and then knocks hard using his frozen fist. The door opens and a woman sticks her head out the front door to survey the damage. She lets Dad into the house. A man sticks his head out and shakes his head.

Dad walks back down the icy steps and his shoes disappear in the fresh powdery snow accumulating on the lawn. He lifts each foot extra high off the ground to clear the snow. He reaches the car after almost falling a couple of times and knocks on the window.

I say, "Who is it?" before unlocking the door, but he doesn't laugh. He opens the door, grabs his Camels, and tells us my mom is on her way and someone's coming to tow his car. Then he waits outside. He lights a smoke.

Santa is quiet now. The only noise is sliding cars trying not to end up next to us, and the only light is at the end of my dad's cigarette. The tip gets brighter as he inhales. Every few minutes, he flicks another butt into the snow and pulls out his lighter to start again.

Ten minutes later, I see headlights approaching. It's Richard. My heart vibrates like it's attached to an electrical socket. Dad's face shows no emotion, but he does flick his half-smoked cigarette into the snow. Richard's bright headlights blind us. I close my eyes, afraid to watch their meeting. My stomach snarls with anxiety. Robert asks what's happening and I tell him Richard is here to pick us up.

Richard parks on the side of the road. Richard makes me nervous. I don't want to look toward him or make eye contact. I'm sure he's aggravated that he had to drive to pick us up in the snow. I think of the nasty Mr. Bumble in *Oliver!* who always screams at the children who ask for more food.

We wait for Richard's door to open, but instead, he honks and motions us to come to the car. There will be no meeting, no epic fight or argument, and no conversation. They will probably never even make eye contact. The two will never meet.

My father opens his front car door without a glance toward Richard and gets in. "Go ahead," he tells us. "Everything will be fine."

He leans back to give us each a peck on the cheek. We pile out of the car and say, "See ya Wednesday." He looks at us and tries to smile.

We head toward Richard's car, and I realize I still have the heart from the Operation game in my pocket. I will return it when he picks us up on Wednesday.

He never picks us up again. I throw the heart away.

CHAPTER 10

Bar Mitzvah Boy

Mom tells us one morning that we're going to have a talk. She leads Robert, Lori, and me into her room and locks the door. It's been years since the three of us were separated from the rest. We're never allowed in the bedroom, so there's serious news to come. Lori and I are now close to twelve. Mom seems nervous, because she's rushing. She slams the door behind us. When we walk in the room, her bed's not even made, so something must be wrong.

The last serious conversation we had with Mom was about getting bar mitzvahed. She never talks to just the three of us without Richard, so Mom must not want him involved.

Since he moved in, I've mostly been in the bedroom for punishment. Usually, Mom and Richard will ask me questions about why my grades are so bad. I say, "I don't know," and we go in circles because they say, "I don't know is not an answer," yet I insist that it is my answer. The truth is, I don't care.

Sometimes the belt is whipped across my butt, but it no longer bothers me. The first time Richard threatened the belt, I thought he was kidding. The red welts that showed up on my rear weren't a joke. Mom would leave the room and he would hit me. Then she'd pretend nothing happened.

Mom doesn't want to make things worse, so she goes along with Richard's rules and punishments. The last time I was summoned, it was so Richard could explain why my bar mitzvah is important to the future of the Jewish people. Richard's always bashing the Jews but forces us to attend Hebrew school. He says rabbis are people not smart enough to do anything else, and cantors are just singers who weren't good enough for Broadway and not smart enough to be rabbis.

Mom never went to temple as a kid, so she doesn't understand the torture. Twice a week, I go to Hebrew school. Sitting for another three hours after regular school as the teacher rambles on trying to teach us a language with no vowels is worse than math class. On Saturday, we are required to attend the morning services and don't get home until the afternoon.

Being the only Jewish kid on my baseball team means missing Saturday games and going late to weekday night games. I wear my uniform to save time and sit in class wearing baseball cleats. When I'm late, I don't get to play the whole game, even though I'm the team's top hitter and made All-Stars. I understand why it's so hard for Jews to become professional athletes. They're stuck in Hebrew school.

We also have bar mitzvah lessons with the cantor. He is the one teaching us our Torah portion and trying to get me to focus. He doesn't spit like the rabbi so that's good. The worst part is singing in front of friends and the entire congregation. I'm unhappy and terrified about the whole event. All my Christian friends have to do to get presents is watch some fat fake Santa crawl down the chimney. They don't suffer through Hebrew and humiliation. There are even Jewish families that act like Santa comes to their house. That's not right, either. We will never get a tree—no way. And to top it off, Dad killed Santa.

Eventually, Mom and Richard promise to let me quit Hebrew school and pay for drum lessons if I go along with the bar mitzvah. The whole becoming a man deal is never discussed. For me, the goal is no more Hebrew school.

Today, Mom's behavior feels different. She has the three of us in her room but won't meet our eyes. The bedroom has a huge bed and smells like Richard's aftershave. The walls have some modern art paintings that look like some kindergarten kid has vomited colors on canvas and signed it. There are no dogs playing poker like Dad has—and Mom always hated. It makes me nervous to look around the room, so I bury my bare feet in the shag carpet and look down, hoping Richard doesn't show up. Mom has a couple of books on her nightstand, one of which is *Everything You Ever Wanted to Know About Sex but Were Afraid to Ask*. It's painful and disgusting to think that Mom and Richard might have sex. *No way.*

Mom tells us she has some news. She attempts a fake smile and announces that Richard has agreed to adopt us and become our real legal father. Isn't that exciting?

Is she kidding? What is happening? Richard can't really want this. Did she have to talk him into it? There's no way Dad wants this, is there? My mind pictures every scenario, like a slide projector making the clacking noise as it clicks from one image to another.

Mom acts like she's just told us we won the lottery. She looks disappointed when we don't react. When Mom asks how I feel, I say I don't know. She says that's not a feeling, but in my mind having no feeling *is* a feeling. It's the feeling of no feeling. What does she expect?

Instead, I ask, "When do I get to see Dad again? It's been a long time."

She stares at me and doesn't answer. Mom delivers her lines like an actress: " Now that I have adopted Richard's kids, Richard is adopting you so we'll be one happy united family. We will all even have the same last name." Her fake smile returns.

"Happy? That's a joke. I'd rather be adopted by Frankenstein— the real one, not Herman Munster."

Mom gives me a tired look and snaps, "Richard's your *dad* now. He considers you his *blood* children."

I look at the floor without speaking and no longer care. There is no mention of Allen. He's been gone for years. He stopped calling even on our birthdays.

It's safer to block any sign of feelings. And that's what I feel for both "fathers"—nothing. They are *not* my dads. They both suck.

I don't understand how adoption is going to help me. Richard is not going to be nicer because now he'll be my legal dad or give me rides to my baseball games or let me take drum lessons. I still don't understand why Mark and Gail take guitar and piano lessons, but I can't take drum lessons until I finish my bar mitzvah. Even Lori took guitar for a while.

My mind spins. How am I going to tell my friends why my last name now has eleven letters and is impossible to pronounce. It's humiliating.

Mom continues delivering her scripted lines about living happily ever after, but she's not convincing anyone—not even herself. This is no fairy tale.

"Steven," she yells, "Where is your mind right now? This is important, life changing. Your dad will be disappointed if he finds out you're not even paying attention. This is a big deal."

I hear Mom talking, but I'm pitching a stickball game.

"Steven, pay attention! Where do you go?" Mom says we'll be evaluated by a head doctor and that the judge has to approve the adoption. I keep wondering: *It's not like there's a choice here, is there?*

Maybe Dad will show up for my bar mitzvah. I doubt he's invited, since most of the guests are friends of Mom and Richard's. We never talk about him. It's like he died, or we are pretending he's dead. We aren't allowed to be sad. All I feel is the feeling of no feeling—*which is a feeling, right?*

Maybe he just forgot our birthdays. I know he doesn't like to call the house, and I figure he doesn't want Mom to bug him about money. I guess I could call him, but I wouldn't know what to say. Mom and Lori like to talk on the phone, but I don't make many calls. Dad isn't good on the phone either. When he used to call, our talks were short because he never says much. Whenever he did call, Mom would spend more time asking me about the call than the time the call itself took. I do miss Grandma Annie and Pappa Charley and Uncle Jerry in Bayonne. Mom claims they can visit anytime, but I don't believe her.

Mom tells us she has an agreement with Allen and that he *wants* us to become Richard's kids. She says, "He *agrees* it's the best thing for all of you." *The best thing? What does that mean?* I'm sick of these so-called agreements. Mom and Dad can't agree about the color of the sky. Everything is a fight. But it's easy for them to make decisions *for* us—even change our names—without *our* agreement. I'm tired of the constant bickering. Allen's gone and will no longer have to pay child support. We will be cut from his life. We will be dead to him.

Mom stops talking and asks me again how I feel about adoption. I shrug my shoulders and say, "I don't know," and at least this time she doesn't bother telling me that "I don't know" is not an answer. Then I ask if we're done, and before she answers I'm out the door. My mind relays my answer. *I don't care and feel nothing.*

Just leave me alone.

CHAPTER 11

Judgment Day

One morning a few months later, Mom wakes me up and tells me we're going to the courthouse today to see the judge. She explains the judge will ask us questions and then he'll decide if Richard will be our "real father," and if so, we'll take his last name.

She asks if this is what I want, and I say, "I don't know," then mumble, "I guess so. It's not as if I have a choice."

She stares. "Richard's your father now, your dad is gone. You will tell the judge this is what you want, right?"

I nod my head, but it feels detached from my body. It's like when we went to the counselor, and he asked if I was happy. I told him I guess so and he said this isn't a guessing game. *It's a mind game.* I shrug my shoulders, say "I don't know," and he leaves me alone.

Mom keeps calling this day "the big day," but when I peer out my window, I tell her the big day looks just like yesterday. I know she wants me to act excited, but spending hours trapped with Richard anywhere is a bad day, not a big one. Missing school is a plus, but it's not like we're going to Palisades Amusement Park. Plus, I have to get dressed up and wear the itchy pants and tie, which I hate. I don't know how to tie a knot, which means Richard will have to come near me and might even touch my neck. I'm always worried he's going to lose his temper and choke me. I hate when the barber touches my neck with his blade like he's going to slit my throat. Richard might want to do the same thing.

Today, he attempts for the fiftieth time to show me how to make a knot, gets frustrated when I don't listen, and then throws the tie in my face. I go to my room to get my clip-on. The clip-on is easy and I don't have to ask for help. Mark laughs when he sees me with it. He returned after one year at boarding school and has been back for three years now. He has calmed down over the years. He's stuck in our family spider web just like the rest of us. And Richard's the spider.

We are going to the courthouse in Paterson to become Richard's "real" children. *The whole thing is painful. A new last name that no one can pronounce or spell? I've never heard of anyone changing their last name. What am I supposed to tell people? All the kids at school are going to wonder what happened and might ask me questions. I will hide within myself.*

Paterson is a city lined with burned-out buildings and is known for multiple murders and drug deals. Fires were started during some riots years back, yet no one has bothered to rebuild or even knock down the crumbling bricks that once housed thousands of residents. I wonder where they live now. Every time we stop, a different person—clothes torn and eyes glazed—runs up to our car and tries to wash our windows. Richard just beeps his horn and tells them to get lost. He says they're bums who sleep on the streets and collect welfare checks. Years later, it will turn out Richard has been collecting his own welfare checks.

Richard and Mom tell us to be polite and let the judge know how excited we are about becoming Eichenblatts. More than anything, I just want out of these clothes.

People who know me understand that I do not like to be touched. This has never been a problem, as no one in my family except for Grandma Annie hugs us, and she's gone. At the barbershop, Mom explains that I don't like anyone touching my neck, and to be careful. When someone touches my neck or my thighs, my entire body gets covered with goosebumps and begins to shudder. During bathtime, Dad would grab my neck and hold me underwater but that was a long time ago. Mom said he was mad sometimes and took it out on me.

The courthouse is an old building in downtown Paterson. We're told to wait outside in the lobby while Richard and Mom go talk with the judge. I sit with Robert and Lori and keep adjusting my tie so it doesn't press against my neck. The lobby has high ceilings and a bunch of wooden benches that remind me of the pew in Dad's office. We sit in silence and pretend like nothing new is happening. A few men sitting on benches near us look like they have slept here.

The smell coming from the man sitting closest to us reminds me of the stench from the toilet bowl when someone forgets to flush. One man tries to stand up but loses his balance and has to grab the edge of the bench so he doesn't hit the ground. He stumbles and keeps looking toward us, trying to say something, but his words are unintelligible. He pulls a paper bag out of his jacket pocket and takes a huge drink.

The man tilts his head in our direction but he doesn't seem to notice us. He takes off his long black coat and throws it on the bench. He unbuttons his shirt, tosses that on the bench, and starts to take his pants off. The smell becomes even worse and we get up to move away. Lori and Robert look shocked, but none of us says a thing. Mom and Richard are still with the judge, and no one else seems to notice. I yell toward the woman at the information desk, trying to get her attention.

The man takes off his boxers and stands there naked. I try not to stare. Lori and Robert stand near me with shock on their faces. A naked man is not something we expected as part of the adoption. I only see naked men when we go to the YMHA and some of the old guys walk around the locker room, their body parts wrinkled and scaly like lizards. It's pretty gross, and I keep my eyes looking upward. I always cover myself and will never let anyone see me naked. The old men smoke cigars and talk with you about the weather or how the Mets did while their fat stomachs and private parts just hang out. I'm pretty certain they stay in the locker room the whole time and play cards and never even exercise. One guy winked at me and said they're escaping their wives and I would understand one day.

The nude man begins to walk toward the planter. He's about to pee when a police officer jumps on him, covering him with a blanket and telling us to move away. We laugh, but more in shock than anything else. *What's next?*

I remember Mom explaining our birth certificates will soon list Richard as Dad. Suddenly, I feel naked and exposed like the man now held prisoner by the police. Is this *real* or am I dreaming again?

A stern-faced woman with thick glasses then walks out and asks for the Nestle children to follow her. Her words are like a gut punch. A wave of uncertainty and sadness washes over me. It's the last time in my life I will be called Steven Nestle.

The woman instructs us not to be nervous, which makes me more nervous, and leads us into the room that she says is the judge's chambers. There are pictures on the wall of the judge with people my mom's lawyer tells us are famous. I don't recognize a single one. In every photo, the judge has the same plastered smile on his face. A uniformed police officer is also in the office. He looks older than my grandfather and has stains on his shirt. He wears a gun but it sits low in its holster, beneath the place where his large stomach meets his thighs. If he ever has to use it, he'll need to lift up his huge gut with one hand and grab the gun with the other.

The woman says his job is to protect the judge. There's no way this guy can protect anyone. He doesn't bother to look in our direction and leans with his back to the window, holding a legal folder. He appears to study the folder, not realizing the reflection from the glass behind him reveals a magazine hidden inside it. He reminds me of Pappa Charley. I wonder if I will ever see him again.

The lawyer introduces us to the judge, who looks bored. He says, "Nice to meet you," and then asks a bunch of questions about Richard, who he says will be our "new father." Before I can answer, he's on to the next question. He asks Mom and Richard to leave the room. I hope he doesn't ask about my grades or Hebrew school. Instead, he asks if I play sports and who are my favorite teams. Tug McGraw is still a Met and, my favorite player. I feel like we're friends. I say the Mets, and the judge stares, his nose scrunched up, and waves me off with his weathered, fat hand.

He mumbles, "The Yankees, kid. The Yankees. Didn't your father teach you anything?"

The judge looks away and asks my sister some questions but before Lori even speaks, he asks Robert how old he is and whether he understands what's happening. The Judge nods as Robert mumbles, but he's not listening so it doesn't matter.

This is happening now because Richard and Mom want us all to have the same last name on my bar mitzvah day. I think more about this change. I dread the moment my friends and classmates find out and start asking questions. *And what happens to Steve Nestle? Is he no longer a real person? I wish I could jump on my old Sting-Ray and ride away.* I just want out.

Dad's not going to save the day and stop the adoption. He must not know the truth about Richard. I mean, if he did, he'd be here, right? It's my fault for not telling him. He would have done something.

The whole thing is confusing, although I answer yes to all the Judge's questions, knowing the decision is made. Richard's behavior stays a secret. Richard knows how to pretend he's a great dad and compared to my first father, he might be right.

The judge pronounces us Eichenblatts and asks the officer to get Mom and Richard. The judge then mutters, "Good luck," stands up, and walks through the secret door behind him.

It's over. The whole matter took less time than it took for me to attach my clip-on.

Mom says "Congratulations!" and Richard pretends to be happy. He even shakes my hand. To celebrate, he'll take us out to eat. Robert asks to go to the Montclair Diner where they make French toast with powdered sugar and syrup, but Richard doesn't want to sit down and wait for food. He takes us to the only McDonald's in town.

I order a chocolate milkshake, large fries, and a Filet-O-Fish sandwich. I like the Filet-O-Fish but ask if they can make it without onions and tartar sauce. When the lady says it will take a while, Richard tells me to just wipe the sauce off with a napkin. He says we don't have time for special orders.

Mom starts to argue, but I'm no longer hungry and just want to get out of these clothes and away from them. I want to burn this stupid clip-on tie. On the drive home, Mom tells me that it's now time to call Richard Dad. She tells us everything will work out and we are lucky to have a fresh start. I'm focused on cleaning my fish filet of nasty tartar sauce but will not be calling Richard—or anyone else—Dad.

My parents say it's a special day, but not quite special enough for the Montclair Diner or my special order Filet-O-Fish. I'll just bury Dad and the Nestle family in the crowded graveyard of my mind. They will remain forever frozen in time. My roots, the ones sprouting from the ground at birth, have now been dug up and tossed aside. The Nestles will die in my brain. Pretend they are dead. Pretend Steven Nestle never lived. It's easier that way. The feeling of no feeling.

CHAPTER 12

An Accident That Was
No Accident, 1975

The fireworks display exploding in my head after the car crash still smells of burnt rubber and gasoline. It's the Fourth of July, but it's hard for me to be enthusiastic. I love watching the demolition derby when it's on television, but those drivers wear helmets and crash into each other, not telephone poles. Plus, the drivers don't ever emerge bloodied with an eyelid split in half. The explosion today was even louder than the much anticipated but always disappointing finale at the Fireman's Fair.

Leaving the gathered onlookers and the bloodied man, I get on my bike, pedaling home in a daze, not even sure how I get there. My mind blanks and I try to regroup. I don't remember much about what happens when I walk into the house. Mom is yelling about the hamburgers but just stares at me. She explains that they are going somewhere. She says she's leaving burgers for us. Mom's eyes are on me, and she knows something has happened. Still, she says nothing. Everything is a blur and I wind up back in the garage and on my bike.

When I get to Billy's house, we go downstairs to his pool room and start talking. He mentions he smells gasoline, but I don't respond. He cranks up Pink Floyd's "Wish You Were Here," but then switches to Aerosmith's "Toys in the Attic." I need something loud and disorganized. "Wish You Were Here" is more acoustic than angry. My mind needs to blow up and get lost in the screaming guitar solos and yells of Aerosmith's lead singer.

Tonight, we hitchhike to the Fireman's Fair. I leave my bike at Billy's house because the fair's too far to ride. This carnival shows up every year with the same broken rides that look almost as bad as the carnies who run them.

Thankfully, we see one of Billy's neighbors and they pick us up. When the traffic builds close to the fair, we thank the driver and jump out at the stoplight. We can hear the humming sound of distant generators playing their own symphony, interrupted by occasional screams of riders going upside down on the dizzying pendulum ride or rickety-sounding roller coaster. As we get closer, the multicolored spotlights get brighter, and the occasional whiff of manure from the kid's petting zoo, mixed with the sweet fragrance of fried dough cooking in the huge grease pots, leads us toward the ticket booth.

I'm distracted listening to the carnie hawking tickets to see the four-headed alligator with three tails or the bearded fat lady. The guy is screaming. His words whistle through the gaps where his teeth used to be.

"C'mon, thtep right up and buy thickets to the thhow... "

We laugh as his words come out wrong, like he has a lisp. The gravel in his smoker's throat sounds like he has a horse in there. Last year the alligator had three heads and four tails and turned out to be some tiny lizard thing in a glass jar. The fat lady doesn't appeal to me, but there's always a rumor that one of the tents has a peep show where beautiful women strip. We've never found it.

As we begin our walk into the main area, the smell of gasoline running the generators near the bumper cars blindsides me, and I flash back to the sound of screaming tires and the crunch of the car striking the telephone pole. It doesn't seem real, but the stink of exhaust fumes still consuming my clothes reminds me it wasn't a nightmare. It's been an interesting day.

The same workers, looking mostly dead, show up each July with fewer teeth and more tattoos. They look defeated, moving each week from one parking lot to another, packing and unpacking the same rides and recognizing the town by the local dive bar. Richard says to stay away from them because most are criminals.

The carnies work hard despite their cigarette breaks, or when they sneak away and take a swig from the whiskey bottles they think they're hiding. A couple times Billy and I have grabbed the bottles and taken a shot, but it's like drinking gasoline. We used to go to the fair and pretend to be a family but Mom and Richard would fight before we even left the driveway. The only time we were ever together and didn't fight was at the bar mitzvah.

***

I think back to that day over three years ago. The bar mitzvah party was at our house. It was one of the rare times we were allowed in the living room and the plastic coverings were off the furniture. Other than stealing my gift envelopes, Richard placed his arm around me and said he was proud. His breath reeked like the carnies' whiskey, and I quickly turned away. He had never touched me before without it being a punishment, so I knew it was all a lie.

We kids had a small party that night with pizza and a rented jukebox. Most were mandatory invites from the bar mitzvah class. My sisters did invite some of their gentile friends to our party. They wanted to play "spin the bottle," a kissing game. Despite Lori saying girls like me, I'm too shy to talk to any girl. The thought of kissing one terrifies me. When Terri London, a girl I've liked since first grade, spun the bottle and picked me, my body froze and I wasn't sure what to do. No one explained this part. She could probably hear my heartbeat. Terri didn't know, but I had never kissed anyone, other than my grandmother who always forced me to kiss her cheek. Sometimes I kiss my dog, Sam, but never on the lips.

I'm reminded it's still the Fourth of July. I wonder what Terri's doing. Maybe she's at the fair. Billy's much better with the girls than I am. Lori says he's gorgeous, like a model. She always wants to go with me to hang out at his house. Maybe when we go back to Billy's after the fair tonight, I'll tell Lori she can come over if she brings Terri and some other friends.

Terri is a cheerleader and the prettiest girl in school. The bar mitzvah kiss must not have gone too well, since we never repeated it. That was three years ago. Despite our one-kiss romance, I am afraid to talk to her. My friends say she likes me and my sister says to call her—but what if her dad answers? Fathers scare me. I dread her dad answering. No boys call our house to talk to my sisters. No one wants to deal with Richard.

Mom stopped pushing me to call him Dad and seems satisfied that Robert and Lori do. Calling him Richard isn't an option. We aren't allowed to call adults by their first names. Once, a neighbor's dad said to call him Bill, like the other kids did. When Richard found out, he screamed about respecting my elders. The rules inside the house are tough, but there are few rules outside. On school nights, it's common to stay out past midnight and come home without anyone noticing my absence. Patrick, Billy, and I hitchhike all over town and sometimes hang out at Willowbrook mall.

Most mornings, the three of us meet behind my house, smoke a few joints, and then walk to the bus stop. We even leave school during lunch and get high. Sitting buzzed in classes like geometry and Spanish that require attention hasn't helped my grades. My D average is not getting me into Harvard.

My Jewish friends stopped inviting me anywhere long ago. Most of them, like Barry Cohen and Sam Miller, pulled away when Richard showed up. Their parents didn't want their kids near him. They'd seen him start the fight in the temple, which didn't help.

My sports career ends because driving me to football or baseball practice is not a priority. Mom and Richard tell me to figure it out. Richard says it's not like I'm going to be a pro athlete.

My bike works, but it's too cold in winter. Hitchhiking means standing outside in my baseball uniform and waiting to get lucky. It's embarrassing, and when some of the other parents ask if I need a ride, I refuse. At one point, the coach began driving me, but that made me uncomfortable. A couple of kids from the football team ask me to join one season, and their dad even offers to drive me. They don't understand my situation. Asking people for favors means I owe them.

Richard takes from everyone and doesn't care. He says he's doing them a favor by allowing them to help him. How does this make any sense? Richard encourages Mark to play football and gives him rides. So much for all of us being his real children.

Richard tells Mom that I'm not tough enough for football, despite knowing the coaches want me to play. I'm not fast, but I do have good hands and can throw the football farther than almost anyone in my grade. Richard seemed to get some satisfaction when my entry into the NFL's Punt, Pass, and Kick competition got lost in the mail and I couldn't participate. It's still a mystery because I remember putting it in the mailbox. Richard told me to shut up about it, since there was no way I could win.

Richard supports Mark in his sports, buys him a Lionel train set, and builds go-carts for Robert and Larry. Mark still catches the brunt of Richard's anger, so it's better if he does nothing for me. I don't want to owe him anything.

Lori has a boyfriend and smokes cigarettes. Mom and Richard were upset when she joined a Drum and Bugle Corp. I had no idea what that meant since she doesn't play the drums or bugle. Mom says she twirls a flag and hangs around gentile kids from the bad side of town. We have a backyard pool that Pappa Ben paid for because it was cheaper than camp. When Lori invites her new friends over to swim, Richard tells us to stay away because it's probably the only bath they'll take this year.

Lori gets in trouble a lot, and some nights Mom goes out and looks for her. Richard says Lori's friends are losers and drug addicts. They are actually cool kids who happen to like music, not sports. Neither he nor Mom know that many nights I'm with my friends getting high. We drink and smoke, listen to music, and talk about girls. I usually sneak home before dawn through the basement door. They never notice the pot smell or alcohol sweating out of me or that my pockets are filled with bags of weed to sell. I never study and my grades are terrible.

My mind keeps drifting away from the fair until Billy pounds me on the back. "You OK, buddy? You seem distracted."

"Distracted? Not really. But let's go back to your house and listen to some tunes."

We begin walking toward our favorite hitchhiking spot. We walk past Foodtown and I point and say, "Fuck Foodtown."

During tenth grade, Foodtown hires me to work in the produce department. One of my friends, Tony Bruno, is hired too. We constantly fool around, playing catch with oranges and apples, and then begin stealing food. We love chocolate Devil Dogs and Ring Dings, so we put packages of them in a produce box near the dumpster, like its garbage. It's a great system, and soon we start loading the boxes with six packs and wine bottles. Tony drives, so we load his car up after work or arrange for a friend to pick up the goods. It's truly a great system—until we get caught, and later, fired. I knew it was wrong but it didn't matter if the police got me. It's Richard who worries me. But fuck him. I don't even like beer; I just loved the mission and the cash when we sold the six packs.

Sam's my dog's name, and he loves me. It's also the boss's name. He's an Italian guy who says his uncle is in the Mafia. He didn't like it when I told him my dog's name is Sam, too, but everyone else thinks it's funny. Sam works hard but he's always bragging about all these women from his bowling league who want him. Sam's chunky, and his brown, kinky hair looks like he hasn't washed it for years. Plus, he smells like the boys' locker room.

Sam doesn't even have the balls to fire me in person. On my sixteenth birthday, he sends Tony to let me know we're both fired. *Doesn't he know it's my birthday? Isn't it illegal to fire a kid on his birthday?* Tony comes by the house and makes the mistake of ringing the front doorbell. Richard immediately tells him to go around back, and I go outside to meet him.

Tony, who's a muscle-bound Italian kid and star football player, looks at me. I've known him since second grade. He's one year older than me, so can drive. He's tough. Not even the Italian gang kids from the T-Bowl Mafia mess with him.

"Ike, that fat shit Sam fired us both!"

I grimace, "It's my sixteenth birthday! He can't fire me on my birthday, can he? I want to kick his ass."

Tony agrees to drive me to Foodtown so I can confront Sam, maybe even fight him. Tony's excited, but he pauses. "That'll be great, Ike, but Sam's almost twenty and he's tough, even if he is fat."

When my last name changed from Nestle, my friends began calling me Ike. I'm one of those people who always has a nickname. Kids called me Ness and later on, it would be Ike, and years later, I became Chief. I figure it's because there are always five Steves in every class. Everyone says I don't look like a Steve. Not sure what that means.

Sam outweighs me by at least a hundred pounds and once beat me in an arm-wrestling match in less than ten seconds. I look at Tony. "Fuck him, I'll kick him in the balls and run away. He's too slow to catch me."

Tony drives me but warns me again that Sam is going to kick my ass. It doesn't matter. It's important to show Richard I'm a man and can stand up for myself.

We pull up and park near the entrance so we can make a quick getaway. I run to the produce section and look for Sam. When I see him, I call him a fat ham slammer and try to throw a punch. Sam turns out to be much quicker than expected and grabs me in a chokehold. He laughs in my face, his beer breath spewing from his mouth, and tells me to leave before he hurts me. I squirm to get loose, but he's wrapped his thick ape arm around my neck and won't let go. It doesn't go well for me.

When other management shows up, he loosens his grip, and I tell him to fuck himself. He just smiles. Richard's always preaching about standing up for yourself like a real man. *Why do I always want to impress him? I hate him.*

The truth is, they were right to fire me. After I'm fired, Richard says I can work taking care of the tennis courts. He isn't mad because he says Jews don't work in grocery stores, they own them. The court job is easy, and no one bothers me. Most days, I go once in the morning and again late afternoon.

I'm still thinking of Foodtown when Billy yells that we have a ride. He's been standing close to the road with his thumb out while I've been... distracted. The tennis court job had been good— until today.

We wind up back at Billy's house. I see my bike and suddenly wonder if Allen Nestle survived. It feels like a gut punch. I begin to mount the Schwinn. It's been a long day. Billy looks at me and asks, "Steve, what's on your mind? You're acting weird. We didn't even stay for the Fourth of July fireworks."

I look at him, my best friend, and begin pedaling away. Then I turn and shout over my shoulder, "I did see fireworks today...I'll tell you some other time."

Billy turns and walks back into his house. I do talk to him about that day... but not for forty years.

CHAPTER 13

The Boxer

The accident replays in my mind with no off switch. Images of the blood-soaked man with his dangling eyelid show up at random times. I can be thinking about the weather, and his face appears. Sometimes, I'll be talking to some kid at the school lunch table and I'll see "the face" instead of his. The symphony of sounds created by the crash has receded the way a great song slows down to a stop, only to restart in my nightmares.

This morning——I'm anxious to grab the Sunday paper. My grades stink, but I'm taking an eleventh-grade class called "Letters to the Editor," and any student who gets published in *The New York Times* gets an automatic A. My teacher says it's impossible, and no one from our school has ever done it. I want to prove them wrong. This week I sent a letter to the sports editor about

Muhammad Ali, the greatest boxer of all time. If it's going to be published, today's the day.

Since it's winter, I freeze my butt off running down the driveway. The paper sits in the middle of a deep, half-frozen dirty puddle. An A grade means no more assignments until the next term, and plenty of time for partying and unsuccessfully chasing girls.

Shivering, my bare feet sink into the slushy mix of melted snow and ice. Shoes would have been smart, but I like challenging myself. I bend down and snatch the blue plastic bag and begin to race toward the back door, trying to outrun the pain of freezing toes. Flying through the door, I head toward the bathroom where no one will bother me. Heart thumping with anticipation, I'm disappointed when nothing shows up in the Letters to the Editor section. Shaking it off, I pick up the Sports section and stare at the picture of a gorilla with a sign saying "Beat Army," and hundreds of uniformed Navy midshipmen marching on the field. The gorilla must have worked, because the headline proclaims a "Navy Shutout." My mind flashes to the Army game attended with my former father.

We had terrible seats and were late, but Army was playing Rutgers, Dad's college before going to Michigan State. I try to remember more details, but have almost forgotten what Dad looked like, other than at the accident scene.

Turning to the inside page of the Sports section, I see short letters, but no mention of Ali. As I close the paper, one last letter catches my eye. I look two, then three times. There's a reason I recognize the words:

Where Would Boxing Be?

To the Editor:

Where would boxing be without Muhammad Ali? Boxing is a great sport, but it has only three or four major fighters. What would happen if Ali retired? The only fighters left are a weary Joe Frazier, a defeated George Foreman and a battered Jerry Quarry.

Muhammad Ali makes boxing. He will always be the champion, regardless of the official title.

Steve Eichenblatt
Wayne, N.J.

I reverse my steps and put the paper back where I found it on the driveway. At least I'll have one good grade this semester.

***

The rest of my junior year at Wayne Hills rolls along without much trouble. One spring afternoon, Patrick drops me off and I discover Mom isn't home. Neither her car nor Richard's are in the driveway. This is good news, so I burst through the front door.

The other kids are in the kitchen, fighting over what's left of Mom's spaghetti. She must have left in a hurry because it's still in the massive stainless steel pot she uses to cook pasta for nine people. The sauce is in a smaller pot and has dripped everywhere and on everyone. All seven of us break house rules by grabbing food out of the cabinets and stealing Mom's hidden supply of Peanut M&M'S. With red sauce spilled across the floor and splattered like blood on the cabinets, the kitchen looks like a murder scene. Empty cereal boxes and half-eaten Pop-Tarts cover the table and countertops as if the neighborhood black bear broke into the kitchen.

Cindy smiles, despite the huge red sauce stain on the front of her white T-shirt. Mark holds an entire garlic bread loaf in his dirty hands like a running back holding a football.

Larry keeps trying to grab a piece, but Mark keeps pulling the bread away, just out of reach. Mark's having fun, but Larry's upset. He's about to take a swing at Mark, and that won't end well. Mark is twice his size and has hurt him in the past. No parents are here to control Mark.

Gail, normally quiet, yells, "Mark, just give him a fucking piece of bread!"

Her words surprise me. Now her blue eyes widen, and she stares through me.

"Steven, are you going to do anything? Or are you just going to let Mark bully him?"

Surprisingly, she is serious and looks like she's about to slug me. It wouldn't be the first time. When we were around eight, we were sitting in the orthodontist's office, where she had to get her braces adjusted for the fiftieth time. Mom had given up on me after I lost three retainers and was deemed irresponsible.

I look at Gail sitting next to the fish tank and wonder: *Do all dentists like fish? Do they think torturing you with their dental drill while shoving their huge stubby fingers down your throat will be easier because there's some half-dead fish swimming around in the tank?*

Gail thought I was staring at her braces, and said, "Stop staring at me or I will beat you up."

I laughed. "Do you want to fight?"

"Yes."

We didn't say anything else, but when we got home, we walked to the side of the house. She tried to throw a kid's plastic football helmet at me and missed. Then she punched me, which didn't hurt, so I hit her over the head with the helmet. It might have been a Jets helmet, but it could have been a Giants. I guess it doesn't matter. Mom then yelled, "Time for dinner," and the fight ended. Richard punished me for hitting a girl and reminded me I was a loser.

Now Mark throws the bread towards a snoring Sam, who is on high alert. In slow motion, the bread falls and Sam snaps it up, inhaling the entire loaf faster than the new Hoover vacuum cleaner Mom uses. I'm not even sure it hit the ground.

We all begin to laugh about Sam, but then Lori looks at me with a slight smile on her face. "Steve, guess what?"

I hate it when Lori knows something and won't tell me. I take the bait. "What?"

She hesitates, knowing she is torturing me.

I snap, "Just tell me! What's happening? Tell me!"

Gail jumps in: "Dad's had a heart attack and is in the hospital. Someone called Mom while she was making dinner and she went to see him. We don't know when they'll be back."

Heart attack. Wow. I'm shocked, but don't care. *I'm not sad, or worried, or concerned, or even afraid he might die. I'm more concerned about the garlic bread and whether Mark saved me a piece.* I feel nothing for Richard, that's my only feeling. I can't decide if this is good or bad news. I'm leaning toward good, because maybe we'll be rid of him.

After a few hours, Mom arrives home. She leaves the car outside without pulling into the garage. Mom walks in the house and announces, "Your father had a slight heart attack. Don't worry, he'll be OK. They're going to check him out and he should be home in a couple days." She looks around the kitchen and sighs, "Kids, it was a close call."

I roll my eyes. *Mom is acting. She can't be upset, can she?*

Mom continues, "Girls, clean up the mess. It looks like someone was stabbed to death in here. Steven, you take out the garbage."

A grunt escapes. "Why do the girls always clean the kitchen, while I'm a garbageman?"

Mom sighs, "Not tonight, Steven. Richard says the girls belong in the kitchen and the garbage is your job. The rest of you need to go to bed."

I grab the garbage and walk toward the back door. It would be great to throw Richard's body in the trash like the dead dogs at the animal hospital. Life would be easier without him. The part of me that doesn't wish he had died wishes he'd never existed. *You can't really die if you never lived, can you? That works.*

Sadly, a few days later, Richard returns. Mom forces us to welcome him as if he's a returning prisoner of war. She holds open the front door for him as he shuffles inside, bent over and holding a hand to his chest. He ignores us as he goes into the bedroom, only stopping to bend down and pet the snoring Sam, who doesn't bother to wake up.

In a couple of weeks, Richard regains his strength and goes back to work. Something has changed, though. He and Mom speak in whispers and act like they're hatching a battle plan. He won't talk about his heart, and Mom doesn't say much these days. She casts her eyes downward when she sees me, as if she feels bad about something. The something will soon destroy my senior year.

CHAPTER 14

Kidnapped

"School's out forever"
— Alice Cooper

The highlight of the year has nothing to do with girls or family. One December morning, Billy meets me in the woods, and we take a few hits off a small pipe he has loaded with hash, then smoke a joint. We walk to the bus stop at the edge of our neighborhood on Colfax Road. We take our traditional seats in the back and the bus begins the five-mile drive to the school. As we get closer we begin to hear police sirens, and then watch as fire trucks honking their horns speed by us. When the first trucks pass, we don't think much of it. But the number of police cars and fire trucks keeps growing, the choir of their sirens screaming together like warriors storming into battle.

I look over at Billy. "Wouldn't it be cool if our school was on fire?"

He laughs. "Yeah, it'd be great."

The other riders begin shouting, "The school's on fire! The schools on fire!" Some cheer. There's shouting and shoving as kids compete to look out the window. The kids crowd the aisles and wedge into window seats to get a closer look, noses pressed against the glass. We stare out in disbelief. Flames and black smoke billow through the morning sky. The school *is* on fire.

Sirens wail, and waves of soot stream from the back of the school near the auditorium. Fire trucks line the circular driveway. We watch as firefighters carry hoses over their shoulders, gripping axes in their gloved hands like they're preparing to cut down trees.

Without warning, our driver pulls into the school entrance and stops at the far end of the parking lot. He leans over and extends his arm, pulling the door lever, which releases compressed air and creates a familiar hissing sound. The door is open. Cold air from the outside floats into the bus and we get our first whiff of smoke. It begins to envelop the school. The driver, a retired sanitation worker who rarely speaks but stinks from slugging his thermos filled with whiskey, watches, saying nothing as we pile out. As usual, he closes the door after us and pulls away. His blank face, with not a single distinguishing feature, remains utterly undisturbed. He acts like the school burns down every day.

There's a huge lawn connected to the parking lot, where everyone has gathered. Its once lush springtime green is now patchy brown as a December chill turns the weather from fall to winter. Students are everywhere, including a few who try to climb up the large flagpole in the middle of the lawn. There are benches nearby dedicated to old students and dead people no one remembers.

Hundreds of kids mill around while the teachers try to organize us into class lines. *This is crazy.* Firefighters have dragged their hoses onto the roof and begin to dominate the flames like a great defense shutting down a tiring offense. *The Giants' defense sucks this year.*

Billy grabs me and says, "Fight, look there's a fight."

"Let's go," I say. "It looks like Joey."

We run to watch as two senior students circle each other in the middle of a ring created by the students who've gathered to watch. There's usually nothing more exciting at school than a good fight—except an actual fire.

Billy and I are too excited to speak. Neither of us can believe that instead of some boring math class, we get to watch the school burn *and* these boys fight.

They continue to circle each other as kids scream, "Kill him, kill him, punch him, punch him," but the teachers jump in and the fight ends without a single blow being struck.

It's been a great morning. The air is cold enough for our breath to show, although mine and Billy's reek of marijuana. We all become quiet as more fire trucks arrive. The buses line up to take us back home. Billy and I decide to get on a different bus and go to Patrick's house. His parents won't be home. We all hope this will mean no more school for weeks.

A few days later, we learn school will be canceled through Christmas break. Half the building is gone or ravaged by smoke and water damage. For days, we relive the moments riding in the bus when the fire trucks sped past us, their sirens wailing.

I didn't know it, but it would be years before I set foot on campus again. I was used to the feeling of no feeling, but looking back, I realize this was closure with no closure. The last page of this chapter in my life was about to be ripped out. I never did get to say goodbye.

***

In April, Mom and Richard gather us all in their bedroom for an "important family discussion." I have no idea what the topic will be, but I guess it's going to be some lecture about college admissions or summer plans. I've received several warnings from the school guidance counselor that if my grades don't improve, I'm headed to technical school or community college. The thought of technical school is funny, since I'm unable to use any tool the correct way.

Mom looks at us and says she has some exciting news. I hold my breath and look around. Everyone's listening. We're all clueless.

"Kids, your father and I have made a decision, and we want to let you know together as a family. Your dad has quit his job at the chemical plant. No more driving to the Bronx."

This is news, but big shit. Who cares where he works? There has to be more. And it can't be good.

Mom continues, "And we're moving—to Florida." My stomach drops. All of us look like we've been sucker punched. "We've bought a house in Sarasota, and you'll finish school there next year and get to live close to the beach." She looks around. Silence. "We are happy," she chirps, "and know you'll *love* Florida. Tomorrow," she pauses to let her words sink in, "tomorrow there'll be a For Sale sign going up in front of the house."

My mind explodes like I've been hit with a left hook by Muhammad Ali. Panic rises through my gut and I feel like I'm going to puke. *Florida! Fucking Florida?* This can't be happening. This. *Can't.* Happen. Words rush from my mouth overriding everyone else's questions. I don't even recognize the angry, loud voice coming from inside as if someone else has taken over my being.

"Bullshit. No way! Mom, what do you mean? We can't move. It's our senior year of high school! I'm not going anywhere. What are you talking about?" My brain swirls around faster than my words, so I stop talking. Everyone is surprised I've been so loud and angry. I continue, "It's bullshit. I'm not moving. No way. We deserve a vote. This is our *hometown*."

Mom looks over at Richard, who just smirks. "This isn't a democracy. You'll get used to it," he says, leaning against the bedroom wall doing the twitching thing he always does with his legs. "It's time you thought about someone other than yourself. You have brothers and sisters who might like Florida. Besides, it will make you stronger."

Nothing Richard says makes sense, but there's no reason to respond to him. It's over.

Gail starts to cry, and I feel bad for her. Larry and Cindy stare with blank faces, not understanding the significance of the news. It's hard to know how Robert feels, but Mark's blue eyes are lit up, and his jaw is clenched. He's angry, and so am I.

Mark bursts out, "What about the football team? Coach said I'll be a starter."

"Yeah," I add, "Mark's a starter! It's not right!"

Moving right before my senior year is unfair. *Where the fuck even is Sarasota?*

Lori mutters, "Are you serious? What about my boyfriend?"

Mom looks again at Richard, who's losing patience, his face reddening. Before he can explode, she says, "Your father's recovering from a heart attack and has to move to a place where he has less stress and can enjoy life more. This isn't a choice. We have to move for your father's health—doctor's orders." Now Lori starts crying. This "discussion" is not going as they planned.

True, Richard hasn't worked much. He must be feeling better, though, because he's playing tennis almost every day, and when it's too cold outdoors, he goes to the indoor courts. I've also seen him take out his golf clubs and head off for the driving range. I want to say, "He doesn't seem too sick," but stop myself.

He does have a history of faking illness or injury. He didn't look hurt to me when he went to court after a car accident claiming he injured his back. Each day before court, he put on a back brace and old glasses to testify. He claimed he was going to get a bunch of money from "the bitch who hit me," which was confusing, since none of us knew he'd ever been in an accident.

When he returned from court, he slammed his bedroom door and I could hear him punching the wall. He screamed about how his lawyer sucked and it was "all that cocksucker's fault." Mom said the jury didn't believe he was hurt, and the insurance lawyer said Richard's back brace looked brand new, like he never wears it. All through the proceeding, Richard was playing tennis and hitting golf balls, just like always. Years later, as a lawyer, I represented Sears and hired an investigator who secretly filmed a man—who claimed to be totally disabled—cutting a tree down in his backyard. I could imagine Richard getting caught doing the same thing.

Waves of nausea hit me again. *Florida… ?*

Desperate, I ask: "What if I can get Patrick or Billy to let me stay with them so I can graduate here? What about Sam, is he coming?"

I look over at him, sprawled on the floor, his chin resting on his paw and his eyes open. He looks concerned but hasn't voiced his opinion.

"See, Elaine, how fast he abandons his family?" Richard laughs. "He's just a follower who cares only about himself and his fair-weather friends."

He glares at me. "It's not like you're the valedictorian. Your grades are pathetic. You don't play sports. You don't do shit. You're all going, so get used to it, and if you don't like it, tough shit! We are done. The discussion is over." *Discussion? That was no discussion.* Richard marches out of the room. I hear him slam the front door and get into his car. Maybe he'll crash. I hate my parents.

Friends find out and offer to let me stay with them. I beg Mom but know it's a waste of time. It's hard to imagine leaving Wayne—my hometown—and worse, to consider living in a strange town over a thousand miles away. I've been a Jersey boy almost my whole life. I'm no Floridian.

I lose my final appeal to stay. One of my friends told me his mom called my mom to tell her she was happy to have me stay with them—but no chance. Mom never even told me about the call.

Richard soon reports that we're moving a few weeks after school ends. *A few weeks! What about my summer plans? They don't know, but my friend owns property near the Playboy Club. We went last summer and snuck in, looking for Playboy Bunnies and Playmates until we got kicked out by security. We even went into their indoor pool. No Bunnies, but still, we have plans to go again. I just got my New Jersey driver's license and am planning on buying a car.*

Richard's self-satisfied grin makes me realize he takes pleasure in my pain. I don't care about Sarasota. I don't care about the new house. My summer is fucked. My senior year is fucked. My life is *fucked*.

It hurts, too, because I've just started to become more confident, to have more friends, and some girls even seem interested in me. It's taken me eleven grades to gather the courage to call a girl on the phone, and now I'm back to square one. Someone told me Florida girls are beautiful. *Hope so*.

In the months following the accident, I continue working at the tennis club, always parking my bike as far from the damaged pole as possible. Sometimes, when the sunlight hits the scattered pebbles near the crash site, shards of glass sparkle, reminding me of a broken diamond hidden in an abandoned mine. *I wonder if he too is broken, alone in some hospital room*. It takes several months for the pole to be repaired, but no one notices or cares.

On occasion, I catch myself staring down the road, eyes vacant, bracing for the sound of screeching tires and imagining the smell of engine fluid and burnt rubber. The skid marks stick around like graffiti on school walls before fading into the roadway. I imagine a pile of cigarette butts near the dumpster behind Dad's office where he goes to smoke. *I don't even know if he still smokes. Should I care?*

Once winter comes, the shards of glass no longer sparkle and the diamonds disappear into darkness. Years later, I'd discover there was a surprise attached to the pole, but there was no way for me to know that back then. Most of the time, thoughts of the accident were relegated to memory—like childhood snowstorms, cold and unrelenting, until they evaporate into nothingness. All thoughts of Allen disappeared as the cruelty of a forced march to another state to start my senior year dominated my existence.

***

July 1, 1976, is our last night in the house that has been the one constant in my fractured life. We are being strong-armed out by a dictator. We have no voting rights. Memories of those first years are dulled and have long been covered up like coats of paint over faded wallpaper. But the battered walls still hold the history—and evidence—of a violent past.

Decades later, I return to my childhood home and ask the owners if they'll let me inside. Surprisingly, they're the same people who bought the house from us. The man recognizes me, even though it's been years. The house seems tiny, but when he walks me upstairs, I notice a hole in the wall next to my old room.

"I can't believe the wall still looks like this. Why didn't you fix it?"

The man studies me and shakes his head. "Your father was tough. Holes where he lost his temper were all over the place. I didn't repair this one. Kept it, so my kids would know what violence looks like."

I look at him, concern in my eyes. He catches my gaze and shakes his head.

"All I know is, the walls tell a story, and it's a bad one."

The man doesn't know how many holes he can't see, including the ones I carry in my heart.

I begin to leave, but he senses my unease. "Is there something else you want to see?"

My mind races. "Yes, my old closet, where I kept my books." *Maybe there's some still in there.*

"Sure, go ahead, I'll wait here."

Taking the stairs two at a time, my sneakers squeak on the wooden floor as I enter the bedroom that had once been mine. The spacious room living in my mind is the size of a small prison cell, the kind they use for solitary confinement. *Is the room smaller because I'm bigger?*

There are no posters on the wall, or dirty clothes on the floor. Although Mark is long gone, the faded echo of Richard's voice haunts me. I hear him now: "Go to bed! Don't force me to come upstairs. Shut up before I make you shut up!"

Some memories are tough to delete.

***

My mind returns to June 1976. We're leaving New Jersey in a couple more weeks. I'm lying on my bed, carefully studying the 1976 *Sports Illustrated* Swimsuit Issue. It stays hidden under the mattress, so Mark doesn't steal it.

Mom enters the room without knocking and stands over me. I can feel her brown eyes staring, but don't acknowledge her. She's in her white tennis dress and has just come from the Wayne Racquet

Club. She's chomping on an apple and waits to finish the large piece occupying her mouth before she speaks. I hear her swallow and know what's coming. It's about my books.

"Steven, how many times are you going to read that magazine?" Her voice sounds serious. "If you studied algebra the way you study those girls, you might have actually passed the class."

She takes another bite of her apple, spraying juice onto the green shag carpet, where it disappears.

"They're not just girls, Mom. It's *Sports Illustrated*, not *Playboy*, and they're swimsuit models."

I stare intently at the bikini-clad beauties lounging on Baja Beach, in Mexico. "Mom, algebra is bullshit. Why do I even have to take it? It's not useful."

She's not here to talk about my grades. She wants to know if I've made a decision about my books. "Steven, we have decided you can take ten books. That's more than anyone else. Most of them you've read a million times, anyway."

"Seriously? Mom, PLEASE, I will use my own money. They're mine. I can't just abandon them."

She begins to lose her patience. "Steven, if you don't choose which books to take, your dad will choose for you. And I don't think you want that."

I don't, but I refuse to concede.

I look up at her. "No way. I'm taking all my books. Well, the algebra book can stay."

She sighs, shaking her head and mumbles, "You don't make things easy for me."

I watch as she removes the apple from her napkin and takes a final bite. My finger twitches, a natural response to apples. *When I move, my scars come with me, a constant reminder of a prior life.*

Then Mom's gone. I hear her walking back down the stairs and calling for Richard. When I get home from school the next day, my closet is empty. The only books left are my hidden copy of *The Happy Hooker*, tucked under my mattress, and my algebra textbook. I have lost the battle of books—for now.

***

I know the owner waits downstairs, so I make it fast. I turn to face the walk-in closet that housed my favorite books—my friends. I spent many hours sitting in here with them, feeling safe. My clammy palm grips the familiar metal doorknob and the door creaks as the trapped, stale air swooshes over me to reveal the darkness of an empty, bookless space. Feelings of sadness and anger hit me at the same time. The smell is unfamiliar, like the room has been sanitized with crime scene cleaning chemicals.

My feelings and opinions were never considered or sought during childhood. *So who was the selfish one?* Although there were no chains binding me, I was not free. I didn't have any more choice than Roman Gabriel did the day he was traded to the Eagles. I had to take his poster off my wall. Our family was departing, and I was dragged along... leaving my books behind.

***

In memory of my favorites left behind:

Crazy Legs McBain
Ragged Dick
PT-109
Sports Illustrated Swimsuit Issues, 1970–76
Jaws
Exodus
Honest Abe
Tom Sawyer
Harriet Tubman and the Underground Railroad
The Amazing Mets
The Chosen
Profiles in Courage
Lou Gehrig
Jackie Robinson
Babe Ruth
Jim Thorpe
The Catcher in the Rye
The Source
Centennial
Instant Replay
All Creatures Great and Small
The Godfather
The Exorcist
The Diary of a Young Girl
Ball Four
Papillon

Rest in peace.

CHAPTER 15

Florida–An Unwanted Misadventure

On July 2, 1976, the entire family boards the Amtrak Auto Train somewhere outside Washington, DC, bound for Sanford, Florida. The seventeen-hour train ride is stressful. Richard fights with Mom nonstop, so maybe they'll divorce before we even arrive. Of course, Mom and Richard have first-class seats while all the kids ride in the "discount" section. I'm happy to grab the last row—for an easy escape—but it's a rookie mistake, because the seats are next to the sole bathroom designated for the lowest class passengers. The stench each time someone cracks open its narrow door blows right into my face. It's fine, they can keep their shit in first class—all of it. I'm pissed about the move to Florida. *Fucking Florida!*

***

The train begins to slow as the squealing brakes engage with the tracks and it rolls to a stop. Looking out, my eyes pressed to the glass, I watch people with expectant faces as they nervously wait to hug their loved ones. Lots of little kids wearing church clothes run around the station while their parents wait for Grandma or some random relative who's likely to smell like moth balls and will force them to drink milk. I'm not sure Sanford, Sarasota, or even the state of Florida is prepared for us.

When I finally step off the train, I'm overcome by a warm blanket of damp, humid air that clings to the skin beneath my clothes. It's like a fucking steam bath here. Mom never mentioned the heat. The summer sun bombards my face, forcing me to squint. I'm not sure what's in front of me and don't care. *Fucking Florida is fucking hot.*

It must be 150 degrees outside, with zero breeze. Mom drives the station wagon, which is loaded with suitcases, and the girls. She's a fast driver. Richard reminds her that she can't afford another speeding ticket. She reminds him that he's been in four accidents. He snaps back, "But none of them were my fault!" They were all his fault.

As we head out of town, there are chain-link fences holding back large pit bulls who chase the train as it rolls past, growling like they smell fresh Jersey meat, until their chains jerk them up short. Most of the houses are identical one-story concrete blocks painted either gray—or grey. They all have flat roofs and gravel driveways. Some have flagpoles flying the American flag, while others fly Confederate flags. Don't they know the Civil war is over?

We drive southwest along Interstate 4 and stare at the citrus groves occupying both sides of the road. The delicate, sweet smell of orange blossoms relaxes me. I imagine peeling off the outer layers of a ripe orange and biting into a plump and dripping slice, tasting the juice as it floods my mouth.

Every few miles, we see roadside stands offering fresh strawberries and blueberries and cold glasses of lemonade. There are colorful billboards showing bikini-clad strawberries, advertising the upcoming Miss Florida Strawberry Pageant.

We stay strangely quiet, like prisoners being transported to Florida's death row, home of Old Sparky, the state's notorious electric chair. Since I consider myself a student of famous assassinations, each state's killing method fascinates me, but nothing beats Old Sparky—not even a firing squad.

Signs point toward the beach, but we turn in the opposite direction. Eventually, Mom pulls the wagon into a circular driveway in front of a Brady Bunch house on steroids. It's a split-level with a high-pitched roof that connects in the center, resembling a small church. There are palm trees close to the house, which sits on a one-acre lot covered with grass and orange trees.

I don't see the Gulf of Mexico anywhere.

"Hey, where's the beach? I thought we were living near the beach."

Richard looks over. "Shut up. Stop complaining. You need to find a job. Don't worry about the beach."

***

School starts in August, a month earlier than it does up north. I'm able to find a job at the Sawmill Inn, a popular restaurant in town. No one else, including Richard, has found work.

Florida seems like a foreign country. I've seen wild boar, armadillos, and too many alligators to count. The lizards are all over and keep getting into our house. They spend a lot of time humping each other, which interests Sam, who made the trip with us. He shows rare speed chasing them around but has never caught one.

Mom is afraid of snakes, so she freaks when she sees a dead coral snake in our driveway. She screams at Richard that she wants to move back to Jersey, not knowing I put the deadly snake there after finding it flattened on the road. In New Jersey, I loved catching snakes and salamanders and scaring Mom. Once, when Richard wasn't home, Mom threatened to call the police when she saw three or four snakes swimming in our pool.

I feel alone and refuse to make any effort to find friends. Mom tries to encourage me, but she's never been the "new kid" who is shy, insecure, and angry.

One of our old New Jersey neighbors, Steve Fontaine, comes down to visit Larry for a week. He and Larry are both thirteen. Larry gets picked on by Mark because he's small and wears glasses. Mark teases him and calls him "four eyes." Larry loves working on bicycles and has a crazy streak, jumping his bikes off the ramps he builds in the driveway or even across a part of the lake. Most of the time, he lands in the water with mud all over his glasses and clothes, but he keeps trying.

Larry's great with tools and always willing to change my bike tire or lend me one of his bicycles. I don't ride much now that I have a car. My prized Schwinn bar mitzvah bike was left behind in New Jersey. I imagine some teenager garbage-picking it from the trash pile. Once, I took a whole stereo system from the garbage, and it still worked.

My best day in Florida was buying a car. I saw an ad for a 1970 Oldsmobile Cutlass Supreme and asked Mom for a ride to the seller. Instead, Richard took me. We went to negotiate with some old, retired cop from Indiana, who had us meet him at his "retirement village," which was actually a Bradenton trailer park with shuffleboard courts and a swimming pool the size of a large bathtub.

When we show up, there are blue-haired women in the pool treading water using plastic balls, probably getting ready to abuse waiters at that night's early bird dinner. Nana Ruth and Pappa Ben hit all the early bird specials. Once they took me, and Pappa grew angry when his matzo ball soup bowl was not filled to the top. He demanded the waitress take it back and refill it. Pappa says the gentiles will steal from you.

As we pull into the park, a man wearing bright turquoise polyester shorts yanked up above his waist and a pink golf shirt tucked in at chest level comes strolling over. The gallon of Brut cologne he's bathed in arrives first. I see hearing aids tucked behind his hairy ears. He apologizes for being late, but he had to shower after an intense shuffleboard match.

His thick-strapped leather sandals are set off by black socks that highlight pale, white skin. The man looks me over, then grips me in a painful, bone-crushing handshake. He's trying to intimidate me, but Richard's watching so I can't show weakness.

Richard stays in the car because he wants me to "man up" and do it myself. The old guy says said he's willing to let the Cutlass go for $1,250. When I ask what he would take, he squints at me. "Are you trying to Jew me down?"

I stare at the old man, angry, and decide to walk away. He calls after me, "I was only joking." I think of Pappa Ben negotiating the number of matzo balls you should get in a cup versus a bowl. This isn't the first time someone has said this to me. Richard might kill him if he knew. Richard is not one to back away from a fight if someone mocks his religion, or bullies one of his kids. He's determined to teach us to stand up and fight back. This is one of the good lessons we learn from him.

The man sees the anger in my eyes, "Sorry kid, I didn't mean to offend you. OK, we have a deal for $1,050. You can even keep the plastic flower attached to the antenna if you want it."

I smile and think about my grandmother. Nana Ruth has a fake rose attached to the antenna of her Dodge Dart because she constantly loses her car in the parking lot of her hair salon, which she boasts has a nail technician. I am uncertain what a nail technician does but haven't cared enough to ask.

***

Since I'm the only kid with a car, everyone asks me for rides. Mom gives me gas money to run errands for her. Larry is thirteen and is always begging me to take him to the local junkyard so he can look for bicycle parts. During the week when his friend, Steve

Fontaine, is visiting from Jersey, he and Larry pedal over to the Forest Lakes golf course, about two miles from our house. They're jumping their bikes over the sand traps when Larry notices an empty golf cart and can't resist. He and Steve get in and start doing donuts on the greens of the eighteenth hole when they see police lights, and the cops start chasing them. Steve escapes... but Larry does not.

I'm in the kitchen when the Sarasota police call. My parents must pick Larry up from the juvenile justice place. It's basically the kids' jail. I hear Richard shout into the receiver, "Keep him, he's not welcome at home," but then he decides to go get him.

Later, we hear the doors open, and Larry walks in the kitchen, followed by Mom. She isn't happy. We wait for Richard, but he doesn't walk into the house. Mom tells us to go outside, and even wakes up Cindy, who's asleep in her bedroom. Sam follows us. I step out and see Richard, illuminated by our outdoor spotlights, piling Larry's bikes up on the driveway and slamming them to the ground as he spreads them out. It's a circular driveway that has a separate portion connected to the garage, so there's plenty of space. He starts jumping up and down on them, screaming, "You think this is funny, Larry, huh? Answer me. I will show you something funny." Richard lifts the bikes up again and slams them down and then turns and hurries into the garage. He's foaming at the mouth like a rabid dog.

I figure he's coming out with a hammer. Instead I hear the engine start. His Buick Electra 225 has to be one of the biggest cars ever built. We stand on the grass—out of the way—as he backs out of the garage faster than usual, squeals the tires, and turns the car toward the bikes. *He can't be serious.* Richard sticks his head out the window and looks at Larry, who tries to hide his tears by covering his glasses with his hands. "Larry, lift up your head and be a man," Richard barks at him. "You think this is all a big joke, don't you?"

Larry's shaken, and none of us is sure what's next. I just know Richard's out of control.

He glares at each of us, one by one. "Watch what happens when you do something stupid." He pulls the shift lever into reverse, and the car starts moving backward. For what feels like thirty minutes, we stand there as he runs the bikes over with the car, rocking back and forth on top of the crushed metal, until the pieces are spread like a stack of flattened pancakes all over the driveway. He's determined to prove his point. The sound of the car tires rolling over the bicycles—like bones snapping—is sickening, but the joy in Richard's face is worse.

I hear someone mutter "shit," and see Steve Fontaine, his face twisted in a crooked grimace, looking terrified. The headlights of Richard's car are beaming into his eyes, and Steve holds his hand up to block the glare. Tears are rolling down his cheeks, and I try to console him. Steve is on a plane back to New Jersey the next morning.

I look at my brothers and sisters. Mark just stares, a slight smirk on his face. Robert and the girls look sad. Sam hangs his head. His tail is down, and he seems upset. Mom has walked just far enough away that she doesn't have to watch, but knows she's not allowed to leave. I wonder why she doesn't do something to stop this man—why she's *never* done *anything*. Larry's her son, just like I am. It's been years since the adoption, and we pretend Mom and Richard are both our birth parents.

When he's done, he looks down his broken nose at Larry and Steve Fontaine. "Now clean up your mess. I want every piece of your bikes in the garbage can before you're allowed back in the house."

I help them pick up the pieces. I tell Larry he can get rides from me in the Cutlass whenever he needs them. I'm furious that Richard destroyed his bikes. Of course, the golf carts and running from the police was bad, but Richard's smirk, his mocking tones, the revving engine, and the sound of the bikes crumpling under his tires all ring in my head.

Living with him is worse than ever because he's unemployed and always home. Every day, he waits for us to screw something up so he can erupt like a volcano. It gets old. Why does he always have to be such a fucking asshole? Larry's a good kid. I'm tired of living in a house where a good day is measured by whether or not you can avoid one of Richard's temper tantrums. My rage fuels the blood around my heart and a fire starts to burn inside, replacing fear with the courage to fight back. I'm tired of Richard's shit. Anger comes faster these days and I miss my friends. I don't even know where to buy pot.

CHAPTER 16

The Fight—My Senior Year, 1977

"I am leaving, I am leaving
But the fighter still remains"
— Simon and Garfunkel

Today, my gut churns with increasing anxiety because my Florida driver's license is supposed to arrive, and Richard loves to hold mail hostage. To make things worse, Larry is waiting for me to pick him up at the juvenile detention center. He finishes his court-ordered community service today and needs a ride. The pickup area is behind the concrete, single-story gray building, next to a large dumpster with peeling paint and red-brown rust. The entire building is surrounded by a gated chain-link fence with barbed wire at the top. He's been assigned to pick up trash along the roadway.

I see Larry hanging out near the entrance, and skid to a stop. "Larry, jump in. I'm in a rush."

Larry opens the car door and jumps into the front seat while I gun the engine. His face is smudged with dirt and sweat soaks his blue Sarasota County-issued work shirt. His long brown hair has a reddish hue, which sets off gentle blue eyes. An army of freckles, gathered like ants in formation, crosses the bridge of his respectable nose, which has turned bright red from working in the sun.

I look over at him. "Hey, I have to haul ass to get home and try and get the mail before Richard does. My driver's license is supposed to show up today and I don't want games."

Larry nods. "Good luck with that."

I pull into the driveway a little too fast, and my brakes scream as I push down hard to stop the car. I have a bad feeling.

Larry opens the car door, thanks me for the ride, and runs around to the back of the house. I glance toward the mailbox and see it's open, which means Richard probably has my license. *Shit.* Bob Dylan's "Hurricane," is still playing, so I wait for it to end. It's about a wrongly convicted man, stuck in prison for a crime he didn't commit.

My personal jail has no metal bars, but Sarasota might as well be Siberia. My nightmares used to end before I woke up. No more. Now, every morning, my physical body wakes up in Florida, but my mind walks the hallways of Wayne Hills High, refusing to accept reality. I still imagine being in the cool kid group and kissing my cheerleader girlfriend before class or counting my invites to the top-tier high school parties. None of that will happen now. Not in fucking Florida.

I don't get why Mom stays with Richard. He mocks her and everyone else around him. It's tiring and I'm sick of him.

The move to Florida has not relieved his anger. I need to slip some psychedelic mushrooms into his Fresca to calm him down or kill him. One good thing about Sarasota is there are plenty of cow pastures, so plenty of mushrooms.

Lori and Gail fight all the time. A house with nine anxious, angry, and resentful people is an accelerant for a firestorm. Living in Florida means hurricanes, but the one sweeping our house has nothing to do with weather. I sense a storm coming and think back to *Wild Kingdom*, Marlin warning Jim of impending disaster.

The song ends so I shut the car off and slowly walk toward the house. I just hope Richard doesn't fuck with me.

Richard worked for many years in a tough, crime-ridden area of the Bronx. He had no trouble facing off with the drug addicts and handling robberies at the chemical factory where he worked. There were times when he came home and reported a break-in, claiming all his stereo equipment was stolen. Later, he would show up with a new stereo for the house, bragging how he'd hustled the insurance company. He was always buying things hot. It wasn't until years later that I learned that hot was not about the temperature. They were all stolen goods.

I brace myself and walk in the door. Since we moved here, Richard's been trying to buy a business. Pappa Ben's bank account will provide the cash. Richard monitors the mail for his Social Security disability checks. He also receives Army disability after being discharged early, claiming a stomach ulcer. In New Jersey, we knew Richard's schedule, so we could stay out of his way. Now, he's always home. With seven kids, he can always find a reason for anger. Richard has no boundaries, once telling my eighty-year-old grandmother in a crowded room, "Ruth, my only wish is that I live long enough to piss on your grave."

I take a deep breath and walk into the kitchen where the family has gathered. I just want my license, without any trouble. Everyone stares, and dread hits me. Mom catches my eye and looks down. She knows how important the license is to me.

Richard's standing at the end of the counter, telling Lori she smells like a tobacco plantation. My other brothers and sisters are seated on the island barstools or at the kitchen table. I stand to one side of the counter, two feet from Richard.

There are no greetings. My presence is acknowledged by silence. Mom looks up, her bleary eyes glazed with pain. I look toward the mail pile, but realize Richard is holding an envelope in his right hand.

With his sarcastic tone, he snaps, "You looking for this?"

He leans toward me like he's going to hand it to me, and when I reach for it, he pulls it back.

Mocking me, he says, "You didn't take out the garbage, and I had to do it myself. So, no license until you apologize."

I wonder how hard taking out the garbage is for a man who does nothing. *Such an asshole.* My body tenses, and anger rises through my bloodstream. My mind is boiling now. I can't handle this loudmouth for another second. Enough is *enough.* He's being an asshole for sport. He *enjoys* this. He's *testing* me. I stare at him across the counter and realize I'm bigger than him and am no longer afraid of him. The bomb he's planted inside me finally detonates. "You fucking asshole, give me my license," I shout. "I am sick of your shit!"

Mom yells, "Steven, you know your father is disabled and could have hurt himself taking out the trash! Besides, he has a tennis match tonight. You cannot talk to him that way."

I shake my head. "He can play tennis, but he can't lift a fucking garbage bag? His disability is a joke. And he's *not* my dad. No one's my dad."

These words come out with unexpected power and confidence. This explosion has been building for years. *Years! He's not even shit to me.*

Mom shouts, "Steven, what's gotten into you?" But she's too late. The Steven she knows is disconnected from his body.

Richard takes a couple of steps toward me and begins to say something. With no hesitation or warning, I clench my left fist and punch him hard just under his right eye. He drops the envelope onto the table, and it slides off the edge onto the floor. There is no time to pick it up. I follow with a quick right uppercut, and he falls back but keeps his balance. The speed stuns him, but no one is more surprised than me.

Shock waves paralyze everyone in the room. This is happening. It's been over a decade since he showed up, and I've hated him every minute of it. Until now, I've been afraid. Until now, no one has ever stood up to Richard. *Until now.*

I hit him with a rage fueled by a childhood of watching him abuse my mother, my siblings, and me. This is the man who calls my mother fat and insults her parents, who threw my brother

Mark down the stairs, who kicked me off my front porch into the mud. He's not as slick as he pretends, and he's made a huge mistake thinking my quiet nature implies weakness.

The thud of my fists is all I hear, my punches aimed for the gap between his front teeth, where he makes that stupid whistling sound. Richard's trying to punch back, but he's moving in slow motion, and I'm blocking each jab with my elbow or forearm. He rolls his head away from my fists and tries to duck down, but I swing in a blind fury, connecting and forcing him to step back... back... back.

Mom's face is a frozen mask of shock and horror. My heart pounds, and with the first strike, the butterflies in my gut disappear. A combination of pure adrenaline and hatred powers my rage, and I can't stop. The voice of my subconscious breaks through the years of scar tissue inflicted by abuse.

Richard has called me weak since the day I met him, yet he is the one who retreats. I smell blood. Lions kill by grabbing their prey's neck and throats. Richard's an enemy, like a hyena who goes after the cubs, a jungle bully feeding on the weak or dead. He's dazed, and blood pours from his nose. Some of it is on my hands.

Richard tries to push back, but he can't. My eyes are open, but all I see is a once-scared little boy, now a teenager with uncontrollable fury, burning with anger and disgust. Send me to jail, I don't care. It's worth watching him suffer. My mind has no boundaries. There are no limits to what might happen. *No fucking limits!* And he knows it.

My eyes zoom in on his flattened, broken nose. Mark's nervous laughter sounds like he's swallowing glass as he tries to hold it back. Richard retreats like he's going to surrender and faces me as he backs further into the dining room. Lori's voice sounds distant, but breaks through: "Stop, Steven, stop before you get hurt."

Nice that someone's worried about me.

Mom screams. I hear her fear. "Stop, Steven, you're killing him. Richard, do something, stop this." My mind stays detached, drifting away from my fists, which swing at Richard, acting on their own. I'm a spectator watching from my ringside seat, but I'm also the fighter. Multiple voices shout toward me. I hear them but can't hear them. I see them but see nothing. I understand what the voices are telling me, but I'm not listening. Bob Dylan sings "Hurricane" from the Jensen speakers inside my head: "But then they took him to the jailhouse..."

I love those speakers... and I realize the hurricane is me. This house is my jailhouse and Richard's the jailer. I'm the guilty one, but I must keep fighting for justice. I'm no mouse.

Maybe they're afraid I'll kill him. Maybe they're afraid I won't. I don't care. I grab his neck again as he manages to hit me across the mouth. Years of torment have lit the gasoline in my guts.

Richard reels back and I jump on him, ignoring the crash of the dining room table falling on its side and breaking, but hearing the shattering of an empty water glass as it hits the floor. We lock up like two wrestlers. I scramble to get on top as he continues to flail. For the first time ever, he's afraid of me.

My hands circle his neck and I begin to squeeze with my fingers. He tries to push back, but there's no way I'm stopping. I tighten my grip.

Richard's in pain, but I feel nothing. This is the ultimate feeling of no feeling. I'm untouchable.

Then it's over. Mark and Larry grab my shoulders and pull me off. My heart's a sledgehammer, pounding hard enough to knock a hole through my chest. Richard lays motionless on the floor, Mom next to him. He looks shocked, and has his arms wrapped around his chest. He breathes hard and struggles for air.

I am unconcerned.

Mom walks around the toppled dining room table and shouts, "Somebody help!" but no one volunteers. She hasn't looked at me or asked if *I'm* hurt. She's just fussing over Richard.

It's time to leave.

I feel a tap on my shoulder and turn to see Robert. He looks concerned.

"You OK?"

He sneaks a glance toward Richard, extends his hand, holding my license.

In Florida, no one knows the truth. Everyone thinks we're the perfect family. No one knows there's an underground river of hate that flows just beneath the surface. And today, it bled out.

"Thanks, Robert. I appreciate it."

Droplets of blood obscure my driver's license face. I wipe them on my jeans. The blood's not even mine.

The walk to the car doesn't seem real. My breathing becomes deliberate and sweat builds on my forehead. My chest is still pounding, and my legs begin to weaken as my mind tries to comprehend what just happened. Opening the car door and sliding into the front seat, I glance in the rear-view mirror, and see blood oozing from my now fat lip, which means Richard landed at least one punch. I sit in the car for a few seconds and try to calm down. The fight replays in my mind. I look again in the mirror and try to assess the damage. Not much showing on the outside, but my insides are a different story. I shove Springsteen's "Born to Run" into the 8-track and begin listening. "Sprung from cages on Highway 9..." No retreat, no surrender.

For once, I am my own hero. The Cutlass starts right up and moves out of the driveway. The adrenaline surges through me like whitewater rapids. My guts churn with the turbulence of uncertainty. I don't know what to do next. The pain from my lip reminds me this is no dream. My family probably cannot fathom how I became a human hand grenade.

Fuck Richard. Fuck that bastard.

I rub my fingers against the tiny holes in the coarse green fabric of the driver's seat. The faded cloth is scarred by burn marks from holding a roach between my fingers to prove I can handle pain. Or maybe it was just self-harm.

Fuck Florida. Fuck this fake family.

CHAPTER 17

My Own Hero

Beating Richard loosens up the scar tissue protecting my heart after years of fear. Fresh feelings begin to form. They feel better than the feeling of no feeling. Much better. But they also bring pain. Half of me wishes there could be an actual dad to call, and the other half is happy I almost killed my father. No wonder I'm fucked up.

Calming myself, I drive to Siesta Key beach. As I fly past the endless stretch of pure white sand set off by the crystal-blue waters, my mind travels back to our first day in Florida.

Mom told us all to get in the car, then drove along this same route, thinking its beauty would eclipse the Jersey Shore. I had rolled down my window, taking a deep breath of salty wind, but all I could think of was my own beach back home where violent waves crashed against rough brown sand driving surfers to shore. We would watch the surfers from the boardwalk, eating our saltwater taffy, and then hit the games and roller coaster going out over the water.

The Jersey Shore is sacred. Seaside Heights, Asbury Park—no Florida dream beach can replace those legendary places.

Mom was determined that first day. She thought driving by the beach would change our minds about Sarasota. As she rolled down her window, she yelled with desperate enthusiasm, like an actress forcing her lines, "Look at that white sand, the crystal clear water. It's perfect. Like something out of a movie. And that water is so blue, it could be Acapulco!"

I blurted out, "You mean the place you and Richard went on your honeymoon?"

As soon as I heard the words stumble out of my mouth, I felt bad; I knew she was trying hard. But at the same time, she needed to wake up. "Mom, We don't live anywhere near the beach, so who cares."

There was a chorus of "Yeah, Mom"s throughout the car. She was outnumbered, and suddenly jerked the car, making an angry U-turn, tires spitting up the sand, then pointed the station wagon toward our new home. She was silent as we drove the twenty minutes to where Richard would be waiting. She had surrendered.

***

Now I pull over and park facing the water. As I stare, I try to understand what happened. A dolphin breaks the surface, and my heartbeat begins to slow down. I watch as the large mammal chases panicked baitfish down the beach. Predator and prey, the natural order of things. I guess survival means occasionally crashing against the waves, fighting for your simplest needs and for yourself. It also means freedom.

I stare at the horizon until the sun begins to set. There aren't many people here. There's a couple with a small boy, all holding hands and walking close to the water's edge. They stick together, except when the boy breaks free, running ahead, screaming, "Flipper, Flipper!" He must think this dolphin is the television star. I hear his parents laughing and watch as his dad scoops him up and lays a kiss on his forehead.

I'm in a daze, but Richard will never bully me again.

I look at my watch. It's time for work. I was hired at the Sawmill Inn before school started and have been working there ever since. The manager tells me he's never hired a harder-working high school kid. He promotes me from busboy to waiter in only three weeks. He doesn't know I was fired from my last job and attacked the manager. I've made some restaurant friends and will find someone who will let me crash.

The best thing about the Sawmill is Rhoda.

Rhoda has beautiful, long brown hair and people stare whenever she walks into a room. She's requested by more customers than anyone and knows how to increase her tips. She knows men like her, and some nights she has her shirt unbuttoned just enough for the top of her boobs to show. She tells me to do the same thing, which confuses me. I never know when she's kidding.

One night when we're closing, Rhoda comes up behind me. "Come visit me at my second job."

I turn around. "Where's that?"

She smiles, revealing perfect white teeth set behind thick, red lips. "Wouldn't you like to know!"

Then she walks away and I hear her laughing.

After work, almost everyone goes out to play pool or poker. One night, my innocence is tested when several of the other waiters convince me to tag along with them to the Black Friar, a local strip club. It's one of those places in the corner of a half-vacant shopping center between a laundromat and a gun store. I've never had the courage to walk in, but curiosity gets the best of me.

The Sawmill friends who've brought me don't know I've never seen a fully naked woman, other than in *Playboy* and *Penthouse*. In my trips to the Playboy Club, I never saw an actual Bunny, just some waitresses with fluffy tails. And *National Geographic* doesn't count. I still have my copy of *The Happy Hooker* but there are no pictures.

Once Billy and I snuck into an XXX-rated film. It never crossed my mind that the movie wouldn't show just naked women, but men, too. The sex scenes were shown in slow motion like the *NFL Game of the Week*, and Billy began to narrate. "He scores, he scores, another touchdown, touchdown!"

We both began laughing, but I was shocked. It was embarrassing. I had never seen any kind of sex show. My parents never had a "birds and the bees" talk with me, and I knew little about sex. *They couldn't be having sex, could they? That's gross.*

When we enter the Black Friar, strobe lights flash in circles around a woman dancing on a small stage. Music blares. It takes a minute for my eyes to focus and understand what I'm seeing. The place is smoke-filled, and there are women dancing on tables and grinding on people's laps. I feel dirty, like a coat of slime covers my body. I want to leave. It feels like I'm doing something wrong. My mind battles itself, but I stay.

We take a few more steps inside, and I now have a better view of the woman dancing, using her legs to grab a metal pole attached to the ceiling. She hangs like a trapeze artist and is completely nude except for the G-string that holds her dollar bills. She stares at me and smiles. I see her red lips and white teeth. Tension grips my body. I'm shocked.

I'm having trouble processing this dancer's identity.

It's Rhoda.

She waves at me, like we're at the grocery store. Embarrassed, I turn away and walk back out the front door. My brain churns, though I'm tempted to go back in and watch her dance. She is sexy. Unfamiliar feelings flash through my body, settling below my guts.

When I show up for work after leaving the beach, Rhoda asks about my fat lip.

She knows our family has just moved here, but I never mention anything else. She persists: "Just tell me what happened."

I meet her gaze. "I beat up my father and can't go home."

Rhoda looks at me.

"He deserved it."

Now Rhoda focuses on me with interested, empathetic eyes and says, "I'm impressed. You're tougher than I thought." She grabs my arm above the elbow and squeezes. I feel my body respond. She says, "Stay with me. I have a pullout couch."

My senior year in New Jersey was supposed to be filled with dates, and maybe a prom date. Now, my chance of a real girlfriend is zero, and I've still never been on an actual date. Yet here I am, spending the night with a stripper.

I stay three nights but never advance past the couch. She's a great friend and loves to tease me but keeps her distance.

On my last morning with Rhoda, I use her phone to call Mom. We haven't spoken since the fight. She answers, but her silence makes me think she expects an apology. She's going to be waiting a long time.

She finally speaks. "Steven, what were you thinking? He's your father and now he doesn't want you to come back home. What am I supposed to do? You were being selfish."

Selfish? How the fuck can she say that? I was protecting everyone from the sick asshole she brought into our lives. I bite my tongue. I've bitten it so many times it's a wonder there's anything left.

She continues, getting more emotional. "You know, we had to take him to the hospital. He had to stay overnight for observation because of his bad heart. You know you broke the table—and a few of your father's ribs."

"Good," I want to say. "I actually did some damage." But I say nothing. It's easier to let her blame me. Anger begins to rise, and I remind myself she's my mother and I'm supposed to love her.

"Mom, why do you always defend him? You should be happy someone fought back."

She takes a deep breath, and I know what's coming. "Steven, you will need to apologize before you can come home."

There it is, no surprise. Speaking with surprising determination, I say, "You'll have to bury me before I apologize to him. He started it. I'm happy he's hurt. It makes me feel good that someone finally shut him up. Stop protecting him."

She gets quiet. We both know Richard is not a man willing to accept responsibility for anything.

Mom says, "He will never apologize." I can hear emotion in her voice. She sounds desperate. She's crying but tries to hide her tears.

I am energized. "Mom, an apology from Richard means nothing. He means nothing. He is nothing."

Next comes the guilt trip. "Steven, just come home. He's going to terrorize me until you do. He's your father, and he did raise you. Allen never did anything except neglect you."

Mom's throwing a Hail Mary pass using Allen Nestle's name the way a quarterback throws a desperate bomb into the end zone to win a football game. It almost never works, and it won't work now.

I think about what to say. I believe Richard signed on so he could tap into Mom's money, plus he needed a babysitter for his kids. Pappa Ben is buying him a business. I'm just a throw-in, like the unknown baseball player who finds himself part of a trade as the "player to be named later."

"Mom, he deserved it. I will not apologize for doing the right thing. Goodbye."

CHAPTER 18

Sam the Man

Running out of the house with adrenalin pumping up my heart rate and blood dripping from a fat lip had left no time for goodbyes. I couldn't even explain to Sam what was happening.

During my time with Rhoda, the most emotion showed when I shared Sam's story and our friendship. Raw feelings needed to be pushed back into their hidden compartments.

I smiled as I began to tell Rhoda about the day he showed up, like a superhero ready to save the day. It was love at first pee.

"One day, a few years after the Eichenblatts moved in, Mom tells us she's got a big surprise. I am probably ten and stopped believing anything she said many years before. Surprises were always bad news."

I clear my throat and pretend to be Mom: "'Ahem... Kids, I have exciting news. You are all going to be even happier than you are now.' Eyes roll. 'I'm rescuing an athlete of unmatched speed, addicted to ball sports, a life force overloaded with infectious energy. I promise you he'll bring our family together like no one else—he is the final puzzle piece we've been missing.' Is she adopting another boy?

"I'm too impatient for puzzles and have never reached the last piece. Mom's no artist, but she's painted the *Mona Lisa*. For once, she's warning us something's going to happen."

I stop and look at Rhoda. "This is the abridged version, but let's just say that the picture she painted, and the reality of the thing were so different that she must have been hallucinating. She had failed when bringing home other males, but for once she was successful."

Rhoda gives me a confused look. I continue.

"I guess that he must be a foster kid who's an athlete. If he's smart, he'll run far away—and fast. Maybe he's some kind of therapist who works with fucked-up families.

"Mom was so excited, and I remember all seven kids had gathered on the driveway, waiting for her to get home, and the big mystery to be solved. Eventually, we hear her Ford LTD Country Squire station wagon chugging and clumping up the hill, like it's carrying a load of concrete. Her muffler is shot. Richard claims he'll fix it, but he hasn't. It's been months. The rotten egg smell from the exhaust pipe enters the driveway along with Mom. She stops the car behind Richard's monster Impala, walks to the passenger side back seat, and slowly opens the door. It's like she's afraid a lion is going to charge out.

"We watch as Mom reaches in. I hear loud snorts, and then grunting sounds, like there's a wild pig in the car. We move closer and smell gas—not gasoline. The mystery man has farted. Then we hear a squeal. There's no doubt, it's some kind of farm animal.

"Sam emerges like a movie star walking the red carpet. He's squat and overstuffed, like a sumo wrestler without the costume. He's not the athlete Mom promised—he's more like a breathing cardboard box covered by matted clumps of brown and white fur.

"Sam's head is three sizes too small for his body. Or maybe his body is too big for his head? In either case, his parts don't match up. Sam's family gave him up for adoption and left him at the dog pound. The clock had been ticking. Mom said he was going to be put to sleep."

I stop talking and think back. I remember that my first father used to get paid to work at the pound. He said he was putting dogs to sleep. But then we'd find the frozen bodies. We knew he was killing them.

Rhoda interrupts my pause. "Keep going. Your mind's wandering again."

She moves closer, and I feel her warm breath against my ear, the touch of her long, red fingernails resting gently against my thigh. I try not to notice but my body reacts. Her empathetic brown eyes encourage me to continue. I nod.

"OK, we had been begging for a puppy, but Mom refused. She agreed to take Sam when she found out he was older and housebroken. She wanted to save him. She said it was a trial, not permanent. If only she'd gone that route with Richard.

"When Mom gets him out of the car, she places Sam on the ground the way you might put down a grocery bag. He stands in one place for a few seconds, like he's posing for the bathing suit competition in a beauty contest. Sam isn't bothered by all these kids standing in the driveway, trying to pet him and calling his name. Mom claims he's a beagle mutt, but he's his own breed. It was a funny moment, with all of us trying to understand what or who we were seeing."

I stop and look at Rhoda. "You still listening?"

She smiles and nods. "You're actually a good storyteller. Keep going."

She squeezes my thigh and tells me to relax. My body jumps.

"You really aren't used to being touched, are you?"

"I'm not used to anyone touching me. But it feels nice." I look away, embarrassed, but continue the story.

"Before we know it, Sam is digging his nose into the dirt like an anteater following some invisible scent. He seems determined to stay on the trail, as if searching for a dead body. He waddles to the passenger side door of Richard's car and sniffs the door handle. He doesn't seem satisfied and makes his way to the driver's side. After a couple of sniffs he backs up, balances on three legs, and shoots an impressive river of pee onto the door. We all know then that Sam is home.

"We explode with laughter and look toward Richard, who has been watching from the front porch. He yells at Mom, 'Elaine, get that g-damn piss off my car.' I watch as he turns to walk inside. He's laughing.

"My love affair with Sam I Am, the fattest, laziest, smelliest, gassiest, most beautiful dog of all time began that night. I lay down next to him and begin to read Dr. Seuss's *Green Eggs and Ham*:

> I am Sam. Sam I Am.
> That Sam-I-Am! That Sam-I-Am! I do not like that Sam-I-Am!
> Do you like green eggs and ham?
> I do not like them, Sam-I-Am.
> I do not like green eggs and ham.

"Since Sam eats everything and doesn't keep kosher, he would have no trouble eating green eggs and ham. What dog doesn't love Dr. Seuss?

"We still talk, despite his limitations. Whenever our eyes meet, I can see he loves me. He's still with us but fading."

Rhoda smiles, and I continue.

"Sam's still the favored child. Unlike the kids, Richard even lets him sit on the furniture and in the kitchen during meals. He used to roam the neighborhood and kept up with the local gossip. He lets Sam use the front door and go anywhere he wants in the house. I remind him that this is still a trial, and he can be sent to the pound or traded away at any time. But he knows I love him."

"That's so sweet," says Rhoda.

"Sam's old now and sick. I would bring him over, but I don't want to go to the house. He still loves going places and watching the retirees and their endless games of shuffleboard. The annoyingly chatty seniors, wearing their colorful polyester clothes, always have treats ready for Sam. I miss him, even if it's only been a few days."

I finish and look at Rhoda. She smiles. "Your story brings back memories of my own dog. She was a tiny poodle who would get so excited when I returned home from school, she would pee. It's nice to feel loved."

She squeezes my thigh again, and I relax. Part of me—a big part—still wishes she had taken me into her bedroom. But her friendship proved more important. A few days later, I drop by the house when Richard's not home. Mom asks me to stay. I don't have a choice and agree. We don't discuss the fight. The broken dining room table is gone. No one else is home, which is a relief. Mom tells me that Richard still expects an apology. We both know that won't happen. She tells me we'll "figure it out." *Famous last words.*

Richard shows up later which has given me some time to settle back in. He ignores me, but I can't help but notice the bruises on his face. It brings me some pleasure.

We stay far apart in the house, eat no meals together, and watch television in different rooms. I sometimes feel the gaze of Richard's stare, but don't bother looking because his eyes are cold and impenetrable. He is without feeling. We all pretend the fight never happened. Decades later, my mom acknowledges she was proud of me that day.

CHAPTER 19

Graduation, 1977

Months pass, and Richard rarely acknowledges me. We occupy the same space but inhabit different planes, and he ignores or moves around me like I'm a piece of furniture. No one discusses the fight.

Mom walks on eggshells around Richard and avoids any subject she thinks will cause an explosion. Sometimes, I catch her looking at me with sad eyes, dulled by my refusal to apologize. Overall, the household rules have been relaxed. Even Richard seems tired of policing us. He appears to have been humbled since our fight. I don't say it, but I am damn proud of myself.

Going to college seems like my best option. Despite low grades, I score well on the SAT. It's a miracle I even finished the test, as my brain was in a total stupor after spending most of the night partying and unsuccessfully charming one of the Sawmill's new waitresses. The morning of the test, I had just fallen asleep when Lori pounded on my door. She and Gail drove me to the testing place, and I survived regardless of multiple bathroom trips to puke.

Turns out I'm a better test taker than I am a ladies' man—my SAT scores are high enough to give me choices.

I apply to the University of Florida, Florida State, and the University of South Florida. All are state schools, meaning Florida residents pay almost nothing. I end up enrolling at Florida State.

The school will assign me a roommate. Richard tells Mom I'll probably be paired with a loser and laughs at my choice of Florida State. Most of this he says when he doesn't think I'm listening, since he still barely talks to me.

Sam has me worried, so I spend as much time with him as I can. Our graduation is only a few weeks away, and Sam knows time is short. Whenever his wise, soulful eyes meet mine, it's as if he's letting me know that everything's OK. At least his love is unconditional.

Lori says he'll be walking across a rainbow bridge, but that's a problem since Sam doesn't like bridges. He may have to be dragged across the bridge, just like I'll drag myself across the stage to receive my high school diploma. Mom won't let me go visit my friends in New Jersey unless I agree to stay in Florida for the graduation ceremony.

My plan had been to skip graduation and drive to New Jersey in the Cutlass. The only good thing about the robes is that they're big enough to hide my bottle of Jack Daniel's. Graduating from this school means nothing to me, so they can keep their diploma. I am just glad it's over.

***

Following graduation, I leave Sarasota to start the drive to New Jersey. Saying goodbye to Sam is the hard part. The decision has been made to let him go as he lives in constant pain. His loss will hit me hard when I realize he's not snoring in the corner or sitting under the dinner table, eating our table scraps. But sadness has always been an easy feeling to block out. Richard says it's weak to show emotion or cry.

The Cutlass starts out strong. There are no strange sounds coming from the engine, nor are there any strange odors coming from the radiator. The trouble starts around South Carolina. The smell of burning oil and steam hits me just before the radiator overheats. I've anticipated this problem and brought some water to pour into the radiator. I keep it going, but eventually pull off the roadway and coast into a gas station.

I approach a burly mechanic who spits out a huge wad of chewing tobacco before he acknowledges me. His distinct southern drawl is hard to understand between the constant streams of tobacco juice he ejects into a well-used Confederate flag plastic spit cup.

This guy can spit, talk, chew, and reload without missing a word. He stares, and I begin to think of *Deliverance*, the movie where Burt Reynolds heads to Georgia on a camping and hunting trip and winds up in trouble with the locals. It crosses my mind that Burt went to Florida State.

"Looks like you have quite a problem, son. Where you headed?"

"New Jersey," I mumble.

"Why in God's name would anyone want to go up there? It's just a bunch of Yankees."

When I look up at him, he has a big grin on his lopsided face. "Just joking, son, I see your fishing pole. You must be alright."

Tobacco man manages to get me back on the road after tinkering with the fan belts and the timing chain. He changes the fluids, fills the tires with air, and even fills my gas tank. We become sort of friends, that accidental friendship created when you break down and are stuck talking to a stranger for six hours. He offers me some chewing tobacco, but I decline. I tried it once before and almost puked.

We debate whether Lynyrd Skynyrd is better than The Allman Brothers and argue about the best color plastic worms to catch largemouth bass. I'm a watermelon seed guy and he likes pumpkin. We trade fish stories that may or may not be true. I even tell him about the bass still waiting for me in Pompton Lake.

If the Cutlass even gets to New Jersey, it may not make it home to Florida. My new friend refuses the few dollars in my wallet and tells me to send him some watermelon seed plastic worms instead. He hands me some old calendar page with his address scribbled on it. He explains there's a big problem with the timing chain and the car will need a good mechanic in New Jersey. He's not even sure it will make it that far. The words "timing chain" mean nothing to me, but he writes down his recommendations, along with his phone number.

CHAPTER 20

Timing Chains

Eventually, I make it to Wayne. I drive to Billy's house and will stay there during my visit.

When my friend Joe D'Amato finds out about my car, he calls me and says he asked his dad to help. Joe's dad, a former police officer, scares me.

I explain, "Joe, your dad doesn't need to waste his time on this. I can find someone..." I am interrupted by the sound of an unfamiliar but commanding voice, *Joe's dad.*

"We will pick you up at seven sharp. Be ready."

I hate people helping me but have no choice.

The D'Amatos are a car family. The three boys drive cars with animal names like Cougar, Barracuda, Mustang, Firebird, Cobra, or Impala. The family commands respect and has always been good to me.

Their driveway looks like the pit area at the Daytona 500. There are wrenches, hammers, rotted car parts, and enough tools and old tires to earn written litter warnings from the county. Having hands dripping with grease, and missing fingers with dirt under the remaining fingernails, is a badge of honor in the D'Amato family.

Joe's mom is a guidance counselor, and his dad's now a mechanic for the school system. Mr. D'Amato has this ancient taped-up leather chair, which is off limits to everyone. He has a routine when he comes home, so we always know when the coast is clear enough to sneak beer up to the room. He's a large man with an impressive gut, but muscular and barrel chested, with the rough hands of a working mechanic. Like Pappa Charley, he loves his Budweiser.

Joe's mom calls me "Joe's nice polite Jewish friend," because once when Joe got in trouble for drinking, he told her I didn't drink. I know she feels bad because of my family situation, so she's nice to me. I steer clear of most adults but feel comfortable talking with her. Somehow, she's safe. One time she tells me she brings her dogs to Dr. Nestle. When I don't react, she says, "He's a great veterinarian," and changes the subject.

***

The entire D'Amato family shows up early the next morning to help. They surround my car, tinker, swear, hammer, sing, swear again, and then, with Mr. D'Amato barking orders, we load into his truck. Joe's brothers follow us like it's a parade. I cannot believe they are doing all this work for me.

Joe tells me my job is to stay out of his dad's way. We head to a couple of junkyards in Paterson to find a timing chain from some old wreck stripped for parts. Most of this is done with hard glances and head shakes from father to sons, as if they have their own code. It's not the first time I've been to Paterson, but it's the first time I've ever been in a junkyard.

On my last trip to Paterson, I arrived as Steven Nestle and left as someone else. Paterson remains a Jersey war zone... without much improvement. It's dangerous, yet it feels safe with the D'Amatos.

Mr. D'Amato evaluates the timing chains in the junkyard like a heart surgeon trying to find a new heart. He picks one up, then throws it aside, walking to the next junk car, searching for the best match. He even gets under the cars, moving like a large ballerina, until he declares he has found the perfect match for the Cutlass. We pile back into Mr. D'Amato's truck and drive to his house.

He begins work on my car. I watch him, and nod in agreement when he reports which part is being replaced or tightened or adjusted. I'm a cheerleader who doesn't understand the game, but cheers when everyone else does. Mr. D'Amato doesn't ask me to fetch tools or order me around the way Richard does. There are no rants about stupidity. Mr. D'Amato and his sons work for hours. They fidget, prod, scream, laugh, drop tools on body parts, argue, drink beer, and manage to fix my car. Mrs. D'Amato brings baloney sandwiches made on weirdly white Wonder Bread with mayonnaise. No doubt, much better than the cow tongue Nana Ruth made me eat.

When the car is finished, I make an awkward attempt to offer payment. Mr. D'Amato waves his hand like this is an insult and mumbles, "No fucking way," which causes chuckles. He then leans over and uses one of his giant paws to pat me on the shoulder. I almost jump out of my skin. He looks me in the eye and gently says, "Steve, it's OK."

My face turns bright red, and I turn away, not knowing what to say. His affection is natural to him, yet foreign to me. I feel unworthy of his attention and help but somewhere inside, I experience a warm glow of hope.

***

The D'Amatos declare the car safe to drive. My plan had been to stay a full week, but I decide to return to Florida before something else breaks. The trip hasn't exactly been a success. My fantasy parade and reunion with friends and girls didn't happen. The old neighborhood and most of my friends will have to wait until the next time.

The T-Bowl shopping center is close by. My ex-father's office has been there for decades. He might be working. It wasn't my plan to pull into his office parking lot, and yet, I find myself staring at the faded sign attached to the brick facade of the Preakness Veterinary Hospital. Chicken Galore still flashes with life, and the barber shop where I had my first haircut is still open. Part of me wants to barge into the veterinary office and demand answers.

I leave my car and slowly walk past the office, glancing toward the window to see if anyone's there. I see the church pew, but the office is dark. My mind travels to the past. *Is he inside? Should I knock on the door?*

I walk down the sidewalk past a dry cleaner and stop outside the barber shop. The fire truck chair is still next to the window, where a young boy sits, Tootsie Pop in his mouth, anticipating the next cut. Mr. Romeo, wearing the same blue barber shirt he always wears, examines his work. He next removes the scissors from his side pocket and makes a few cuts over the boy's eyebrows. Then he snips the hair next to the boy's earlobes with the skill of a fine swordsman. There is some comfort watching his routine, the same as it was years ago when it was me sitting in the chair.

Romeo pulls out the hair spray. I imagine the sound as he presses the aerosol can and sprays the boy's hair, gluing each lock in place. The mom sits watching, and just as the barber glances toward her for final approval, his eyes catch mine. My heart stops. *He recognizes me.*

I turn away and begin walking back to the car. Since the barber recognized me, I'm confident that even though I'm a decade older, Allen Nestle will, too. But that day will not be today. I am not ready. Reality is, I'm afraid of facing him, afraid of facing his truth. Afraid of pretending he isn't dead.

***

The Cutlass cruises home with no issues. I now have a working timing chain, but what it does—and why—remains a mystery.

When I get back, I dig the greasy calendar page with the Virginia mechanic's address out of my wallet. It's ripped from an old *Playboy* calendar, but the good parts are covered with dirt. My first stop is the bait store to buy plastic watermelon seed worms, which I send along with a hundred dollars in cash. He bailed me out and deserves to be paid. I invite him to fish with me. Years later, he takes me up on that offer.

Next stop is a local citrus shipper, where I send Florida oranges to the D'Amatos. Richard scoffs when he hears me tell Mom about the work Mr. D'Amato did. They even gave me a hundred dollars to help with gas or emergencies down the road. Richard makes a snide comment about the Mafia, but I just walk away. His words mean nothing to me.

But the words Mr. D'Amato writes in his thank-you note mean the world.

"Steve," the letter reads, "Thank you for the oranges. It wasn't necessary and it's always our pleasure to help a friend. When someone does something nice for you, do something nice for someone else. That is all the thanks I need. Be a good man and a good son. Your friend, Mr. D'Amato."

The power of the right words used for good helps me believe they are true. *Maybe I am better than I think.* Tug McGraw sensed this when he encouraged me, a lonely kid looking for connection. Mr. D'Amato knew this when he wrote the note. Even Rhoda showed me what friendship meant. *Why is it so easy for some people, and so hard for others?*

Mom pulls me aside to tell me about Sam. "Steven, Robert and I took Sam to the veterinarian. We couldn't wait any longer."

I nod and try to force tears that won't come. Instead, I feel numb. Robert and Mom had the courage to walk into the veterinarian's office. Of course, it wasn't Allen Nestle's office—but Sam can rest now. Losing Sam hurts but I won't allow anyone to see my pain.

I'm sad, but Sam will forever live close to my heart. His constant farts and terrifying sleep apnea will always bring me joy.

Today, Sam's picture hangs on my office wall next to my children.

He was family. He will be loved, feel loved, and most importantly, know he is loved.

Wisdom sometimes comes from places you don't expect. Mr. D'Amato gave me permission to be courageous. He is a huge, strong man who knows acting tough is different from being tough. He inspires me with his kindness and fatherly advice. The broken man who was once my dad will be forced to face me.

CHAPTER 21

Reunion, 1979

After last year's car trouble, I decide to fly to New Jersey. Mom doesn't want Richard to know so doesn't even say goodbye when it's time to go. She does slip me some spending money so must not be too upset about the trip. Mom's stuck in a volcano that will erupt. Talking to Richard about where I'm headed could set him off. Lori agrees to take me to the airport.

Someday, Mom will get the courage to escape, and it will be my job to help her. I know that's the right thing to do.

Anxious but excited, I fall asleep on the flight thinking about tomorrow. Most of my dreams are nonsensical fantasy, but the courage to make the dream come true sticks with me. I feel challenged to gather the courage to confront Allen Nestle.

Billy picks me up from the airport and we go to his house. Patrick's working all week, so it's easier to stay with Billy. Uncertainty keeps chipping away at my confidence, but there's no turning back. My whole trip can't be spent worrying about how hard it will be to knock on Allen's door. We go down to Billy's pool room like the old days, turn on some Pink Floyd, and Billy lights a joint. He hands it to me, and I take a long, deep toke. *I'm home.*

The next morning, Billy insists on walking the four miles to the veterinary office with me. I've made this walk many times before—but never to see Allen Nestle.

It's a gray, humid day when we set out, and about halfway there, the sky turns to black and a light mist blankets us. I taste salt from the sweat dripping down onto my lips. We make a brief stop at the Sweet Shop a few blocks down from T-Bowl. Yoo-hoo is not an option. No fishing today. The old bass will have to wait for our reunion.

Billy follows me as we enter the suburban shopping center where Allen Nestle has spent his career. His office is still sandwiched between Chicken Galore, a dry cleaner, and the T-Bowl. The only signs of nature are the weeds growing in the sidewalk cracks. Hurried husbands picking up premade boxes of fried chicken compete for prime parking places with determined moms driving their kid-filled station wagons to the grocery store.

Jersey hasn't changed. The locals can still be heard arguing over parking spaces. My heart is a chemical combination of anxiety, adrenaline, and fear. The urge to take flight nearly overwhelms me, but the voices in my head stand strong; I've flown here already, and I'm not running anywhere.

My mind envisions a grand reunion with warm hugs and Grandma Annie's freshly baked cinnamon cookies, still warm on her metal baking sheet. I wonder if she and Pappa Charley are alive.

I'm curious: How many times did Allen drive by our house, or high school—or the tennis courts—hoping to see us? Calling him over the years was not an option. We walked by his office many times and never stopped. Mom never mentioned him, even when we stood a few feet away on our way to the barbershop or dentist.

Thinking about how close we lived and that we still couldn't see him is beyond fucked up. How is it even possible that a father or a mom could think this is best for the children. Let's face it, his disappearance, Richard's appearance, and everything else that happened would screw up any kid. And according to Richard, I'm the selfish one? Fuck it, why do I even care what he thinks?

Billy and I stand outside the entrance door. This is by far the hardest thing I've ever done. Fighting Richard just happened, so I had no time to be nervous or afraid. This is much harder. This is HARD!

I stand there, waiting. Billy speaks up, "What's the matter? Just go!" I still don't move, so he shouts, "Are you afraid? If you don't go, I will."

I take a deep breath and look at Billy. "How fucked up is it that he works right here, and I wasn't allowed to see him? Just give me another minute. I mean, what if he doesn't recognize me?" I take a few steps back and sigh. "No Billy, I'm not afraid, just hungry. Let's eat first. We can sit at the T-bowl counter."

Billy looks at me. "No way. We aren't going anywhere. It's now or never. I walked four fucking miles through the rain and you aren't going to *chicken* out."

He starts to walk toward the door, "You or me Steve, who's going in?"

He's right. I look at him, and he motions me toward the door.

I draw closer to the office window and see the reflection of an eight-year-old boy with choppy black hair and chubby cheeks. It's the past, and the boy is me. I place my hand on the door. The white curtains in the window look faded and worn, and the lamp sitting on the small desk is the same one my father bought years ago. This is the same waiting room Lori, Robert, and I used to sit in for hours when he was called in for an emergency. From inside, I hear the steps of someone approaching and my stomach turns queasy. I jump back. When the door opens, sharp bolts of nausea shoot through me.

It's not him. A teenage girl leaves the office without noticing us. She's probably one of the high school kids hired to clean kennels this summer. The summers are busy, as pet owners board their pets while on vacation. A few times when he lived with us, the owners would never return. Allen would show up at home with an abandoned dog whose eyes revealed confusion and fear.

Allen had strict criteria that had to be met before he would let someone adopt a pet. He spent hours deliberating the best place for the abandoned animals before he'd sign off on an adoption. But when it came to his own children, even me—his oldest son—he didn't bother investigating the stranger Mom married. He just dropped us off and drove away. We were no longer his problem. He was no longer my dad. He was no longer anything to me.

Jill, his nurse, later became his second wife. I learned about their son, my half-brother, long after he was born.

"Hey, Billy, did I ever tell you I have another brother?" I ask. "I haven't met him but someone told someone who told someone who told my mother and she told someone on the phone and I overheard her."

Billy tries again. "Holy shit, Steve, stop stalling. I gave up years ago trying to understand which kid belongs to which parent, and who is blood and who isn't. Your house was crazy. My family is boring." *Boring? I'd kill for boring.* Billy places his hand on my back and pushes me. "Steve, get going. We can't stand here all day."

I step forward like a death row inmate being led to Old Sparky. My mind is on overdrive and the time has come. I slowly move toward the door and pull it open. The wood creaks, followed by the jingle of familiar chimes announcing a visitor. It sounds the same as it did years ago. There's still the same painting of dogs playing poker, with no children or humans in sight.

Years later, looking back at this moment, I think about how my office is filled with pictures of my children, either together with me or playing football, lacrosse, or soccer, or cheerleading, or fishing. I have every little piece of pottery (mostly unidentifiable) my kids made for me during preschool, and the art on my walls is all from their art classes.

This office has an occupational license from Wayne Township. The grandfather clock in the corner—a gift from Pappa Ben—is still there, and the stink of vitamins and pee mixed with bleach still fills the air. The strong smell of chicken cooking next door oozes through the wall. It's lunchtime, so the fryers are in full swing. I imagine the sizzling sound of french fries being poured into the hot grease.

The familiar "Visitors Sign In Here" notice catches my attention. It's exactly as it was years ago. The stained brown church pew against the wall sits in the same place. Memories flood back. I remember how excited Allen had been when he bought it. It was one of the few times we were in his office with Mom. They were still together when the pew was delivered.

There's no one in the waiting room. Appointments must be done for the morning. This might be a good time to catch him. A small silver bell sits on the counter next to the sign-in sheet, with a blue pen attached. There are two closed doors, one to my left leading into the operating room, and one in front of me leading to the main office.

I walk up to the sliding window and examine the sign-in sheet requesting the patient's name, pet's name, time of arrival, appointment time, and chief complaint. *Steven Eichenblatt. Abandoned son.* The distraction helps, but the butterflies fluttering in my gut wake up. There are footsteps approaching the door from inside the office. The smell of a burning cigarette is close by. When the office door swings open, my stomach drops.

Out walks a tall, skinny, middle-aged man with thinning, uncombed, Einstein hair and wild eyes. Black bifocals sit crooked on his nose. His rumpled shirt sports a cigarette pack in his breast pocket. He doesn't register my presence, takes a step toward the front door, and then halts like he's seen a ghost—which in fact, he has. He almost walks right out the door without saying a word.

He mumbles, "Can I help you?"

This is Allen Nestle.

The first thing I notice are the scars around his dull blue eyes. His voice seems familiar, but the smoker's rasp has added an edge. His skin has a gray tone and is wrinkled around his eyes and on his forehead. He has a dark cloud of energy wrapped around him, and he doesn't smile. This moment is occurring in the slowest motion. Allen has no idea who is standing in front of him.

He asks again, "May I help you? I'm grabbing lunch and will be back later this afternoon."

Time speeds up. Shit, his reaction or lack of reaction is surprising. My heart races again, so fast it might explode, and I feel like there's peanut butter stuck in my throat because words do not come.

He doesn't realize it's me. This isn't a dream, it's not a ghost story, not an imaginary reunion. We aren't in a time machine. The loud sound created by pelting rain brings me back to the present moment. Wind pushes against the front window. Allen Nestle stands in front of me, too puzzled and confused to understand who I am. Something is wrong with him. Very, very wrong. He looks drugged.

Uncertainty grips me as I consider my next move. Once again he breaks the silence, "Do you need something?"

Seriously? This guy doesn't know his son is standing in front of him for the first time in a decade. He looks beat up by life. I could have bailed out right then and walked away. He would never have known it was me. Instead, I say, "Dr. Nestle, it's Steve, your son."

Seconds pass and the ticking of the old grandfather clock against the wall is the only sound between us. The rain has slowed to a trickle. Granted, I've shocked him, but reality seems elusive and his face shows no sign of comprehension. He gasps, "Steve... What, my Steve? You're my Steve?" His question hangs in the air as a lost decade passes through us, but it's just seconds before he understands.

Silence. He's in shock.

Slowly, his dull eyes brighten, and his brain grasps reality. He looks catatonic, not sure what to say or do. I loudly clear my throat, trying to wake him up. Then, he moves toward me, walking with the careful steps of a man worried he's going to fall off a cliff. When he's safe, he drapes his bony arms around me in an awkward half-hug.

He stares, but his blue eyes look vacant. His mind is processing, and the delay must mean he's having flashbacks. We stand there, both uncertain what to do or whose turn it is to talk. I stay quiet, waiting to see what he does. The facial damage from the car crash is easy to see and makes me wonder whether he has other unhealed injuries. I certainly do. *Is he brain damaged or something?*

Words come, but his mumble is worse than I remember. He's still confused. He wants me to call Grandma Annie. I had wondered if she was still alive.

He tries to smile, but that disappears when I ask about Pappa Charley. He looks down, "Charley died several years back from cancer. It was a horrible death. He wanted to see you, Steve, but I didn't know how to find you."

That's a lie. I can't be that hard to find. He could have told me.

I stare at this odd man. When he was Dad, his behavior seemed normal. He keeps looking me over, cheek bones pushing through his thin, gray skin, his head cocked to the side like an exotic woodpecker. He seems uncertain, and his knees shake noticeably, like he's about to fall over. There are long, uncomfortable moments of silence. Sadness and anger rise to the surface. Charley's death disturbs me. I hadn't realized how much I'd missed him until now.

I try to make eye contact, but instead look away and firmly state, "I loved Charley, he was my grandfather. Someone should have told me." I turn to walk outside. "I have a friend waiting." The rain has stopped and the clouds are turning away. The sun shows its face, and a beam of light hits me. Billy gives me the thumbs up. My face breaks out in a grin, and I'm relieved.

I look at Billy. "Fuck, that was hard. Fuck! My grandfather died and no one told me. Worse, his dying wish was to see me. It just sucks."

Billy shakes his head, then looks up. "Introduce me to your old man."

We walk inside the office together and my heartbeat slows. Allen Nestle waits for us, squirming on the church pew in his own waiting room, his ever-present cigarette in hand. It's clear he doesn't know what to do with himself.

I'm not sure what to call him. He's not Dad, but calling him Allen doesn't feel right. So, like with Richard, I won't call him anything.

I look at him. "This is Billy. You've met him before."

Allen looks down at his worn brown desert boots. I can see the shoes aren't tied well, but don't say anything. There's an uncomfortable pause, another moment when time seems to stop. Finally, he looks up, fixing us with his faded blue eyes. *They seemed so much brighter when I was a kid.* "Hey, you boys want to go to lunch?"

His staff members walk out to meet us, and he invites the two women to join in. Both wear long white lab coats that have "Preakness Veterinary Hospital" stitched over the left chest pocket. Each has a plastic pocket protector with number two pencils, a Bic pen, and a dog thermometer. One has a small notepad. I can see scribbles in black ink.

Allen doesn't say anything, so I introduce myself.

"Hi, I'm Steve and this is Billy."

One of the women looks at me. "Yes, we know who you are. And we know Billy because he brings his dog to us." She's Mom's age, and her tone is sharp.

The other one whispers to me, so Allen can't hear. "Steve, it's me. Linda. I used to babysit for you years ago. We lived down the street at the bottom of the hill."

I look closer and realize that her horn-rimmed glasses, oversized lab coat, and frumpy long dress make her seem much older than she is. She looks a little familiar, but my mind might be tricking me.

She continues, "He talks about you all the time."

I'm puzzled. "He does?" I whisper back.

She smiles, "Of course. He even hired my brother once to see if he could take pictures of you, Robert, and Lori."

I shake my head, eyes cast downward, realizing this makes me sad.

"He did? I didn't know that."

Linda continues, "There's a lot you don't know, Steve. He keeps pictures of you three hidden away. I was with him a few times when he would drive by your house to see if you were outside. He never would stop. The day he saw the For Sale sign on the house almost killed him. He made me drive by every day for a week to see if it was still there."

She takes a deep breath. "He's got a big heart for animals. He's a great veterinarian, just not so good with people, even though he means well. He struggles... Well, you'll see. He hasn't been the same since he crashed into a pole on Colfax Road. You might know about that, but he almost died." She lets out her breath, looking towards me as if expecting a response.

My mind drifts, and BOOM!—the slam, screech, crunch of the car crashing interrupts her words. *Maybe she knows the truth. No one knows I was there. No one knows I know. Or maybe...*

I nod in agreement, "Well, we will have a lot to discuss."

She looks down. "I stopped babysitting when Richard showed up. I felt sorry for you, but didn't want to be near that man."

"Thanks for telling me." I sigh, looking toward Allen. He's walking ahead of everyone else. "Does he know... how mean Richard is?"

She stops, placing her hand on my wrist. "Everyone in the neighborhood knew he was mean. He had a terrible reputation."

She takes a deep breath. "And I didn't have the heart to tell Allen. He still has this fantasy going about the perfect family, or something like that. He gets easily depressed. He's not a strong man."

We follow Allen down the sidewalk of the shopping center, past Romeo's barbershop and into a small bagel restaurant. He lights another cigarette and takes a long drag, inhaling for a solid thirty seconds. He asks if we mind but doesn't wait for our answer. He offers Billy one, but he refuses. We cram into a small booth and the waitress comes over. It's one of those neighborhood places where everyone seems to be a regular. She looks at him. "Dr. Nestle, you having the usual?"

He nods. I'm not hungry, but order anyway. Allen's eating pickled herring with chopped liver on rye bread. Billy stares and whispers, "He's eating cat food, isn't he?"

I laugh. "It's Jewish soul food."

I wonder what to say. I mean, isn't he the one who should be initiating the conversation about why he's been gone? Lunch is a blur. Food will not make me happy. Allen pays for the meal—a treat for his staff—and then looks at me with expectation.

"Steve, will you come to my house for dinner? I want you to meet Beth, your half-sister." He takes a breath. "She doesn't know about you," he shrugs, "but I guess she's going to find out."

Before I can answer, he invites Billy, too, but Billy says he has plans. Billy's like the sherpa who helps a climber reach the top of Mount Everest, understanding the struggle and leaving me alone to experience the summit. Allen looks at me, eyes wide with expectation. "What about you, Steve?"

Confusion hits me. He's acting as if we were together last week and this is just my Wednesday visit. Doesn't he understand what he put me through? Next, he'll ask me to call him Dad. *That* won't happen. He has not earned my trust.

Sitting here with him, I realize that this man blackballed his own kids, the way a fraternity expels a pledge who can't meet the standards. *My mind begins to fight itself, and I'm disconnected. Why am I even here? Then I hear my voice answer.*

"Sure, I'll come over. I want to meet my sister."

CHAPTER 22

Little Sister and a Chicken Dinner

We drive to his house in Pompton Lakes. In the car, he lights up another cigarette and opens the window a crack. The car is some kind of Volkswagen, but I don't pay much attention. When we stop at a light, he knocks the ashes out and eventually puts the cigarette in the car's ashtray with its companions. He doesn't say much, but I imagine his brain is churning like the ocean during a hurricane.

After a few miles, he turns into a middle-class neighborhood. The homes are all either split-level, colonial style, or one-story ranch houses. The last time I saw him, he lived in some cramped apartment with one bedroom and a pullout couch. It was a dump. Here, white and pink dogwood trees in full summer bloom greet us on each side of the street, creating a welcoming line.

Kids playing football on the street move to the side as we pass. Some wave, but Allen doesn't wave back. Each driveway has a family station wagon,. Since it's warm out, some of the kids wear bathing suits and are spraying each other with hoses or running back and forth through sprinklers on their front lawns. I can see backyards with plastic outdoor pools, the kind you fill with water during summer and take down as winter comes. *It's hard to picture him running around like the other dads do.* He probably hasn't exercised in years.

We pull up to his house, a split-level similar to the Brady Bunch house. It's still hard to believe he now has two other children. *Did Mom know? She probably did. How many secrets can one family have... ?*

We begin to get out, and he starts shaking his head. "I'll let Jill know you're here, so she can start dinner. She's probably just gotten out of the shower."

Jill appears and I instantly recognize her. She's pretty with blond hair, a triangular-shaped face set off by blue eyes, a small delicate nose, and a pointy chin. Jill's shorter than I am and in good shape. She looks as good as he does bad.

Her hair is still wet, and I watch as she tilts her head sideways, droplets falling from her forehead, jerking her head up and down. Suddenly she smiles.

"Hi Steve. It's been a long time."

She pauses and looks me up and down, still trying to comprehend who she's seeing. "Wow, you're a grown man. Your dad and I are happy you're here. You were just a kid when your mom stopped letting him visit you. It's been too long."

She doesn't get it. He abandoned me. It wasn't Mom's fault. Or... was it?

She pulls Allen aside and I listen as she lectures him in hushed tones: "We're going to have to tell Beth the truth. She doesn't even know you were married before. And we'll need to tell Michael soon before Beth tells him."

Allen mumbles something, but as usual, it's hard to understand. I think he says, "That's fine," but it sounds like "Let's fuck." Either is possible with him. His words don't always connect to the conversation.

Allen is oblivious to Jill's frustration. The weight of living multiple lies weighs on her. When he pulls out a smoke, she snaps, "If you must kill yourself, do it outside."

He shoots me an awkward smile and motions to follow him.

We walk toward the back of the house, and he opens a sliding door. The wooden deck creaks as we both step on a board that looks rotted. There's a small table in between two plastic Adirondack chairs on it. There's an ashtray filled with ashes and half-smoked cigarettes.

The light is fading. Allen motions for me to sit down. He has a pack of Camels in his hand and extends the open end toward me, offering a smoke. The Camel drawn on the pack looks tired and has me curious about the connection between a camel and tobacco, but I dismiss the subject. Doesn't matter. *My mind debates the most worthless shit sometimes.*

"No thanks."

"Bad habit, started when I was in the Army."

He pulls out that same old metal lighter, and I recognize the sound as he clicks the little wheel until a small flame appears. He expertly moves the flame toward his mouth where the tip of the cigarette is exposed. I hear him inhale as the end lights up and he takes a long drag.

"Is it OK if we call Grandma Annie after dinner?"

I nod yes, trying not to cough as he blows perfect smoke rings and watches them disappear into the night. I imagine he's spent many hours out here alone, watching the smoke vanish into the darkness. I listen as a chorus of crickets sings in tune—the music of nature.

Allen listens as well. "Did you know August is cricket mating season, and they chirp loudest when trying to attract women? I actually have a master's degree in bugs. Parasitology."

"Are you serious?"

He takes a long drag. "I really do. Chirping never worked for me when I was dating. Maybe you should try it."

I smile, and for the first time, we share a laugh.

Jill yells from the kitchen, "Dinner's ready!" Allen ignores the ashtray and flicks his cigarette into the grass, using his index finger to punt it with the precision of an NFL kicker. He doesn't bother waiting to make certain it doesn't light the grass on fire. I delay until the embers are no longer visible, then follow him inside.

On the table are two Swanson Hungry-Man Fried Chicken TV Dinners, still in their aluminum trays, each food group with its own geometric configuration. Since I failed geometry, I can't name all the shapes, but I do know that the mashed potatoes sit in a small square, and the slimy mini-carrots that resemble cat food rest in a triangle. The chicken tenders have likely been frozen since the dinosaur age. There is also an unidentifiable dessert, a mishmash of flour and either peaches or apples, or both. Could that be a trapezoid?

The conversation is limited as there is tension dominating the energy between Allen and Jill. I know nothing about their relationship, but something is off. Later I will discover they live in separate bedrooms and are on their way to divorce. After dinner, we walk into Allen's den. I recognize the old, still dirty coffee cup and wonder when he last washed it. During lunch Linda told us about how when she first started working for him, she washed the same disgusting cup. He almost fired her and explained that she had "ruined the seasoning" and it would take months to achieve that level again.

The garbage can next to his desk is filled with crumpled yellow typing paper. Most pages look blank or just have a few sentences on them. There are stained wooden bookshelves that extend from floor to ceiling, loaded with books. Also on the shelves are family pictures. I move closer to examine them. The one that catches my attention is a colorful photo of them standing in front of the Magic Kingdom sign welcoming them to Disney World. *Disney World!*

My heart races. "So you've been to Florida?" I turn and look at him.

He avoids my gaze, shoulders slumped. "Yes, a few times on vacation. I thought about trying to see you, but..."

He seems to hunt for words.

"... it didn't work out."

I hear myself mutter under my breath, "I'm sure you tried hard."

The guy lived five minutes from me for years and didn't bother seeing me. So why would he pretend he tried to visit me in Florida? Am I that hard to find, like a CIA agent?

During the awkward silence, I watch as Allen picks up the phone, dials, and hands it over. In seconds the raspy voice of Grandma Annie bombards me.

She sounds so much older now, with the rough tone of someone who has smoked two packs of cigarettes a day for sixty years. Her voice cracks as she demands to know who's calling.

"Grandma, it's me, Steven!"

There's silence. I imagine the tears forming at the corners of her wise but hardened eyes. She stifles a cry and then blows her nose, a little too close to the phone.

She regains her composure and speaks. "You know Charley's dying wish..." I hold the phone away, not wanting to hear this again. "Listen, Steven." She pauses to take a drag of her cigarette. "Your father loves you and it nearly broke us all when he told us he had decided it was best to let you get adopted. There's so much you don't know, but he got pushed out by your mother. Your father may be in denial about her horrible husband, but I know he's bad news."

She takes a deep breath and continues, "You don't have to respond. Pappa was in tears when he couldn't see you. Then, your father almost kills himself in that *fakakta* car accident. Ridiculous. He hit a telephone pole, did you know that? Meshugana."

She grew up speaking Yiddish, and it takes me a moment to recognize the words

Defeated, I mumble, "No one told me Pappa Charley was sick. I'm sorry."

She sighs, "You come to Bayonne, and I'll fatten you up with some real Jewish cooking."

"OK, I'll come soon." Jewish food bribery is a time-honored tradition.

Before I can say anything, the phone clicks.

I hand the phone back to Allen, who still sits at his desk.

I'm beginning to feel this visit has been a mistake and then, BOOM! Everything changes when Beth, just six years old, storms into the den like a general inspecting the troops. She's wearing E.T. pajamas and has huge brown eyes and a mop of curly hair that, if red, would have made Little Orphan Annie jealous. She carries a stuffed elephant and shoves it in my gut, commanding "Hold Dumbo! Pllleeeease!"

As I take the elephant, she shines her innocent eyes up as if she's contemplating my existence and deciding if she approves. Her energy and light are undeniable—a force of nature.

"Where did you *come* from? Are you my *big* brother? How *old* are you? Where do you *live*? What *grade* are you in? *Why* haven't you visited before. Can you give me a *hug*?"

Laughing, I respond, "You ask a lot of questions, do you know that? Come give me that hug." Joy fills my heart. She's amazing.

When I bend down, she wraps her arms around me and the bonds of our blood connection flow together. She's the first person I've ever hugged effortlessly. She continues to pepper me with questions. It's clear she's never been told of my existence until today.

Beth looks at Allen. "Daddy, let me stay up. It's only fair."

He pours himself more coffee, but shakes his head no.

Beth begins to beg. "Please, pretty please!"

The den door pops open and Jill walks in with a serious mom face. "Let's go honey, you will see Steve again."

"Tomorrow?" Beth asks?

"Maybe not tomorrow, but soon."

But Beth's not done. "Steve, can you kiss me goodnight?"

My heart melts as I nod yes, tears forming in my eyes. I bend down and grab her chin with my hand. "You're amazing, Beth." She smiles as I plant a kiss on her forehead.

My words crack with the emotion of a thawed heart. "Goodnight, little sister."

Allen gestures me toward a small couch. I hesitate, looking at the typed pages thrown on the cushions. It looks like an entire book! There's an open bottle of Wite-Out spilled on one of the pages. Its chemical scent causes my head to spin.

"Why don't you sit down for a moment, Steve. Just push the papers away. Hand me the Wite-Out and I'll put it on the desk. I get carried away sometimes."

I hand over the bottle, push the papers to the side, and carve out a spot to sit. He's saying something about writing but is distracted as he shakes yet another cigarette from the pack he's pulled from his shirt pocket. I hear the familiar click of his lighter again and soon the room is filling with smoke.

My eyes tear up from the cigarette, combined with the lingering Wite-Out chemicals and butane from the lighter. He's oblivious that it smells like a chemistry lab. He slowly sinks into his desk chair, starting a conversation somewhere in the middle. I try to follow as he speaks.

"What could I do? My practice was terrible, I was behind in child support, and every visit had to be negotiated like it was the Camp David Accord. That was the only decent thing Carter ever did. And that mess with Iran and the disastrous hostage rescue attempt. Tragic!"

I say quietly, "Yes, but at least they made an attempt."

He rambles on about Reagan the actor, and the disgraced Nixon, and the political state of the Soviet Union and on and on...

I interrupt him. "What were you saying about the divorce?"

Allen spends a lot of time talking about Pappa Ben being his landlord, and mumbles something that sounds like "it was difficult to be married to your mother." Tuning him out, I look at his desk and see an autographed photo of the poet-singer Rod McKuen, an autographed baseball from Roy White, and a picture of Woody Allen.

He continues to ramble: "Blah blah blah... your mom... Richard... they gave me no choice in the adoption." Then he stops. "So Steve, how old are you again?"

Before I can answer, he says, "You look athletic. I remember you were a good baseball player. Did you play in high school? I figured you would."

I stare at him. *Honestly.* He knows nothing about me, not even my age.

"No, I stopped playing baseball years ago."

I look over as he lights yet another cigarette. "Yankee outfielder Roy White brings his dog to me for care. You really should follow the Yankees."

He sucks a long drag on his cigarette. He's agitated as he launches into a stream of complaints and "not my faults" about his failings in business and with people.

I think he forgets who he's talking to. His words seem like subconscious debates, not conversation. Richard doesn't like whiners and says being a victim is not an excuse for failure. I realize Richard's right. It's ironic, since he acts like the biggest victim of all.

Finally, Allen clears his throat. "I heard Richard was a good father and even president of the tennis club. It must have been fun growing up with all those kids."

I look at him, scars illuminated by the light, eyes glazed red like he's half stoned. This enrages me. I can barely sit still.

"Are you serious? Richard? How could you even *think* that? There's nothing good about him."

Allen's face freezes, the cigarette dangling from his lip. He looks as if I've punched him. There's an awkward silence as he begins to process the gravity of his mistake.

"I... I didn't know. I thought it best for all you kids to stay together as one family. It was easier for everyone. I didn't think you needed *two* dads."

I didn't need two. Just one good one.

"So," he continues, "I stepped aside. It wasn't easy, but it was for you. I did it all for you."

Easier? For me? You did it all for me? What the absolute... He thinks he's a hero. That's fucked up!

Disgusted, and aware that this discussion is pointless, I change the subject.

"So," I ask him, "doing any fishing these days?"

He stares at me, then extinguishes his cigarette. "Nah, never did like to fish. Do you?"

***

Allen surprises me with a story. "Did you know I gave up the chance to play touch football with the Kennedys?"

I'm confused. "How would I know that?" *The thought of this man even touching a football is a little scary.*

"Steve Fayer, my first cousin, lives in Boston. He's a writer—scripts and documentaries. He was invited to play touch football in Hyannis Port. You know they would invite friends to play when they got together for a game. Steve was invited, and it happened to be a weekend I was visiting him. I thought about it, but I didn't feel comfortable going because of a running bout of diarrhea. Pooping on the lawn with the Kennedys would be a tough one to overcome." He pauses, looking to see if I'm listening or laughing. "Mike loves this story because of the pooping."

"Well, Steve went and I drove back to Jersey. Turns out a rainstorm popped up and the game was cancelled. And I only made two emergency bathroom stops on the way home. I know exactly where the cleanest toilets are." He talked as if this was a huge victory for him.

I almost feel sorry for him, but not quite. "Nice story, but I'm not interested in your bowel movements."

How about acknowledging that you shit on your kids?

***

Allen mumbles, so most of my questions are asking him to repeat himself, until eventually he slows down. *How could he think Richard was a good dad? What the fuck? He makes himself believe that so he doesn't have to face the truth.*

Mom once mentioned she suspected Allen used drugs when they were married, and it crosses my mind now. She used to tell me how handsome he was, but now he looks like a walking skeleton.

His clothes hang off him. *I wonder what Jill sees in him. He's only in his late forties but looks eighty.*

Allen tries to talk me into staying over, but I'm ready to leave. This was supposed to be a short reunion at his office. It never crossed my mind that we would spend the evening together.

Man, he's dark and exhausting. I never asked him about the accident. That would stir up hours of nonstop ramblings. He's a hard man to know. Was he always like this? And he says Mom was the one who was hard to be married to!

He's intense, and probably has much more to say but isn't ready to say it. His unease stops me from grabbing all the unanswered questions that hang in the air and throwing them at him, full force.

Our future relationship is yet to be determined.

CHAPTER 23

Disconnection

Despite our momentous reunion in August 1979, any current of heartfelt connection with Allen fades to a trickle. Over more than a decade, there is no rekindling of a father-son relationship, no rapprochement, no reckoning. Our letters grow shorter. I stop calling, because our conversations are dark and depressing. He never seems happy to hear my voice. Maybe I remind him of his failures. He certainly failed me.

My fantasy father never appears. It's clear Allen is incapable of establishing any father-son bond, one where he might give me advice about women or marriage—or just life. He isn't interested in becoming Grandpa Allen to my kids and prefers to remain an urban myth. He's like the sports idol you finally meet in person only to realize they're not deserving of the pedestal you placed them on. Allen is not emotionally equipped to handle adding ex-family members to his life. He suffers from health issues, mostly self-inflicted, and he's a downer.

The disconnection becomes clearer with each successive Father's Day. Our conversations grow shorter until they're just an obligatory exchange of words. "Happy Father's Day." "Thanks." Each year, I debate the right thing to do—and always wind up dialing his number. My conscience acts as an electrical fuse box trying to provide emotional power, but without feeling contact there's no connection. I want to feel love, but he's like an offensive tackle, blocking me from capturing his heart. If I get close, he scrambles away, afraid I might hurt him. He's the one who abandoned me, and yet he's the injured party.

When I knocked on his office door that day my expectations were low. He's a tortured soul, which helps me understand his distance. Still, I'm glad we met and even, for a while, that I thought I understood him. As it turns out, I don't understand anything. His death, when it comes, delivers shocking secrets from his dark past. And my own.

***

Allen Nestle is a short road to nowhere. A new beginning with a dead ending. Our relationship is on life support when he pulls the plug, just like when he left the first time. It's hard to pinpoint the exact moment he disappears, because at first I hardly notice, but one day I realize he's not answering my calls. There's nothing to miss, so I don't miss him. He's vacant, a home without furniture. We speak one last time before his death.

In early 1993, Lori reports that Allen is hospitalized and dying. She'd reconnected with him but unlike me, she called in advance, so she didn't have to introduce herself. Lori visited him several times early on and spent time with Grandma Annie. Her relationship with Allen was different from mine. She bonded over discussions about animals but also struggled to find true connection.

***

Grandma Annie died sometime in the late 1980s. At least, she'd had the opportunity to reconnect with me. I never did bite into a warm cinnamon cookie again, but like her, their warmth and comfort became a permanent part of my memories—a patch of sunlight brightening the darkness of my mind.

After hearing the news about my father's impending death, I deliberated whether to reach out. You might ask what kind of son deliberates in this situation. You might also ask what kind of father abandons his children. Maybe, facing death, he'll be different, more present and engaged.

I imagine Allen Nestle reaching weakly for the phone from his hospital bed. His gray lips tremble against the receiver, as he finally utters the longed-for words that I will forever carry with me. The power of just five words haunts me. I can almost hear them—my heart reaching to reel them in like a large bass. "I love you, I'm sorry."

But instead, the words escape into the turbulent waters of Pompton Lake, never to be spoken or heard.

The only hope of turning this fantasy into a reality depends on me picking up the phone. So one Sunday morning I scroll through my contacts and stop at Allen Nestle (hospital). I stare at his name for a few seconds, recognizing I'm calling him on his deathbed.

I step outside my house and begin pacing in the backyard. I'm barefoot but barely feel my toes scraping the small stones that cover most of the area. I walk to the grassy section and sink my feet between the blades, still trying to decide whether to call. I know he won't appreciate it, but I dial the hospital in New Jersey where he will spend his last, difficult days.

I hit enter.

A nurse answers. "Dr. Nestle, your son is calling. Do you want to talk to him?"

I hear mumbling, and she repeats, "Steve's calling."

He picks up. "Steve? What do you want?" *What do you want?* His tone is ice cold, and I can tell *he* wants to hang up.

"I'm just checking in. Lori said you aren't doing too well."

"Yes, I'll be dead soon. Thanks for calling."

No apology. No last words of fatherly advice. No profession of love.

I hang up, feeling stupid for feeling hopeful. I might as well have been a telemarketer calling to offer the dying man life insurance—or a kid waiting for hours to be picked up by a dad who never shows. It bothers me that it bothers me. I would rather feel nothing, the feeling of no feeling I know so well. He left my goodbye dangling in the dead air of a phone call, already disconnected. I would never hear him say, "I love you."

We remain strangers, and that's how it will end. The truth will disappear with him.

On April 20th, 1993, Lori calls my office to tell me Allen has died. He was only sixty-three years old. I feel only irritation at his timing and the inconvenience of attending a dreary New Jersey funeral. She says it will bring us closure and thinks we might regret it if we don't go. *Regret. That's rich.*

Closure is one of those overrated, polite words that sounds comfortable and convenient to round out a storybook ending or an epic tragedy. It's a lie we tell ourselves so we can pretend to move on. There is never closure, just an epilogue to add to a story that isn't over. I will do the right thing as a father myself and say goodbye to the man who failed to say goodbye years ago.

When I get home from work, I grab my two-year-old son, wrapping my arms around him with the love of a dad who will never let him go.

CHAPTER 24

Funeral for a Stranger

Sitting graveside, close to the George Washington Bridge and Lincoln Tunnel, under the highways of New Jersey, I wonder why I'm here. Maybe it's just the right thing to do. Being here might help me feel sadness, regret, *anything*. It's not like Allen's going to miss me. New Jersey has a singular feel to me, a continuous combination of diesel fuel, bus exhaust, raw sewage, manufacturing plants, smokestacks, and smog. I realize the whole state is not like this, but it's what my mind flashes to whenever I hear the word "Jersey." Of course, there's Springsteen—but he's from Asbury Park.

The Nestles are from the guts of the Garden State, the towns across the polluted river from New York, where the nicest gardens are found in the cemeteries. New Jersey has changed since I was a kid, though, and when the plane lands in Newark, I notice construction and rebuilding taking place all over. I've been told that Bayonne and Jersey City have become much better places to live. They couldn't have gotten much worse.

Driving my rented Ford Taurus, I intentionally weave through the towns on Pappa Charley's bus route—Jersey City, Newark, Bayonne, and Secaucus. I feel the magnitude of his loss. Charley was a big, brawny, tough man who was never afraid to show love for his grandkids.

The odor of Jersey sewage, accented by the fading stink of old Secaucus pig farms, is familiar and oddly calming. Sitting in an urban cemetery burdened by the noise of planes landing and taking off at several major airports, and inhaling diesel fuel from eighteen-wheelers stuck in highway traffic, is a bizarre spot to feel stillness, and yet I do. It's strange, but there's something relaxing about the constant noise. It's like the rain pounding outside my window. The sounds of life will always be present for the dead. That makes me feel better.

Memories return, and thoughts of Grandma Annie's pot roast, boiled for days (or at least long enough to become shoe leather), make my stomach growl. The hunger is real, but there's no pot roast in the cemetery. Her absence saddens me. She and Charley were collateral damage. I'll miss them.

Despite our disconnection, I'm here to bear witness as the man who helped create me is returned to darkness. Some say closure allows you to leave grief behind, as if some magical door can be shut. Allen Nestle's casket is closed now, but he ended our story years ago.

As the rabbi tries to compete with car horns, squealing brakes, and drivers shifting gears, I consider where the hurried travelers are going and imagine families waiting for fathers in nice, suburban homes with renovated kitchens and tidy landscaping. I envision lovers rushing to find a hidden nook where they can smother each other with affection. Maybe there are dads taking kids to spring baseball practice and then out for ice cream after. Maybe there are divorced dads dropping their children off after an afternoon visit, feeling empty and deprived, counting the days until they get to see their kids again.

Few people at the funeral service knew Allen Nestle. Many are from the funeral home, or are Jews needed to meet the required ten for a minyan. A traditional orthodox minyan requires a quorum of ten Jewish men over the age of thirteen for the rabbi to lead certain religious prayers. Since Allen wasn't orthodox, or traditional, women are welcome to join. I'm not sure what happens if there are only nine. Maybe a quick conversion of the gravedigger? We were short a few eligible mourners, so the rabbi must have recruited some Jewish strangers who happened to be visiting other dead people. *Yet another blended family.*

There is no noticeable weeping or sobs from those assembled. Down here in the Jewish cemetery, the rabbi's words commit the dead to God, while the living roll along on the roadway. Do those drivers wonder who has died and assume tears are being shed?

As the rabbi continues the service, my mind struggles to retrieve some good memories, the kind that create stories you retell so many times that your kids begin telling them, too. Maybe, by remembering something we did together, the tears might come. The lost bass is one memory I safeguard like an expensive diamond. But my strongest feeling is dead apathy. Nothing.

The rabbi asks us to rise. Even now, I stop shy of my full height. The need to be small and low to the ground keeps getting stuck in my head. In my house, the safe strategy was simple: If you stayed out of Richard's sniper scope, you wouldn't be hurt. That same instinct has me desperate to avoid the rabbi's eyes, fearful he'll address me in front of people who all wonder who I am and why I'm here. The rabbi glances over to where Beth and Mike, Allen's other children, are sitting.

Beth and I have stayed in touch. She's a beautiful, vibrant young woman now, working as a manager in a doctor's office. Mike is quiet, and we don't have time to talk. He's in technical school, learning to be an airplane mechanic. Years later, we will become close.

The rabbi wishes the family condolences and then stares me down, an imposter parading as a son. When I feel the sensation of knowing glances headed my way, my eyes shift to avoid contact. What could these people possibly know?

The rabbi instructs us to be seated. He has the impatient look of a therapist on the clock, stealing glances at his watch, trying to finish this so he can go on to his next event. This rent-a-rabbi is probably paid well for every event he covers—baby namings, Jewish weddings, a bris. It strikes me as funny that one moment his job might require a solemn burial, and the next a celebration for an amputated foreskin. *How about a funeral for an amputated father?*

I'm not staying long. My appearance is a surgical strike: quick, respectful, and in-and-out—the sooner the better.

Could I feel any more self-conscious? The answer is yes—I just don't realize it at the moment.

It had not been my plan to sit up front; I've always been a back-row guy. Does an abandoned ex-child qualify as a front-row son? I worry that the ghost of Nestle will tap me on the shoulder and ask to see my invitation. One question overwhelms: Is it worse to be abandoned at birth by an unknown father, or abandoned as a child by a father you once knew? Maybe it would have been easier to have never known him at all. That way, it wouldn't be outright rejection.

It strikes me how little I know about this man. Did he have girlfriends before my mother? Did he play tennis or golf or believe in killing animals with guns? Democrat or Republican? Favorite drink (besides coffee)? Favorite food, book, movie? Was he a virgin when he married my mother? Was she? All natural questions a son has about his father's life. But questions never asked are never to be answered.

The only passion I remember, other than Allen's love for the New York Yankees, was his obsession with Albert Payson Terhune, a writer and dog breeder who once lived close to our house. Terhune wrote a famous novel in 1919 called *Lad: A Dog*, which became a movie in 1962. Allen used to take us to Sunnybank, Terhune's abandoned estate, haunted by the ghosts of his dogs. We'd walk the property looking for their gravesites.

A tall, bearded man hands the rabbi a couple of typewritten sheets of paper. The rabbi mentions that Allen's cousin, Steve Fayer, has written a few words. The rabbi seems relieved, as he now has something personal to share and no longer has to run out the clock with a template sermon. He lifts his head and looks out at those gathered with deep concern and empathy. It's clear he has practiced this particular rabbinical look.

The rabbi clears his throat, and Steve Fayer's words cut through the rumble of traffic and even the dull drone of a small plane flying overhead:

> I spent the day after Allen's death reading the letters and articles he wrote for national magazines. While I did that at my desk in Boston, young men and women were running the Boston Marathon, passing by almost in front of my front door.

I doubt Allen knew I had completed the London Marathon a couple years ago.

The rabbi continues:

> I do not often think in parables. But that long race, twenty-six miles from Hopkinton to Boston, reminded me of Allen's life, particularly the later years.

> There are places along the route of that race with names like Heartbreak Hill, long upward climbs that runners dread. Somehow, they summon the courage and the strength to overcome their fears and weakness and push on.

> Anyone who watched Allen Nestle moving back and forth every day to the work he loved, slowly edging down the steps

to his car every morning—first stiffly, then later with one cane, still later with two canes—would have recognized in him another marathon runner, stubborn, determined to run the next stage of the race. Stubborn, determined—to be useful.

My cousin Allen was a hard man to know. He was sometimes a hard man to love. But he was indeed a *man*—who did not easily drop out of the race. Yesterday, I reread an article Allen had published exactly twenty years ago this month, in April 1973. In it, Allen was writing about the end of our grandmother's life. But I also realized he was writing about the end of his own time on this earth. And the message is not bitter. It is, in fact, filled with love. This is what he wrote:

What would Ida think of her now vacant land? She would remember all the families from all the years. And the children. And she would argue, correctly, that the buildings had done their work well. What could anyone expect? To live forever? And don't the most important things of all remain? The land, the earth, the soil, the rocks, the next generation, the seeds that continue the world. She would be content.

That is what Allen wrote. The words, and the love, are a message to his children, and to all of us. May he now rest in peace. May he, too, be content.

There is natural silence as the raw and poetic feelings of the eulogy sink in. *Content...* The word lingers, then vanishes into the Jersey sky, like one of Allen's smoke rings. The frank honesty of Steve Fayer's words is deeply moving, and for the first time, some of those gathered show tears of sadness, maybe even feelings of loss. Who are these people? I wonder if they just love the poetry of

Steve's words, and don't even know Allen. Or are they attending just to fill chairs for the funeral home, to pretend to know a man not worth knowing?

A fat woman next to me shifts in her seat, her body contorted and touching mine as she reaches into her purse for a flowered handkerchief. I shift away just as Steve Fayer extends his hand across the woman and introduces himself. He has thick, curly gray hair, bright, inviting blue eyes, and a welcoming smile.

"You don't remember me, Steve, but we met when you were a baby. I always liked your mom." Steve seems familiar, and his friendly approach is a relief. Then he mentions, "Hey, did you know your dad was a helluva writer?"

Excuse me? I'm confused. Our eyes meet and he says, "I'll send you some things if you have an interest."

Steve tells me a few things about Allen, assuming I know them. I nod, but I'm not sure what he means when he says Allen was a writer. An image forms—the distant, hunched outline of a man years ago, cigarette hanging from the corner of his mouth, banging away at an old typewriter. He used to sit at his typewriter and write in the small apartment he moved into when he left our house, but it never occurred to me to ask what he was writing. I was just a kid.

Now I hear the faint clicks of his fingers hitting the keys and start to smell old coffee and cigarettes. Is Steve Fayer going to send me those balled-up pieces of yellow paper that didn't make it to the wastebasket? The service winds down, and the rabbi is about to begin the *kaddish*, the Jewish mourner's prayer for the dead. I stand, more to stretch my back than to pray. I know this is one of Judaism's holiest prayers, and I mumble along with the rabbi's chant in Hebrew: *Yitgadal v'yitkadash sh'mei raba...* Despite my emotional disconnect, I feel the dark prayer reflects a sad life lived by a lost man.

I'm proud to be a Jewish man, and I'm proud of our history, though my religious upbringing was forced on me and had little to do with spirituality. The prayer moves me. I'm glad Lori convinced me to attend. It's not closure exactly, but it's something.

It's time to go home. My focus is gone, and the image of the unfinished appellate brief sitting on my office desk has become a strobe light flashing through my mind. There's an earlier flight to Orlando. If I can escape, I can get home before the boys go to bed.

It takes a minute for me to sense an unnatural silence. I feel the rabbi staring in my direction. The assembled look around, their whispers drowned out by the roar of the traffic overhead. The rabbi is now asking that the oldest son of Allen S. Nestle step forward for the traditional shoveling of the earth on the casket. I feel foolish. He thinks I'm the dead man's oldest son and is motioning for me to step toward the grave, but I stopped being his son when he stopped being my father.

My Jewish upbringing didn't prepare me for this moment. I'm not familiar with the custom, nor do I know if it's appropriate, given our estrangement. The rabbi must not be aware of my legal relationship—or lack thereof—with the man now waiting for his dirt. After all, I don't understand my own relationship with Allen. Plus, how is throwing dirt on a dead guy an honor? But if I don't do it, I know I'll feel guilty—a seemingly universal Jewish custom. Why can't I stop analyzing everything and just make things easy by throwing the dirt without torturing myself with questions?

Does the rabbi realize this man isn't even on my birth certificate? That I didn't know him well enough to miss him? My skin tingles from the intensity of expectation. The eyes of strangers burn my back. I glance toward Lori, who appears concerned, as if I'm going to do something irrational.

Now would be the right time to cry, but tears won't come.

Can a father, once erased, simply return to being a dad by dying? *Just shovel the dirt and get the fuck out.*

Yet emotions, unlike birth certificates, cannot be erased and rewritten. The bond between a boy and his father is one that is designed to last forever. It cannot simply end by court order.

I rise and notice that next to Allen Nestle's grave site lies my Uncle Jerry, a lover of life and the New York Jets. Jerry was charismatic, quick-witted, and outgoing. Allen never smiled and was dead serious. They will rest forever side by side, probably bumming cigarettes off each other and arguing about the Yankees versus the Mets. Jerry died several years before I resurfaced.

Next to Allen and Jerry is Grandma Annie. Pappa Charley is interred in a Catholic cemetery somewhere. He could share foxholes with Jewish soldiers fighting Nazis during a war where he lost two brothers, but he's not allowed to share eternal life with his wife.

Allen's gravestone will not be put in place until there's a formal unveiling at around eleven months. Jewish traditions are too numerous and confusing to explain, but the delay at least allows for a layaway plan. I'm certain he died with nothing. After he and Jill divorced, he lived alone in Annie's old apartment during the years before his death.

My impatience kicks in—there is a flight to catch. The only connection I need is the one that takes me home.

Time to get this body buried. The bicep exercise can't hurt. I place the shovel upside down in the dirt pile, pick up a respectable amount, and throw it on the casket. Although the traffic keeps building above us, the only sound I hear is dirt hitting wood, and the rush of others to cover him and his misery up for good. I do hope he's finally found peace.

Walking away from the cemetery, my focus is on the future. Soon I'll be airborne, and there's no reason to look back. The secret chapters that Allen carried around with him, like an unfinished mystery novel, are now finished. His life is over, and it's time for me to move forward.

But the dead man isn't done with me yet.

***

In late 1993, months after the funeral, Steve Fayer sends me a large cardboard box, held together by layers of moving tape, and labeled with the words, "precious cargo," as if there's a small child inside.

I cut through the tape and pull back the top. The musty smell of mildew wafts out of the box. The scent lingers like a ghost as the papers inside release the unmistakable aroma of typewriter ink. When I touch them, my fingers stick together, the powdery residue of Wite-Out clinging to them. The chemical smell is now imbedded in my skin.

A personal note sits on top:

November 1993

Dear Steve,

Here, as far as I know, are most of your father's letters, writings, and articles. He was for many years far more successful with his writing than I was, and I thought you might enjoy his work. It has taken a while to go through them and send them so please forgive me for my delay in getting this to you; in these hundreds of documents I have relived the last three decades of my own life. And, as in life, your father has worn me out once again with his energy and his productivity, sometimes three letters in a week. As I read them, I often feel the immediate obligation to answer some of the questions, challenges. There is no mistaking his voice. And his energy seems to have endured and outlived the body we lowered into a cemetery in North Jersey.

Despite this latest trip to Fairview—it was good seeing you and who you have become.

Take care, cousin.

~Fayer

I take a quick look inside. There are hundreds and hundreds of single-spaced typed pages on yellow paper—letters he sent to Fayer over thirty years. There's poetry on napkins, scrapbooks with handwritten notes, and typed journal entries from 1978, written on a 1974 calendar. One of the newspaper articles has a photograph of him sitting at a desk, staring at the camera and attempting an awkward smile. The paper describes a promising writer who's won multiple awards and wants to be the next James Herriot, a British veterinarian with several bestsellers.

My father died a poor man. If the number of people who attended his funeral is a measure of a healthy life, his was not well lived. Allen's legacy is contained within the walls of a cardboard box. His life views, philosophy, disappointments, and shortcomings are all within these pages. His words bleed the pain, making them hard to read.

My funeral conversation with Steve Fayer about Allen's writing surprised me, but Steve was probably relieved to find someone to take the mess off his hands. After a few weeks, I assumed Fayer had forgotten about the letters or trashed them. And now, here they are.

Though a part of me is fascinated, it's hard to find time to dive into all of this paper and make sense of what's been sent. Each page is single-spaced, and most are double-sided. I can see that the writing is scattered and disconnected—like its author. There's no logical order; page two does not follow page one. I take a deep breath and look around at the loving faces of my own kids; their pictures on my office wall capture their joyful innocence. I close the box up and push it into a far corner. It will be years before it's opened again.

CHAPTER 25

Unboxing

A decade has passed. I am two marriages removed from the time Fayer sent Allen's writing and find myself living alone. A recent extended bout with pneumonia resulted in hospitalization and near death. I desperately try to sell my enormous house, now empty except for me. It turns out to be a financial disaster as the only way to sell a nine-acre horse farm in the middle of a real estate crisis is by short sale.

Work stress and personal pressures enclose me like a suicide vest. Sometimes, I feel the sensation of drowning and am unable to catch my breath. However, I'm always rescued by the lifeguard of love for my kids.

Saturday is a perfect day to clean my law office, where there's enough clutter to make a hoarder jealous. Still recovering from illness, but able to drive, I climb into my Suburban and drive to our building, a historic plantation style house in downtown Orlando. My law partner purchased the building with me years ago, and it feels like home.

I look around the office. Most of my legal awards, diplomas, and membership certificates have been stacked up in the corner. My Florida Supreme Court admission hangs on the wall next to a colorful framed Torah quote: "Justice, Justice You Shall Pursue." There is also a striking photo of a fire truck speeding up the Brooklyn Bridge toward the burning World Trade Center. These were firefighters whose families I represented as a volunteer lawyer before the September 11 Victims recovery fund. My mind drifts to the day years back when I entered Allen's office. For him, photographs of family were self-abuse. There were no pictures of him walking his daughters down the aisle, or attending my law school graduation, or holding a grandchild. He was a runaway, his life like a face on a milk carton: "missing."

My photos bring pleasure, not pain. My kids' faces are everywhere, from sporting events, fishing trips, and the many hours we've spent at theme parks. There are signed baseballs, team pictures, and plaques given to me from the many teams I've coached.

The rain continues outside, so I plop down in an office chair. My eyes rest on the boxes in the corner. (Additional ones have arrived in the mail from Fayer over the years.) It's been ages since I've opened any of them. Allen's whole life seems to live inside. Personal, nonsensical journals, unpublished and published stories and poetry. Many of the pages are letters to Steve Fayer, himself a writer, who later won an Emmy for his work on *Eyes on the Prize*, a civil rights documentary.

Steve had warned me there were thousands of pages. For the first time, I begin to remove the contents of the boxes. Allen types down one side, up the other, and then reverses his pattern on the opposite side of the same page. Dates are random. The disorder of his entries reflects the overwhelming turbulence dominating his mind.

My heart races as I search for any sign of my existence in this man's life. There are many sides to the truth, although he has never shared his. It's frustrating, and I realize there's still billable legal work to finish. My eyes scan the pages, and the date on one entry grabs me in a chokehold. I take a breath, understanding history is about to be rewritten. Insanity is becoming reality.

JULY 4th, 1975

PROBABLY ONE OF MY MAJOR MISTAKES IN WHEN? THE REST SHOULD BE WRITTEN IN BLOOD.

I had known for some time that my ex-kids played tennis at the courts on Colfax Road. I had hired an investigator to take pictures. He discovered Steve works at the club and takes lessons from someone I think named Eldon Schwartz. Richard is the president of the club. Probably means he goes after all the lost balls. Lori and Robert are in a drum and bugle corps called The Monarchs.

Lately I had begun driving home that way in hopes of catching a glimpse of Steve, even though I would never stop if I did. Just maybe slow... The rest should be written in blood.

I have driven Colfax 1,000 times. I can make excuses about not looking and here comes the biggie, never use a seat belt.

I glanced at the court, distracted, and my Cutlass '71 attempted to demolish a telephone pole. It happened so quickly I have no excuse. I felt extreme pain, blood, and was knocked unconscious I think. I broke the steering wheel with my chest and the windshield with my face. I don't remember much. I saw a sliced pancake of my flesh hanging but immediately looked to my eye. It could have been hanging in my lap but there it was staring at me. Then the blood began to flow. (It was two weeks later that I found out I had three cracked ribs and a collapsed lung). I wavered in and out of consciousness. What surrounded my eye would eventually take 200+ sutures by a plastic surgeon. The tattooed agent we call the Angel of death. The accident and no seat belt.

The car was damaged beyond repair—financial position unbelievable. The weeks after the accident I had to go into the office with one eye sewn shut and numerous cuts and abrasions on my face. Scabs all over my head and face make me seem like Frankenstein. Swelling prominent pain everywhere. I can barely breathe. Try explaining to patients and others the story of a bleeding father trying for photos of lost kids and almost killing himself for a glimpse of them. Try selling that story. Perhaps I write soap opera? One day I will put the book together.

BUT THAT IS NOT THE WORST PART... The paramedics had me propped against the car. I was getting my head wrapped and my eyes covered. I felt them grab the wallet out of my pocket. Just before my mind faded into unconsciousness, I caught a glimpse of a dark-haired husky teenager. Steve?

Can this be true? I pause and reread his faded words: "I caught a glimpse of a dark-haired husky teenager. Steve?" *What?*

My memory fights to maintain clarity as the bitter scene plays on the screen of my mind. The answer has been in these cold files all along, waiting like a patient pet to be let out of its cage. Emotion embraces me like a warm hug.

He knew.

For forty years, the accident disappeared into my mind's black hole as if it never happened. It hung like a tiny knot stuck in my memory. I almost convinced myself it was a bad dream. What would have happened if I hadn't gone to the tennis courts that day? He wouldn't have seen me, wouldn't have gotten "distracted," and wouldn't have crashed.

I survive by squashing reality, even when my subconscious smothers me with the sound of screeching brakes. Despite his injuries, he knew I was there.

He knew.

Allen carried his scars on the outside, while mine are only internal. When we spoke, we were like death row prisoners talking about the weather without ever mentioning the execution date. His avoidance of the subject must mean it tortured him.

I continue reading. Allen's unmistakable voice floats off the written pages. Weeks before the accident, Allen had sent a letter to Mom asking for a picture of his kids:

July 20, 1975

Can things get worse? I had written to Mrs. E, asking for pictures of the kids... I forgot the clincher. A few days later, I received my letter, unopened with a printed message on the outside. LEAVE MY CHILDREN ALONE. NEVER BOTHER US AGAIN. I shouldn't have written the letter. The cruelty of the letter is inconceivable—except the world is full of Richards. Little men who take power and hurt. It makes me want to tear his balls out. Can things get even worse... I received a bill for a new telephone pole! The letter is written by the lawyer for the tennis club and signed by the club president, Richard Eichenblatt. Three grand is what the insurance company will pay. I send it to them.

I decided to accept the honor and name the new pole The Allen S. Nestle Memorial Pole. One day I grab Linda who works for me, go to the hardware store and buy three metal letters... ASN. I sneak over one night and nail them into the pole. The ASN Memorial Pole. The letters are probably still there.

One month later I received a large glossy of the three kids from Mr. and Mrs. Eichenblatt. A beautiful picture of my ex-three. Which was all I wanted. Is the fact I had the accident the reason?

The evidence grows stronger. *Mom and Richard knew about the accident.* Who knows what else they knew?

Allen's detailed notes prove that a simple photograph would have stopped the bleeding, because the accident would almost surely not have occurred. *They sent pictures and also sued him?* The story is insanity. *Letters nailed into the pole? Could that be true?* I contact Linda, Allen's former employee. She is now a retired microbiologist living in Evansville, Indiana.

She writes, in part:

I vividly remember the accident your dad had on Colfax Road. He knew you played tennis and cared for the courts and began driving home that way in hopes of catching a glimpse of you. He desperately wanted to see you but even when he knew you were there, he would not stop. The adoption precluded him from seeing you while you were a minor. Sometimes he would use the excuse of driving me home to head that way. The first time I saw him after the accident, he had one eye sewn shut completely, broken ribs, and cuts and abrasions all over his face and arms. He was lucky he did not die. I found out he saw you on the tennis court and hit the pole. It upset him so much that you saw him and must have known who he was. He remarked at times how it would make a great movie, father almost dies trying to see his son only to have his son save him. The car was totaled and the telephone pole had to be replaced. When he was healed up and things quieted down, I took him to the hardware store where he bought little metal letters. He nailed them to the phone pole. For all I know, the little silver "ASN" may still be on that pole.

My heart shakes. The fact that Mom knew disturbs me. Mom and Richard may not have stabbed Allen with a knife, but they killed him. I picture a desperate, damaged mind attached to a broken body, with a hammer in his hand. He's determined to make his mark, to take ownership, to stay connected, to prove something to himself—or me. He kneels in the dark, taking possession, eager to get the last word. According to Linda, the letters *may still be there.*

July 27, 1975:

Dear S.C.

How many tears can a normal eye surrounded by a centennial of scars shed? When one is almost literally dead should one give a fuckety fuck—fuck his literary career?

Can shock after shock to both physical, mental and financial being be shrugged off? Rejection. Debts. Three broken ribs added to a Frankenstein eyebrow...but I live. I breathe....

***

The conspiracy of parental indifference will not be passed on to the next generation of survivors. I was diagnosed with post-traumatic stress disorder years ago, and the therapists didn't even know about the accident. They assumed it was childhood trauma and abuse. Allen's feelings push a faint breeze of emotion through my body. *Such* a wasted life!!! Anger rotates with sadness which rotates with resentment as mixed feelings surge through my brain.

***

How many times have I wondered how my life would be if he or Richard had been different? For years, I watched other kids with their parents. Friends who ate dinner with their families, and whose dads taught them about things like shaving, sex, or how to balance a checkbook. I try to have feelings for Allen, but my heart fights back. He left me, but now he wants to love me. He's fucking dead. My feeling of no feeling remains.

And yes, he did lose his temper with me; he was no saint—he never writes about that. He doesn't mention forcing me onto a stool in his veterinary hospital, striking me as he cut my hair with dog clippers. I can hear him, probably drugged:

"You look like a girl. I will take care of this right now."

I said nothing and tried to be strong, the sound of his clippers circling around my ears. *Bzzzzz*. I kept moving my head to get away from the noise.

The metal blades click together. I wait for him to cut a piece of my ear off. The sound brings back the toxic odor from the bleach he used to clean the operating room. It's like a hospital smell, or a dental office drilling sound, that never disappears. Animal urine, vitamins, bleach, and a disturbed veterinarian with dog clippers in his hand—not the best way to spend time with Dad.

I try to push past the shit. *What was he thinking? Mom says he would lose patience with me during bathtime and hold my head under water or drag me across the floor by my arm. Maybe he was worse than Richard? Not possible.*

Allen's pages are published in magazines, scrawled on napkins, torn from spiral notebooks, written on yellow typing paper, single-spaced with no regard for format or number of words on a single page. His writing can be dark and depressing: pain, death, families torn apart, pet euthanasia, and the Yankees. He writes poetry, descriptions of his dating life, and random thoughts scratched onto cereal boxes. Occasionally, he might get paid for a story acceptance, but the money was minimal.

Even now, sitting in my office, the stale coffee from his dirty cup and the whiff of his cigarettes seem too real to be my imagination. I decide to bring this box home, an interesting house guest. I can't wait to dig in, like an archeologist or archivist making discoveries as he preserves ancient history.

Hurrying out of the office, I'm on autopilot, so disconnected that I'm not even sure who's driving. All I can think about is finding the answers to decades-old questions. How must he have felt the moment he hit the pole? Had he first seen me sweeping the courts? Years later, he never mentioned the accident. Maybe it was too painful to speak about? The events of July 4, 1975, were never discussed. Yet he knew I was there.

He knew.

CHAPTER 26

Back to the Future

I sit down at the kitchen table while the coffee is brewing and begin to read:

> It is March 5th, 1976, and I am not dreaming. This is the planet earth and I am extricated in a brain drain. I leave Colfax Road and turn down the street to my former residence. FOR SALE! I am shaken by this event, which will change the future in which the former children seek out their former father.

Allen knew about the move and still didn't reach out. He couldn't find the courage to be anything except a desperate stalker, watching from a distance, driving past our house or the tennis courts, trying to catch a glimpse. How many times over the years must he have gone down our street or by our school or past the ball field where we played? *Did he watch our house like some divorce detective looking to bust an unfaithful spouse?* Reading his notes makes me wonder: If he hadn't crashed that day, would he have stopped the car? Or just slowed down, like he wrote? Did he have some plan?

According to his own description, he had taken Valium. Was he too drugged to understand that his ex-son had saved him?

> March 5th, 1976
>
> I am despondent and confused. It turns out they are all moving to Florida. Because of Mr. E's health? His coronary was obviously a factor but the change of location and such can only be financially possible because of the grandparents. I absorb this and try to accept the common sense attitude that since they haven't seen me in Wayne, it's like they've been in Florida the whole time. Better to pretend they are dead.

In New Jersey, Allen had patients who would update him. He listened to gossip about Elaine and Richard or reports of kid sightings. The shocking news of our move to Florida stripped away his remnant of connection. It's no coincidence that several of his employees lived in our neighborhood, giving him an excuse to ask questions or drive down our street.

> August 6th, 1976
>
> The simple fact is my ex-kids know where I am. They know they can call and are probably in the shopping center all the time. Let Richard and Elaine live their lumpy lives. Jill blames them.

We were kids. *He* should have called *us*.

Skimming pages, my attention is grabbed by another mention of "Hellow, Yellow."

May 7, 1976

Getting the kids to read Hellow, Yellow will undoubtedly get me into trouble. Yet how can a vow of love, of future rainbows be a problem to the Eichenblatts? I know any contact is a no-no so I shall have to play it cool.

May 14, 1976

Still meditating about whether to send them a copy of Hellow, Yellow or forget it. Best to wait, perhaps for years. THE POWER OF THE PRINTED WORD. If these words have power.

"Hellow, Yellow," which I spotted that day on the back seat of Allen's car, is a mystery that may never be solved.

Allen also writes about my visit in this letter to Steve Fayer:

August 1979

Dear Steve,

[...]

It is worth going into detail about Steve's appearance... I was going over to the library—to Xerox copies of the article for query letters—and I'm into my waiting room heading for the door and somebody walks in. I really didn't look closely. A bearded youth. I said, "May I help you?" Surely a classic bit of dialogue considering.

He said, "I'm Steve."

No, I didn't say Steve who. I took him into the office and tried to be casual as he did although it was a heavy moment. It was an awkward half hour and that was the only awkward time we spent together. He spent part of almost every day with me. In the beginning it was hard to keep from popping out with tears—happy tears. Toward the end of his visit it drove me crazy that we are alike in so many ways, that we enjoyed each other's company so much, that I was able to tell him of my love for my first three—something that somehow became wiped out for all those years—because there I was, right where I always was. The last night before he left we talked until two in the morning. I kissed him goodbye.

I must interrupt. Allen's version and mine, like many eyewitness accounts, are different, but that doesn't mean they both aren't true. It's like a fish story that just gets better and bigger with each telling. He might think my world-record bass that jumped off the hook at Pompton Lake was actually a small sunfish. And I might think his beloved Rod McKuen albums were shit. Never heard of him? To each his own.

Ever since Steve reappeared at my office I have felt we have something special. Yes of course fathers love sons and sons love fathers but I mean more than that. I don't even know how to express it. I remained low-key when I was with him, but inside was on a real high. I surrendered a lot when I gave in to his mother. I did it for the three of them. It had nothing to do with Jill or Beth or Mike. I took so many knives in the back, but none of that could guarantee any feelings when we did meet.

I search my memory to tell me the particular moment in time I should have gotten together with my ex-kids and their mother and had an adult, mature meeting to explain what was happening, why I signed the papers, etc. It doesn't hurt hearing about your family—what hurts is wondering how I screwed up—how the three of them could be in Wayne all those years and be ghosts.

It goes without saying I miss them as much as before. I am very happy about what has happened, a new emotion. It is not yet time for them to read "Hellow, Yellow" but someday we can cry about it together—happy tears—in a real way.

I'm still sitting at the kitchen table, when the coffee pot calls my name. Standing, my legs feel tight, but caffeine will kick in and I can jump back in time, my own *Back to the Future*. If I stop reading now, it will be like putting a great book aside without reading the ending. I grab a Florida State coffee mug out of the cabinet and pour myself a cup. I drink it black, taking a long sip and ignoring the hot liquid that burns my throat.

July 6, 1976

Biggest news of the weekend was the daring raid of Israeli commandos in Uganda. Ridiculosity is a small animal practitioner, 46 years old with 14 years of experience, sitting tense as usual simply because the phone might ring. I think of past due bills and pain. Yankee games have featured the heroics of Roy White.

Allen is always struggling. The guy is a mess. The journal flows like a traumatic beach novel that's impossible to put down. Each page reveals a new plot twist or tragic ending to an ongoing drama. These are the words of a man whose shell has been busted open, and I get to look inside. There's a river of despair just below the surface, an underground current of electricity waiting for the next fuse to blow. His written words express everything he never said out loud. I never hear his voice, but he's screaming in my ear.

> I want my kids, especially the Florida bunch, to care for me. I want them to know me. I want them to love me—for being me, the fucked-up veterinarian, sometimes writer, etc. that I am and always will be. I know they will like me when we finally all get together, not because we are of the same blood, but because of something I carry around with me all the time. Love.

I take another sip of my now cold coffee. What? *Love!* I search the paragraphs with fresh eyes now, shocked awake by Allen's pronouncement. My mind processes his words singing from the pages. A person no longer breathing cannot be written off as dead. Allen's voice is loud—and loving. Though he was never able to express them to me directly, his feelings are crystal clear.

I hear him.

I am listening.

My inner voice, the discouraging, fearful one that holds me back, won't shut up. This voice tried to stop me from walking into my father's office when I was twenty years old. It convinced me not to go to a doctor when I had pneumonia, almost killing me. I could have gone out on so many more dates. This voice has stopped me for years from taking chances.

Allen focused on the empty slices of his life instead of the full ones. He couldn't see that we were his gold medals. He didn't have the courage or strength to fight for us. He simply surrendered. Loving fathers sacrifice their lives to protect children from evil. Love was not a word ever heard in my house growing up. Allen should have shared his feelings, no matter how difficult. He should have visited us instead of killing us off. No one fought for us when we were too young to fight for ourselves. Allen allowed himself to be junked, like one of those crushed cars at the D'Amato's junkyard. I mix feelings of anger and empathy the way you might mix a gin and tonic—bitter and sweet in the same emotional moment. The voices inside me never agree, until now.

I am a relentless seeker of truth as a lawyer, yet I know nothing of my own family's truth. Allen writes like he knows my hands will be holding the pages. It's an intimate feeling, as if he's looking over my shoulder. He writes about death with powerful acceptance:

HEAVEN

No tears. Dead is dead. The thing I feared above all was blankness, whether it be of my own mind or it be the paper sheets beyond my reach. If I was going to be able to survive in heaven I must write. This was going to be a new start. I didn't want to cause trouble but I ache with longing. A piece of coal, a brown paper bag, a chewing gum wrapper, anything to occupy my time. I would have written in blood, if I had any. I was a practical soul and I still am a practical soul. It may sound disorderly to express myself that way but we don't measure time in heaven.

ALLEN S. NESTLE

In "Death Time," a short story from 1966, he writes of a long hospital stay for either a mental breakdown or a disease related to deer ticks. He's still married to Mom. His words trigger a new image of six-year-old Steven starring in the slideshow playing in my mind, the memory finally set free from its rusted, locked archive.

Sadness comes to the surface as I remember being the only child left on the yellow school bus for day camp. The rest of the campers have been picked up by their parents. I like the sweet smell of diesel fuel, and watch out the window, feeling the vibration of the idling engine, and sitting on my knees for a better view.

On this day, Dad's supposed to take me to a swimming class. The bus driver grows impatient and stomps on and off the bus, the door hissing as it opens and closes. Dad never shows, so the driver takes me home. I sit alone, wondering where Mom is, and am greeted in the driveway by our next door neighbor. She tells me Dad has been hospitalized.

Reading Allen's story, I whisper to the six-year-old Steven, that he will never have to wait for Dad again.

"Death Time" continues:

Use death as a message for the living. And writing myself into oblivion could serve a useful purpose. As a practicing veterinarian, I am familiar with death. I fight death. I win. I lose. I also dispense death swiftly, painlessly, immediately. I push the syringe into the vein and the eyes fade with surprising speed.

Pathos is not exactly a pleasure. I should have wept and embraced the children. But I would only have frightened them. I was learning to be a spectre. I wished that I believed in ghosts. Then I could theoretically watch over them. No, I didn't believe I would return. Mine was a one way journey.

The deer ticks politely waited as I said my farewells. Self-destruction was plausible. I reminded myself that my children would be my legacy. No posterity or plump maggot could ever destroy it.

I never thought of destroying others. There were a few I knew who deserved it, but they all had turned faceless. It was too late to become a Mafia hitman and leave a respectable sum behind. I didn't worry about my veterinary practice. The money I owed my father in-law would make sure he sold the practice for a profitable price. How romantic it would have been to join such immortal heroes as a mountain climber whose ashes were tossed into the air at an appropriate time. Or the soccer player who wanted his remains scattered on the home portion of his favorite soccer field. Unorthodox rites such as cremation couldn't be assured. Elaine would probably do the usual thing. For the kids' sake.

My silent rage at the situation vanished. I am making my peace.

I hurriedly wrote a few notes. To my wife:

GIVE MY KIDS THE LOVE THEY DESERVE. THE LOVE YOU NEVER GAVE ME.

Later she would call it a suicide note.

I decided on an epitaph. I would have preferred to be cremated but I decided the children should have a site to visit, to mourn, I hoped. A simple stone would suit me. There would be a chronology. Born June 17, 1930 Died. The date was no problem. That would be filled in. What about some simple phrase? Like GOODBYE. No heart rendering needed. Or some religious homily. HE FOUGHT THE GOOD FIGHT. JESUS CALLED AND HE RESPONDED. HE LIES IN THE ARMS OF JESUS. Oh Christ no. The engraving:

FATHER

I was definitely under control. That he did his best.

Allen's taking me somewhere I can't yet discern. Many of his stories ride the invisible line that separates insanity from brilliance. I picture Allen and Richard on a seesaw, with Allen as love on top, and Richard as hate on the bottom. Occasionally, Allen is coherent, and the desperation in his voice bleeds through the typing. There are handwritten pleas for help, and paragraphs discussing his life as one big failure. He writes of the loss of his children as if we had been killed in some tragic accident. He forgets that he made a choice, while we had none.

CHAPTER 27

Butterfly

"Butterfly" was written in August 1972, years after he had disappeared. None of us knew Allen was a ticking time bomb.

After six weeks of what might be called a drought, the divorced father salvaged a Sunday visitation with his three children. It was the first Sunday in August, and July and part of June had been dry and dreary. Even the constant visits to the pool adjacent to his apartment where other children splashed, content in this suburban oasis, had been painful. The legal hang-ups now in progress had made the period a desert, the green hills, and grass surrounding the clean-looking pool only an illusion.

Now, it hardly mattered that the invisible strings were still in place. The weather, all of the cool and happy imagery the pool represented, the suntanned kids jumping in and out, cannonballing off the small board—the conditions represented the best Sunday the father had ever experienced. He sat by the edge of the pool, sunglasses hiding his tears, trying to smile as the three kids he loved so dearly cavorted, occasionally waving to him.

How sky blue the horizon seemed! How gallantly green the trees off in the distance! The sun's rays darted into the clear water, spring-fed and marvelously refreshing, radiating joy and health. And though the father knew it was only a brief interlude, the good life—so rare in suburbia as far as he was concerned—suddenly seemed possible. If every Sunday were like this one...

The father tries to store up this scene for the future. A future, which bodes of legal documents and child support and walls. Walls which time and circumstances were forcing into his consciousness no matter the facts of biology. Blood types do not a father make.

It's hard to understand his pain writing about lost children when we were never lost.

He was like Marlin, sending his loyal assistant to check for danger, a hitman on photo safari, stalking his prey to catch a rare glimpse of an unsuspecting victim, or then taking his picture. His greatest fear was facing the truth, or worse—us.

One day, I saw your new "Daddy-Richard" and his children, all four of them carting trash to the side of the house and it seemed as if I needed a sledgehammer on my head, that the trouble was because of the new family unit being formed, so rapidly. Richard was fixing up the cellar before your mother's and my divorce was final. He took over my office before the ink was dry on my writing.

Did you know I had a twelve-page separation agreement worked out with the lawyers so that I could always look out for you kids? And in the short space of time that you and the boys all climbed in the back I had a vision of that expensive legal document that was incorporated in the divorce agreement turning to mulch, compost, or manure for your lawn.

Turning pathos on instantly is not easy. How pathetic a figure I could make myself. All I wanted was to stay close to your innermost thoughts and see you as often as was convenient, and that is a quote from the old agreement, before I became your ex-daddy.

I drove down the street and around the circle, away from my former home but with my three children. That was a strange thing. Even when I saw you kids three and four times a week, I missed you on the days we didn't get together. And on the nights you slept over, the three of you inside the one bedroom of the apartment and me out in the living room, I was in a castle and was supreme. How about that? You see, I wasn't always such an impotent factor in your life. I was it.

These stories are creatures that lived in his imagination—stories he told himself. He was not, as he claimed, my "ex-daddy," but became no daddy at all. Regardless of his intentions to remain a solid presence in his children's life, he failed.

***

I learn more about my family history during one hour of reading than I have in my entire lifetime. It's no surprise that there were secrets hidden in the corners of both families. After all, Allen's disappearance and Mom's marriage to Richard required layers of deception and convenient misdirection. He must have learned from his own father, Gus, who was introduced to me as Uncle Bill. They hid their relationship from Annie by lying to her and to us.

***

Blood doesn't make you a father or grandfather. Love does. Otherwise, you're just a sperm donor.

CHAPTER 28

Another Father's Funeral, April 2009

"Stairway to Heaven" cranks through my headphones. I am pumped to start a 10k race. Our law firm represents a high school basketball coach who suffered a heart attack during a playoff game, causing significant brain damage. We sponsor the race to raise money for a handicapped van and medical expenses.

Without warning, my tunes are hijacked when Madonna interrupts Led Zeppelin. I recognize Lori's ringtone.

I answer, which shuts up Madonna.

"Lori, I can't talk. Gotta run."

"Steve, Dad's dead."

"Good, we can celebrate later."

The last "death call" Lori made was in 1993, before cell phones became an appendage.

Richard's death is not a surprise. He's had worsening heart issues the last few years. Once Lori hangs up, I start the race. I feel loose. Taking deep breaths, my head bobs with each step. *Yes, yes, yes, it's about FUCKING time. YES.*

My 10k time is my personal best. I won't be making the Olympic team but am curiously motivated by Richard's demise. Allen's death was different. I was not motivated but indifferent and not even disappointed. While driving home, my shirt soaked with sweat and body sore from the run, Lori calls again to try to convince me to show for the funeral. Like before, she persuades me to attend. Any pain I am experiencing has more to do with leg cramps than sadness. I will not miss him.

Over the years, Richard and I learned to coexist. There were times he made an effort to get the family together. Somewhere inside that cold heart, there was a need to stay connected. But our only meaningful conversations were related to the Tampa Bay Buccaneers. We talked about nothing, and I felt nothing. And yet, he is part of me the same way shrapnel stays in a soldier's body. The flame of his sarcastic tone taunting me to "be a man" has been extinguished, but my anger still burns.

***

Fuck it.

Showing up for the funeral is still the right thing.

Lori provides details. It will be a quick trip. Richard didn't leave boxes of family history. There are no pictures with his kids from past life events. He does keep his promise that his children will receive equal shares of his estate, but those turn out to be equal shares of nothing. His last hustle: His promised estate of riches does not exist.

Richard's death and the thought of attending his funeral stirs me up. It's been more than a decade since all seven kids have been together. I'm dreading this. There's bound to be problems. Several of my family members rarely speak to me. It's going to be awkward, but we are still a family, even if a dysfunctional one.

I enter my home, grab a Gatorade, and sit down at the kitchen table. I'm still recovering from the run but decide to take a few more letters out of Allen's box.

Allen's writing exposes his dark philosophy, chronic emotional and physical pain, and daily habits. He also has several journal entries about taking Valium but keeping it secret. *Is it a secret if you write that it's a secret, or is it a cry for help?*

Allen's words also drip with wisdom. They are his absolute unshackled truth. My mind fills with the irregular clacking as I picture Allen who finger-pecks the keys in an unrecognizable, unorganized pattern, creating a symphony of words that land gently on the pages to form sentences, the way notes—played loudly—reach your ear, music becoming song. Each magical letter will pop up on the sheet until words, then paragraphs, then pages appear. It's Richard who died, but it's Allen who visits me from the dead. His love is the current that flows through every documented thought:

> We carry an enormous history around inside us. We forget chapters. We remember chapters. Mostly we forget chapters, that's why it makes so little sense sometimes.

> I explained to my mother, successfully, that voices from the past are the greatest consolation the living can have. All memories aid the premise that the past is always there. I know that sounds corny and vaguely metaphysical or overly sentimental, but where would we be without memories?

> —Allen S. Nestle

I find a newspaper article from December 1972. The headline reads, "Wayne Man Wins National Short Story Competition."

What was I doing while Allen was writing his stories? *That was the year I made the Police Athletic League All-Star team. Did he know the All-Star game was played three blocks from his office? Did he care?*

There are other feature articles about his short story honors and his body of work. One columnist writes, "A doctor's compassion and a writer's talent won first place in a national competition. He studied and taught journalism for two years at the New School for Social Research in Manhattan."

The vision of Allen standing in front of a classroom, muttering half sentences while balancing unfiltered Camels and coffee does not add up. Later, I ask Mom about this, but she's not impressed. She didn't care enough to be curious. The man she married was a mystery novel whose last chapter may never be written. Solving the puzzle of a confusing man when half the pieces are still missing keeps me digging into the boxes of his soul, left behind like an old safe with no combination, just a riddle to solve. *Is "Hellow, Yellow" the answer?*

Although Allen seems to share every piece of himself, including his sex life and bathroom habits, he can't bring himself to share "Hellow, Yellow."

In the newspaper, there's a picture of Allen, probably in his forties, with a proud look on his still unscarred face. There are photographs of two young kids, and pets in the background. There is no mention of a prior life. No mention of me. He looks like a normal person. The media doesn't always tell the true story, just the one that sells.

I return to the article that discusses his writing, his awards, and the novel he's trying to publish:

> [Nestle] admires the new frank journalism, an attitude he promotes in his creative writing classes... Finding expression in both the arts and sciences, he reaffirms the axiom that it's not what you do but who you are that counts... Dr. Nestle lives with his wife and two children, Mike, three, and Beth, six months, on Hamburg Turnpike and has practiced in Wayne since 1962.

We are edited out, left on the floor like crumpled pages that need a rewrite. We weren't simply forgotten, like when an actor wins an Academy Award and forgets to thank their spouse. We were *erased, dead to him.* At Allen's funeral, there'd been rumors of weird behavior and a drug problem. I heard he'd made several suicide attempts, including one where he was found unconscious on his office floor. In a letter to Steve Fayer, he describes what turned out to be an intentional overdose:

> Dear Bearded Soul Cousin: Wed, Oct SOMETHING
>
> Yes we are SOUL COUSINS. I look lousy? I could say I've been in the hospital 3x in a year and a half and have lost my pectoral muscles... I am in constant pain from my arms. I am what they call psycho-physiological. One afternoon, I staggered across the office and passed out on the floor of my office. A high school girl found me laying, knocked out with broken glass from a frame knocked over during the fall. I was shipped to the hospital and the shrink. ASN

Those stories did not make the paper. The photo of his peaceful face, his bright blue eyes peering out from behind his desk, hid the tormented soul living in his body. The stories don't mention bizarre behavior, for which he was hospitalized several times over the years.

***

Richard's funeral is coming up, yet it's Allen's story that's bringing some piece of me to life. It's a great drama with surprises, tragedy, despair, with the final chapters to be written. It's the story of a father's love, loss, and the consequences of divorce. Allen also wrote about presidents Carter, Reagan, Nixon, and Ford. I learn about his military experience in France, his work as a scientist, and his effort to gain admission to veterinary school. I read details about his personal life no son should know. He was a man who could not connect through spoken words, yet became endearing, open, and loving on the page. He was vulnerable yet kept people at a distance. He was awkward and he knew it. Maybe it was from years of self-abuse, or his manic personality. On paper, he's more alive than he was while breathing. He jokes, writes out his budget, and debates whether Reagan will be a good president. He worries about the Yankees and Roy White. His unique observations alternate between absolute brilliance, anger, vulnerability.

***

It takes a marathon of emotional energy to read the work. Every sentence has meaning. He takes me into his subconscious, his closed compartments now purged onto paper:

> This writing a book is torture. Supply information but not too much. Build plot lines. Make everything fit.
>
> Words are linkups of the soul, words that will never see the ink of a book press or even be preserved, but words that make me actually a prophet, a lover, a more understanding person, if only on the inside.
>
> At times I am merely a collector of pages, at other times my writing provides a glimpse into the brain, the times, the differences in each of us that are ordinary but somehow revealed in this way. What I write has never been seen before on the pages of books by glorious creative artists. For there is a similarity in the depths of the human that by its very commonness gains significance.

Later, he contemplates his reason for writing:

> Maybe I use the writing for a release. Maybe I ought to drink and screw around instead of faithfully filling my coffee cup and pounding the Selectric. Maybe I ought to pound my peter. But then I will only get another erection. Maybe I'm role-playing...
>
> We Jews, always seeking glue for the foreskin on our shoulder...

I read a letter he wrote in 1979 (but never sent), after our meeting in his office.

September, 1979

Dear Steve my son,

My brain cells have been tossed around and around. They haven't recovered. I cry tears of happiness. I want to be able to tell you I love you. I was there, always there. You just didn't see me. Someday you will have to tell me what you expected, what you must have thought.

I can't remember your calling me "Dad." Of course I don't care what you call me. (I really do, but it's how you think of me that matters, and I hope now you will think of me often.)

I could not express my feelings when we did meet. I don't know if I will send this letter, but I will keep a copy and send it to Fayer. One day you will read it......

.......I have known for a long time that fathers and mothers take things for granted and kids and parents go their separate ways. But when one is deprived of the other, suffers a great loss, and then finds it again...

It felt wonderful to be able to see you. It feels wonderful to be able to write Missing you. It's confusing to miss you when I have never stopped missing you.

Tell me how you feel.

Love,

D

No one explained Allen's death to me, but I no longer need an explanation. His death certificate could have said: broken man, broken heart. Richard's says heart attack. Both died of heart failure. Is it a coincidence? Richard's funeral is a non-event. Done.

CHAPTER 29

"Hellow, Yellow," August 2009

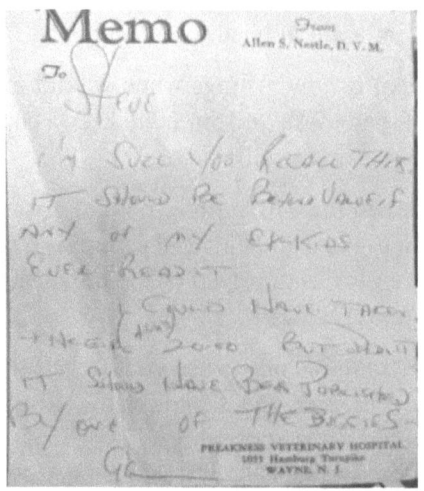

Sitting at work, my new paralegal brings the latest mail to my office. She usually weeds out the junk but today hands me an old magazine article with a note attached.

She looks at me with curiosity in her eyes. "I was about to toss this but realized there's a couple of handwritten notes attached. It looks old."

I say thank you and ask her to close my office door. The smell of her strong perfume makes my eyes water. I pick up the note.

It's from Fayer:

Steve,

I am not sure your father wanted you to ever read this, but he also left it with me for safekeeping. I think he wanted you to have it so you'd know his side of the story. I will understand if you want to send it back.

SC (SOUL COUSIN)

From Allen to Fayer

I'm sure you recall this but it should be beyond value if any of my ex-kids read it.

I could have taken the 20.00 but should have been published by one of the biggies...

Allen

***

Hellow, Yellow

by Allen Samuel Nestle

A yellow-toothed horse with golden wings, carrying a most precious burden, attempts to fly toward the rising sun. He falters. He struggles. His wings melt away. The three children on his back vanish. I roll from the couch in my lonely apartment onto the rug littered with torn pieces of yellow scrap paper. Dozing, my monochromatic fantasies continue.

A 747 glides in for a landing in the forest behind my apartment. Its spotlights reach within my sleeping eyes and I stir as the pilot who has delivered the huge jet, its nose lettered, "HELLOW, YELLOW," stands above me, grinning with his teeth which resemble the winged horse. He is wearing yellow goggles and matching jumpsuit and carrying a clipboard which glistens with the color of my dreams.

He makes no small talk, merely hands me the keys to the plane, fashions a bicycle clip to his ankle, and pedals expertly out of my apartment on a child's three-wheeler. In such situations there are no dimensions. The phantom Chinese pilot exits from the apartment without opening the door.

I rouse myself to life. I open the blinds and look out on a patch of suburban forest, beautiful in its autumn foliage, taking in all the colors of the leaves. The greens and half-greens, the yellows, the reds. A scene of chirping birds and dying leaves. I force myself not to stare at the yellows.

Yellow. A color that has become both dear and hateful. Refreshing and nightmarish. Yellow, since a few nights before, injected into my brain with the crowbar of fatherhood lost. Yellow, forever nostalgic.

I study the remaining pieces of legal-sized yellow scrap pad. Oh, the drivel I had written and written before I faltered. Before I acknowledged that love was not fighting and harassing one's ex-wife over cars and custodial problems and visitations. Love was making things as normal as one could for one's children. Tearing the trio between their mother with whom they lived and their father who they only visited had finally reached its end. For various reasons I had raised the tattered banner of surrender.

I won't go into the drivel of our civilized divorce. If ever a term is contradictory, that is. And when my former wife remarried and the spectre of adoption was raised I fought. Fighting a mother with custody and control means constant war, constant defeats.

I had not involved the children. I made their nights at my apartment one of games and hijinks. I became a stand-up comedian, savoring each giggle, each wrestling match, each second of everything and anything.

I called a psychiatrist about the problem. Was it better for the children? Could I handle it? My life was centered around their visits, their activities. We seemed close, closer than before. But what was best for them? Was a father in residence better than a part-time buddy?

His answer was cruel, but over the years since I have seen them (and it is five years although we live in the same town) his advice was correct, if more than impossible to follow.

He said, "Pretend they are dead."

I had no comeback to that sort of counsel.

I read *The Father's Book*, by Charles V. Metz. He had faced a similar situation. In it he wrote, "God help the father who wants to kiss his children goodnight and can't."

I expected no help from God but it was some comfort to know that other fathers had done the right thing and survived. I stalled. I promised that I would think about it. In the meantime,

I picked up the kids and dropped off the kids, cheerful, joking, as far from my real self as a person can be. If the kids, aged eight (twins) and six, knew what was pending they gave no sign. If they didn't want a new daddy they gave no sign.

It is a falsehood that fathers can't love their children as much as mothers. But was that any consolation? Did it help Stella Dallas, standing out in the rain watching her daughter marry well, that it had become possible because of her mother's love? I like to think the answer is yes. I must.

I had the three of them sleeping in the bedroom of my apartment. Two in the bed and one on the floor in the sleeping bag, which they usually fought for. I sat at my desk basking at their presence, taking in and storing, if you will, the sound of their movements. As usual I felt a sense of contentment. They were there with me. It seemed like the most important thing in the world. And it was to end.

I consoled myself. Their genes would always be the same. My blood was half theirs. And though their last names would soon change, I would know better, as Shakespeare had known centuries before. And though I had gone through the days of decision with a constant burning sensation, my mouth tasting of rot and mildew, my heart pounding erratically with never-ending sleepless nights, I had decided.

This was to be the last night. I listened to music. I toyed with the yellow pad, writing long, confused, piteous "legal" briefs, tearing them to shreds as I finished. I was like the condemned man hoping the sun never rose.

I rolled a blank sheet of yellow paper into the typewriter. But I had run out of words. I stared at the blankness of the paper, lost in a trance of finality.

Suddenly I saw my son standing at my side, yawning and blinking, his eyes sleep encrusted and squinting from my desk lamp, the only light in the room. His hair seemed to have a halo above it, his brown curls so much like mine, gleamed golden. We grinned at one another. Father and son sharing the joke, playing the game. I don't say he was reading my mind although it turned out it seemed so. He presented a portrait that will be fresh in my mind until I die. When he has children of his own, to me he will always be that sleepy six-year-old looking for an excuse to stay up with his father. An ordinary situation. Until it is taken away.

I pretended annoyance.

"OK, what is it? You have to go to the bathroom? You want a drink?" He went to the bathroom. He guzzled a drink. But he didn't return to the bedroom.

"What now?"

"I want to say a poem," he announced between yawns.

A 3 a.m. burst of creativity? I called him on it. I rolled a fresh piece of yellow paper into the machine. "OK, shoot."

There was a few seconds delay. I knew, or at least I thought I knew that it was just an excuse not to be tossed into bed. Then he said, "A Poem."

I typed, "A Poem," and waited. When he looked like he was asleep on his feet, I turned off the machine and was just about to carry him off when he blinked, opened his eyes wide and said his poem.

And then, he fooled me. He did have a poem.

And here it is:

"Hellow, Yellow. Hellow, Yellow.

A poem.

Say hellow, yellow

And you're not alone."

I carried the six-year-old poet into bed, the words of his poem already inscribed into my flesh. The color yellow would give me nightmares in the weeks, months to come, as their absence became as much a part of my life as their presence.

In the morning they giggled over their cereal and as I straightened up the apartment and gathered their few belongings for them to take with them I heard some discussion about whether the young poet had indeed written a poem the night before.

"Of course he had," I said. It was a great poem. It is not surprising that the poet himself did not remember he had written it, or more exactly, he didn't remember the words. I told him it was a poem I would always treasure.

I dropped them off at their home, my former home, acting as if it was an ordinary morning. As far as they knew it was.

A poem is no substitute for the love of a six-year-old or the legal loss of three children. Of course not. But thanks to the poem, to the encouragement my young poet gave me in the middle of that last evening, I shall never be alone again.

And again, thanks to the poem, I can hope that my dreams will change to a reality. That some decade or other my children will know that my love has smoothed their life. That they have a father whose yellow nightmares will change someday before he dies to a golden rainbow—where he won't be alone.

The End.

***

"Hellow, Yellow" is a short story from *AIM* magazine. It was published in 1973 and, though the print has faded, the story's message overwhelms me. It's about his last night as my dad. Above the title, the publisher used the teaser, "In a broken marriage, love is making things normal for one's children." It's hard to process the words. My eyes are fixed on a simple black-and-white illustration, depicting a man with his back turned away from his three children, two boys and a girl—a man pretending those children are dead.

The story sends shock waves through my body. Trying to remember our version of the "Last Supper" means mining my brain for long buried memories. My head involuntarily shakes in disbelief as I begin to read again. My heart thumps. My mind keeps repeating the same question: *What the fuck? What the fuck? What the fuck?*

Adrenaline surges, but I'm not sure how to direct it. Sadness should come but doesn't. Happiness is not an option. Maybe it's exasperation that he shared our story with the world without telling us. Or maybe it's my own surprising detachment and indifference that pushes his truth away. I should be vulnerable and produce tears. But my sadness is that I'm not sad. We were just young kids. I get up from my office chair and begin to pace, my eyes focusing on a photograph. I'm feeling the feeling of no feeling.

It's me, standing at the edge of the ocean, the bright yellow sun shining from high overhead, as three of my kids, all laughing, are draped over me, holding tight, the deep blue waves turning to foam as they break against my ankles. I remember that when the water hit me, I pretended to lose my balance, causing the kids to scream, "Dad, Dad, DAD!" and attach themselves to me like superglue.

The reflection from the white sand catches the joy in their faces, knowing I will never let them go. Energy jumps from the picture frame, reminding me how deep a parent's love for a child should be.

Since I'm at work, any emotions will stay hidden. No one—myself included, apparently—knows my history. How many other secrets will this dead man confess? The words "Hellow, Yellow" have always seemed familiar. Now, flashes of his apartment and the posters on his wall break through my mind. I see Raquel Welch, wearing a tiny cavewoman outfit, hidden on the inside of his bathroom door, causing her to steam—as if she's taking a shower with him. I remember the time he caught me reading a *Playboy* magazine hidden in his closet.

Losing his children, and the self-inflicted torture of his own last supper, was a disastrous event, but we weren't consulted. How could a loving dad drop off his innocent children curbside, next to the garbage pails, deliver his usual peck on the cheek, and mumble goodbye? He acted like he would see us in three days, not three decades.

The lawyer inside me analyzes his decision. *Was this a conspiracy of deception in the name of love, or personal convenience?* We were held like hostages with no choice but to follow our captors' orders. *Did he succumb to the financial blackmail caused by his failure to pay child support? Was there evidence he was an unfit father? Or were we an obstacle interfering with a new relationship? Was it the perfect storm, resulting in his own drowning?*

His daily suffering is evident. We didn't just lose a dad, but an extended family who loved us. Did Allen, or any of the adults, consider how the additional loss of loving grandparents, aunts, uncles, and cousins might affect us? By "pretending" we were dead, the Nestles became dead to us, never mentioned or discussed. We were stripped of our identity, reborn and baptized into the Eichenblatt family.

I stand up and turn to look out my window.

All I can see is Allen staring back at me with the sorrowful eyes of a man killing off his own son. *Pretend they are dead! That's his excuse?*

It must have taken a family conspiracy to execute the plan of his practical death. His memory was like an insidious tumor, shrinking away over time, but leaving a few cells as a reminder that the cancer could return.

After a while, I forgot the sound of his voice. The one I heard in my head became silent, like a phone number that's disconnected. The smoke from his Camel cigarettes no longer bothered my eyes, and the sound and smell of his constantly brewing coffee machine disappeared. I forgot his eyes were blue.

***

Looking back, we were kids with no voice and no choice. Kidnapped by divorce. The four original Eichenblatt children lost their mom months before they moved into our house. She and Allen were thrown into the junkyard of history. No pictures, no discussion, no empathy for lost parents. That psychiatrist's advice destroyed him. I wonder if Allen misunderstood the advice or just invented it to make himself feel better. If a psychiatrist gave that advice today, he would be sued for malpractice.

From his writings, it's certain that Allen never recovered. He stalked us. He asked for photos. He remarried and redivorced. He endured major depressions. His finances were a disaster. He numbed his pain with Valium and an unknown array of veterinary medications. He attempted to take his life several times until his body surrendered, no longer willing to fight. He died alone, without hope, no family at his bedside, a one-game bingo barker, his voice forgotten.

CHAPTER 30

Love is Love

How could an intelligent man think it was the loving thing to kill off his kids? Was he also a hostage, forced to make a deal that required him to sacrifice us? Still, there was an aura of spirituality around him that has stayed with me since his bloodied eye stared me down.

Maybe the best way to reach him is to write a letter. We could be pen pals, like the ones we had in elementary school, sending letters off to soldiers in Vietnam and never expecting a response. Even then, some part of me knew my pen pal might be a dead man. I always wondered where those letters went. Allen was a prolific letter writer, but he never wrote to us. *How many letters did he write but never send? How many emotions did he feel but never express? There are unfinished letters among his journals and correspondence. Some are addressed to us but never sent. Why?*

Writing allows me to transport the thoughts floating around in my mind onto paper. Allen may be dead, but he will receive my message. It's not easy to write. Perfectionism is the enemy of the rookie. My own rituals for writing expose my insanity. I have hundreds of fine point pens that must be used with a Black n' Red hardcover notebook while listening to Led Zeppelin or Springsteen. Sometimes, I listen to mellow '70s hits, but usually it's heavy metal. My self-diagnosed obsessive compulsive disorder forces me to be ritualistic when setting up my writing space at five o'clock each morning.

While I write, my own coffee machine sizzles, then begins dripping as it fills up the glass coffee pot. It's usually some exotic brand imported from Costa Rica or produced ethically in an African village that turns out to be in China. Recently, we purchased a Keurig coffee maker, which reminds me of the small Styrofoam cups of coffee offered at the tire store while waiting for a bill that exceeds the cost of the car. *Why do you have to replace all four when only one is flat?* I miss the old coffee maker, with its gurgling and choking noises as the hot water percolates through the coffee beans.

Allen locked himself in his den for hours, like a bear hibernating for the winter. He might emerge for food but would return and lock the door so no one dared bother him. I imagine the faint sounds of his stereo playing "Strangers in the Night" by Frank Sinatra, or an album featuring some obscure Yiddish singers. The music went well with the clicking of his fingers striking the typewriter's keys until the bell chimed and his IBM Selectric reset itself.

Writing each morning starts slowly, but once I get moving, the letters somehow find their way onto the page without the inconvenience of thought. Words eventually appear, turning into sentences that become paragraphs, and finally entire pages. While Allen had to fix mistakes by applying Wite-out, I can hit the delete button or cut and paste. No wasted paper, or journal entries typed on last year's calendar.

I take a deep breath before beginning, but then stop.

What should I call him? Dr. Nestle? Sir... Father... Dad? It's been a long time since I've called him Dad, and now that he's gone, it's probably too late. It's a word—like love—that has to come from the heart to mean anything.

My fingers find the keys, and I begin:

Dad/Allen Sorry it has taken so long to respond to your letter of August 20, 1979, but it took 20 plus years to reach me. Let's not forget you didn't mail it but left it in the box Fayer sent. Hope you are doing well considering the circumstances. You were miserable those last few years so may be happier dead. The last time we spoke, you were breathing, but there was no life left. Our conversation was short.

Living in a coffin even if you are dead can't be much fun. I am claustrophobic so will need Valium before they bury me. Or, I can opt for cremation but I'm not a huge fan of being burned up. Plus, the thought of someone carrying my ashes around or leaving them on a shelf somewhere makes me anxious. These days, I can't sit in a dental chair or ride an elevator without starting to panic. I have quirks that show up with no notice. I am addicted to my pedometer, and can't rest until I have walked 10,000 steps, even if it means pacing in the bathroom to hit the number.

My life has had challenges, many earned by making bad decisions. You struggled with Mom, but at least got close enough to get her pregnant. I'd be nothing without you. Like actual nothing since you're my sperm donor. Weird concept. Losing you as a kid makes me determined to make certain my kids know their dad and that they know I love them.

Marriage has been a challenge for me. Growing up (and this is not an excuse) did not provide me with the best male role or relationship models. My first marriage ended more than 20 years ago. My ex and I have done the best we can to maintain stability for the kids. We both made mistakes, but the kids always came first.

After my first marriage, I married someone who had been a friend. That didn't last. We did have Cole, who was worth the pain of a second divorce.

Financially, divorce has been a disaster, but my law business is strong. My law partner is a special person and close friend. He has supported me through chaos and we have had great success. We have helped many people and worked to help families facing catastrophic tragedies and dysfunction.

Staying miserable in a miserable marriage is bad for everyone. Good people become domestic terrorists and the kids are collateral damage. Money is not a motivator for me but the stress of paying decades of alimony and years of child support takes a toll. Mortgaging my kids like you did is shameful. "Hellow, Yellow" helps me understand your version but it's not an excuse. You write about loving us, then discard us. Makes no sense unless it's not true.

I wonder why you never tried to see us. We were just minutes away. We didn't know what was happening. We were your kids, you were our dad... it still hurts...

Enough for now,

Steve

I put the letter aside. It's not like Allen's waiting for mail. Writing to him brings back feelings of anger, desperation, and indifference. *Why does his love even matter? What does it even feel like?*

***

"Hellow, Yellow" is an attempt to explain why Allen dumped his kids. Allen's sharp mind crafts poetic sentences without the confusion of his mumbling, disorganized speech. His writing jumps from one topic to the next without the need for a logical connection. Maybe that's the brilliance of it.

Yes, he surrendered his right to be called Dad, but Richard didn't deserve to be called Dad either. He treated it like an empty job title—no need to do the work. Mom failed to persuade me to call him Dad, and he held that against me. He died without ever hearing me say the word.

Divorce sucks. That's the reality. Family counseling might have helped prepare me for Richard but was not considered. When hurricanes come, you have time to prepare. Mom's marriage to Richard was a tsunami that turned my life upside down. We kids were thrown together like prisoners forced into a cellblock: no selection process, no voice, no vote, and no love.

My mind wanders. *What kind of psychiatrist tells a father to pretend his kids are dead? And what kind of father accepts that advice?*

***

Love is not about blood, it's about love. Adoption is not a blood transfusion. Biology can make you a father, but it doesn't make you a dad. Being a dad means feeling the wonderful warmth pulsing from your heart when you look at your kids. It's late-night diaper changes or running to the twenty-four-hour pharmacy to pick up Tylenol or Pedialyte. It's throwing the baseball even when you're ready to collapse. *One more throw, Dad, just one more.* It's telling your children that you love them every day. It's showing them how to love, to be affectionate, to be vulnerable. I have not been a perfect dad. But my shortcomings were not because I didn't love them but because didn't always know how to show it.

CHAPTER 31

My Worlds Collide

"Death cannot stop true love—all it can do
is delay it for a while."
— William Goldman, *The Princess Bride*

Allen Nestle has been gone for over thirty years, but we're closer than ever now. His published works, agonizing journal entries, and declarations of love are all his words, but they do not describe the strange man I remember. He's a complicated, brilliant, tortured soul who was unable to express his feelings outside of the written word, but his words will live forever.

> Dear Dad,
>
> I wanted to share some great news. No, it's not the Yankees. I haven't followed baseball for years. After struggling through a few post-divorce relationships, I found myself alone. Loneliness was not an issue, as my kids, friends, hobbies, and work kept me busy. Plus, it helped to take a break and reset my life.

It's too complicated to explain, but our world has become virtual. It's an easier way to find people to date, but it's never easy to find "the one." When I was a senior in college, my few relationships lasted long enough to have fun, before walking away. Other than sexual connection, I had little to offer. I never could consider anyone a girlfriend.

My life changed when one fall Saturday of my senior year, I volunteered to work in the Seminole Booster box. Missy and I didn't know each other but we were both members of a student club that would serve drinks during FSU football games. While serving drinks one game, my eyes kept drifting toward one particular girl with long, curly black hair and an engaging smile. She had dark, inquisitive eyes, and I noticed several of the booster club members flirting with her. She was wearing a garnet and gold vest over a dark blouse and tight khaki pants. She was beautiful and somehow I found the courage to introduce myself. I may have taken a few shots to gather my charm. *Liquid courage.* We talked the rest of the night like we'd known each other for years. Over the next months, we grew close and became an official couple. Missy met the family, even Richard, and everyone approved.

Over time, it became apparent we both had our own journeys to take, and mine was law school. Plus, my personal baggage became too heavy for her to carry. I had problems with connection and intimacy. We drifted apart and had stopped speaking by the end of my first law school year.

One morning, almost forty years later, I woke up and saw a message from Missy, who now went by Melissa. She contacted me through Facebook, a social networking platform. I was a twice divorced man and she had never married.

Melissa and I began to "message" each other. It's a way to talk without speaking. She was a single mom and successful businesswoman hired by the federal government to provide wellness programs for the Coast Guard. When she hit forty, she decided to become a mom through an anonymous sperm donor. Zach, her son (now mine) is the love of her life.

Melissa lived in Miami, so was hours away. She commented that it would be funny if we dated again. By now, you probably know where this story is headed. It was time to re-meet in person.

Have you ever had that "feels like I saw you yesterday" feeling? Our reunion was like having my best friend return from the dead. No offense, as I respect most dead people. We hadn't seen each other for almost forty years, yet there was never an awkward moment. We were supposed to have dinner, but instead spent hours talking. Crazy, but I had never mentioned that you existed or explained that Richard was my adoptive father. She knew nothing about me except what she could see on the outside.

When I began sharing, she sobbed and said that she had always suspected I was carrying trauma and might be the victim of sexual abuse.

It took forty years for me to find Missy again. My determination powered me through the emotional marathon of divorce, child custody, and financial despair. It's as if she was waiting to see if I could cross a finish line of sorts. And I believe that love lost can be reclaimed if we are willing to sprint the last miserable mile.

Reconnecting with Melissa was like winning an Olympic medal. She has her own incredible story to tell. Love found me. Turns out it never left me. We parted decades ago, but she wasn't the one who was lost. My heart's internal compass was pointed the wrong way until I learned to read it. It's a romance story custom-made for the Hallmark Channel. Two students fall in love, break up, and make their way back to each other forty years later

We began spending time together—this included Zach, who was ten. Becoming a father figure to a fatherless child felt like no coincidence. Zach didn't have to say it, but it's hard to watch other kids with their dads. The child in me identified with that sense of emptiness. We made the decision to marry, and it was one of the happiest days of my life.

Our wedding reunited not only Melissa and me, but all of your biological children. Robert, Lori, Beth, and Michael stood with me for one picture. I can attach it to this letter.

One of my favorite books is *The Princess Bride* by William Goldman. It's a love story, a fairy tale about a farm boy who spends his life fighting to find his true love.

There is a line where he says, "I have always told you I would come for you. Why didn't you wait for me?"

She says, "Well, you were dead."

He responds, "Death cannot stop true love—all it can do is delay it for a while."

Forty years later I know what true love is—and have finally found it. Remember, love never dies—in death your feelings are stronger than ever.

Steve

Epilogue

I take a moment to myself. Dads aren't perfect. It's hard for me to discipline or punish my kids. If my mistakes are from loving too much, I'm happy to make them. My determination to prevent a repeat of family tradition inspires me. My dad's father left him, and my dad left me. The pattern stops here. Throwing the kids in the crossfire of divorce changes the trajectory of their lives. History will not repeat itself.

Growing up, I refused to acknowledge pain or allow any sign of vulnerability. Toughness was a requirement. It took several decades for me to learn that the opposite is true. Showing vulnerability is strength; acting tough is a charade.

Repressed memories are part of self-protection, helping to toss trauma overboard in an attempt to bury it in our mind's deepest oceans. Allen buried us by pretending we were dead. He turned his back on us, and we weren't even invited to our own funeral. I buried the car accident and kept the secret for forty years. My mind won't delete that terrible day but I use it to inspire me to be a Dad, not a stranger or worse, a stalker.

Allen drove the streets, desperate to catch a glimpse of his ex-children. We had moved on with our new "father." Looking back, my own brothers and sisters don't know my childhood story.

We were blended together like cast members on a television show, forced to play supporting roles in a script whose head writer left love on the cutting-room floor. Everyone has found some happiness and success. Mark and Larry are both successful businessmen, Robert retired from the printing business and recently became a grandfather... Lori has four children and is happily married to a wonderful man. Gail and Cindy both became strong moms with successful careers.

It's impossible for me to comprehend the desperation that drove Allen Nestle to leave his own children. "Hellow, Yellow" is a nice story, but it's not an excuse. Both fathers still push me. Richard's fading voice challenges me to be tough, or tricks me into thinking I won't amount to anything. Allen's abandonment pushes me to be a better dad.

Every day, past trauma motivates me. We need to change the messages we send ourselves. Abused kids struggle to understand it's not their fault; that they are the victims. Yet, you will never find a hint of happiness if you allow your past to become a chronic disease, forever preventing you from becoming the person you were meant to be.

You might be a victim, but you do not have to stay one. It's your choice and I chose to fight back. Use those voices in your head as a sword for good, not as an excuse for failure.

Allen's words throb with a life force that finally carries his love to a place where my heart can feel it. I hear his voice and know he loved me. Love is almost dying just to catch a glimpse of me. Maybe I shouldn't have left the scene that day. Maybe I should have told someone. His blood and mine blend together like a strong Bloody Mary, a happy mix of emotional spices and mind-numbing alcohol.

I search for the yellow. It's not easy, but we both want to connect. Everyone makes mistakes. His might be unforgiveable to some, but I can forgive him.

He will never be forgotten: He's. My. Dad.

I communicate with him through words he'll never read, but I know the message will reach him.

Dear Dad,

This is Steve, again. It's still hard to call you Dad, but my brain sees your face when the subject of fathers comes up.

You have grandkids. I have five children: four boys and a beautiful daughter. One day, they will know our story, but they do know they have a Grandpa Allen. The kids will hear about overcoming mistakes, forgiveness, and love—the love I now feel as your son, the love you left behind for us to discover.

The best way to honor you is for me to be the dad you could never be to your own kids. My kids will know the power of a dad's love and will receive some extra hugs for you even if you weren't much of a hugger.

My mission as a lawyer is to help families of dysfunction and victims of abuse. I tell our story so parents understand that there are lifelong consequences to impulsive emotional decisions. The chaos we create can be maintained by understanding help is available... There's so much I didn't understand until Steve Fayer sent me all your journals, stories, and letters. Today's world is tough to navigate alone. We still need the support of those who love us.

I spend hours reading your words, my brain locked in a time machine transporting me to those precious few years before you left. Living the transcript of your life, I feel myself walking the thorny path of your chronic pain, your tormented mind, the one less traveled, the one you chose because you thought we were better off without you.

Sacrificing yourself by killing off your kids is not fatherhood. Parents do not abandon their children. And I know now, you never totally abandoned us.

We were in your heart, but you chose distraction from the truth. Stories of bingo and dating tales had me laughing, while your dark side and despair brought tears. You allow me deep into the brilliance and desperation of your vulnerable brain.

Before now, no one knows how many hours I spent hidden in the basement closet, buried in books, afraid the man who became my father would find me. The truth is, Richard never looked for me, but you did, and almost died doing it. Our two lives, woven together like chapters in a book, have become one.

Outside our house, the dogwood tree we planted is in full bloom, its white flowers providing a perfume of honeysuckle, the abstract, geometrical pattern of its branches reminding me that life may seem random, or unpredictable, but even the trees need to find the bright rays of yellow sunshine. Yellow is no coincidence, it's a color in your rainbow, a symbol of hope.

Finding you, my dad, allows me to leave the closet of my mind, knowing the mirror will no longer reflect the scared little boy who once hid there, but a man who has become a father himself, a man whose five kids call him Dad.

The world changes all the time, but the meaning and feeling of a dad's love do not. Your children know now that what you did so many years ago, you did for love.

As I write, my eyes close while the blinds in my mind open. I see your patch of suburban forest, beautiful in its autumn foliage, taking in all the colors of the leaves. The greens and half-greens, the yellows, the reds. A quiet time interrupted only by the sound of chirping birds and the wind blowing the leaves off the trees like snowflakes, but they are not dying. I wait for the sound of screaming tires and crunching metal against the tree, but it never comes.

The words you wrote in "Hellow, Yellow" echo once again:

And again, thanks to the poem, I can hope that my dreams will change to a reality. That some decade or other my children will know that my love has smoothed their life. That they have a father whose yellow nightmares will change someday before he dies to a golden rainbow—where he won't be alone.

My imagination captures the image of "Hellow, Yellow"'s illustration, and I watch as a father, his back once turned, faces three children, arms wrapped around them in a tight embrace, like he's never going to let them go. You can't see his face but I know tears begin to roll down his cheeks.

Dad, some say rainbows are messages of hope and love from the angels. Maybe it's true. When I open my eyes, there's a momentary flash of yellow light and I watch as your autumn leaves of greens, half-greens, reds, and yellows fade to gold. Your nightmare is over. The love we feel for each other is real. It's the feeling of feeling.

A golden rainbow appears, so you can stop searching your dreams and know you will never be alone.

I love you.

Your son,

Steve